THINKING
TRANSLATION

For details of the Teachers' Handbook and cassette of oral texts
please write to:

ROUTLEDGE LTD
ITPS
CHERITON HOUSE
NORTH WAY
ANDOVER
HANTS SP10 5BE

ROUTLEDGE INC.
29 WEST 35TH STREET
NEW YORK
NY 10001
USA

TITLES OF RELATED INTEREST

The French Language Today
Adrian Battye and Marie-Anne Hintze

A History of the French Language
Peter Rickard

In Other Words: A Coursebook in Translation
Mona Baker

Redefining Translation
Lance Henson and Jacky Martin

Handbook of Commercial French
C. Geoghegan and J. Gontier Geoghegan

Translation Studies
Susan Bassnett-McGuire

THINKING
TRANSLATION

A Course in Translation Method:
French–English

Sándor Hervey

Reader in Linguistics, University of St Andrews

Ian Higgins

Senior Lecturer in French, University of St Andrews

London and New York

First published in 1992
by Routledge
11 New Fetter Lane, London EC4P 4EE

Simultaneously published in the USA and Canada
by Routledge
a division of Routledge, Chapman and Hall, Inc.
29 West 35th Street
New York, NY 10001

Typeset in 10 on 12 pt Times by Fotographics (Bedford) Ltd
Printed in Great Britain by TJ Press

British Library Cataloguing in Publication Data
A catalogue record for this book is available
from the British Library

Library of Congress Cataloging-in-Publication Data
A catalog record for this book is available on request

ISBN 0–415–07815–6
ISBN 0–415–07816–4 pbk

To

Willie Cardwell
Elizabeth Clingan
Colin Connolly
Fiona Duffy
Lisa Elliott
Sarah Evans
Jane Gadsden
Jill Gamble
Linda Ingram
Hilary Jackson
Belinda Kelly
Richard Littledale
Karen McBride
Mairi MacLeod
Dana Robbins
Mark Sutton
Peter Turberfield
Louise Whitlaw

1986–87 – The Elite

Contents

Acknowledgements

We owe considerable debts to a number of friends and colleagues who have helped us in the preparation of *Thinking Translation*: to Adrian Gratwick, Ian Mason, John Minchinton, Siân Reynolds, Maurice Shepherd and Isabelle Scott, whose advice and criticisms have solved a number of specific problems; to Bernard Bentley, Cathy Davies, Paul Gifford, Nicky Haxell, Mike Loughridge, Peter Read and Jim Supple, for their constructive participation in teaching the prototype courses from which the book has evolved; and to Ann Cottrell and Ann Pearce, for the patience, good humour and alertness with which, bearing torture by a thousand commas, they typed the first and final versions of the course respectively. We owe a particular debt to Jim Supple, who read the manuscript and made many invaluable suggestions for its improvement. Finally, we owe an unquantifiable, but real, debt to the many students whose participation in, and reactions to, the successive versions of the course have helped to shape it.

Introduction

This book is a developed version of a tried and tested course in translation methodology for third-year undergraduates in modern languages at the University of St Andrews. The course was first designed for students of French, and our main focus is indeed on translation from French into English. However, the French course has been so successful that parallel versions adapted for German–English and Spanish–English translation have been developed and are currently taught at St Andrews. In other words, underlying the French-oriented version presented in this book there is a common course structure applicable to, and easily adapted for, other modern languages. On pp. 4–11, we outline suggestions for ways in which the same format can be used to organize versions of the course for German and Spanish.

Let us briefly dispose of a few basic assumptions that underlie the structure we are advocating. First, it is not a disguised version of a 'grammar-and-translation' method of language teaching. Our focus is on how to *translate*, not on how to speak or write French. It is assumed that students already have the considerable linguistic resources in French that they need in order to benefit from the course. It is also assumed that they have learned how to use dictionaries and, where appropriate, data-banks. Naturally, in using their linguistic resources to produce good translations, students inevitably improve those resources, and this is an important fringe-benefit.

Nevertheless, our main interest lies in developing useful translation skills and, generally, in improving *quality* in translation work. In this connection, the point should be made that this quality depends on the translator's having an adequate command of English as much as of French; indeed, Birgit Rommel, head of the Übersetzer- und Dolmetscherschule Zürich, has lamented the lack of mother-tongue training in universities, concluding that: 'Great stress is laid on improving foreign language proficiency, but excellence in the mother-tongue – the translator's target language – is, quite wrongly, taken for granted' (Rommel, 1987, p. 12). As Rommel's comment also suggests, it is normally assumed when training translators that higher quality is achieved by translating into the mother-tongue than into a foreign language; hence the predominance of unidirectional translation, from French into English, in this course.

Second, the course is not intended as a disguised version of translation theory, or of linguistics. 'Theoretical' issues do inevitably arise, because translation practice and the involvement of linguistic resources in it are so complex. However, such issues are not treated out of theoretical interest, but out of direct concern with specific types of problem encountered in translating. That is, our slant is *methodological* and practical – theoretical notions have been freely borrowed and adapted from translation theory and linguistics merely with the aim of facilitating and producing a rationale for problems of methodology. Throughout the course, we have provided instant and simple exemplification of each theoretical notion invoked, and linked these notions instantly and directly to practical issues in translation.

Third, the course has a progressive overall structure and thematic organization. After beginning with the fundamental issues, options and alternatives of which a translator must be aware, it examines a series of layers that are of textual importance in translation (from the generalities of culture and intertextuality to the nuts and bolts of phonic or graphic details). It then moves, via a number of semantic and stylistic topics (literal meaning, connotation and language variety), to a consideration of textual genres and the demands of translating texts in a range of different genres. Our aim has been to produce an integrated approach to the various aspects that need to be discussed in the context of a methodology of translation. While we cannot claim that this approach is exhaustive, it does have a wide scope of coverage and a coherent organization.

Finally, our claim that the course systematically and progressively builds up a methodical approach to translation should not be taken to mean that we are offering a way of 'mechanizing' the process of translation by providing rules and recipes to be followed. On the contrary, we believe translation to be a highly creative activity in which the translator's personal responsibility is constantly to the forefront. We have, therefore, tried to emphasize throughout the need to recognize options and alternatives, the need for rational discussion, and the need for decision-making. All the material in the course – expository and practical alike – is intended not for silent consumption, but for animated discussion between students and between students and tutor. (In fact, we have found that many of the practicals are best done by students working in small groups.) Each chapter is, therefore, intended for tutor-student *discussion* at an early part of the corresponding practical; this is because we are not trying to inculcate this or that particular theory or method, but to foster the view that, whatever approach the translator adopts, the most important thing is that it should be self-aware and methodical.

While the course we are presenting is a progressively designed whole, it is divided into a series of successive units intended to fit into an academic timetable. Each unit consists of a chapter outlining a set of related notions and problems, and an accompanying practical in which students are given a concrete translation task, working on material to which the notions and problems outlined in the chapter are particularly relevant. The first fifteen units are designed to be studied progressively, in numerical order. There are, however, four further units, which can be studied (preferably in the order given) at whatever points in the course seem most appropriate to local conditions. These are Chapters 16–19, devoted to four different 'contrastive linguistic' topics. In these four cases, the amount of expository material varies from chapter to chapter; in some, the chapter consists almost entirely of practical exercises.

With the exception of some of Chapters 16–19, each unit needs between 90 minutes' and two hours' class time, and students are also required to prepare in advance for class discussion of the chapter. It is important that each student should have the necessary reference books in class: a monolingual French dictionary, a French–English/English–French dictionary, an English dictionary and an English thesaurus. Some of the practical work will be done at home – sometimes individually, sometimes in groups – and handed in for assessment by the tutor. How often this is done will depend on local conditions; we have found that once a fortnight works well. When an exercise is done at home, this implies that some time should be devoted in the following class to discussion of the issues raised. (Fuller suggestions for teaching and assessment can be found in the *Teachers' Handbook*.)

From consideration of the progressive overall structure of the course and its modular arrangement, it is easy to see how versions of the same course outline can be designed for languages other than French. With the exception of the contrastive topics in Chapters 16–19 (which, for another language, would need to be replaced by different contrastive topics that loom large for that language), adapting the course involves the provision of illustrative material for each chapter and of suitable texts for the practicals. We outline below a suggested format of courses for German and Spanish. A version of both these courses is currently taught at the University of St Andrews. For the preparation of the German course outline, we are indebted to Dr J. M. Loughridge, Department of German, University of St Andrews. We are similarly indebted to Dr C. Davies and to Mr B. P. E. Bentley, both of the Department of Spanish, University of St Andrews, for their collaboration in devising the Spanish course outline.

N.B. (1) A number of the practicals in the course involve work on texts that are not contained in the present volume, but intended for distribution in class. These texts are found in S. Hervey and I. Higgins, *Thinking Translation: Teachers' Handbook* (Routledge, 1992), which can be obtained from the addresses given on the opening page of this book. (2) The oral texts for use in practicals are available on a cassette: S. Hervey and I. Higgins, *Thinking Translation: Oral Texts*, which can also be obtained from the addresses given on the opening page.

OUTLINE OF GERMAN COURSE

Practical 1

1.1 Intralingual translation
Genesis 3, v. 1–10, *The Holy Bible*, Authorized Version.

1.2 Gist translation
500-word extract from a news report in a German newspaper.

Practical 2

2.1 Strategic decisions and decisions of detail; translation loss
Binding, R. 1954. 'Unsterblichkeit' from *Gesammeltes Werk, Band I.*
  Hamburg: Hans Dulk, pp. 168–9.

2.2 Speed translation
500-word newspaper article in German to be converted into 300-word
  English article.

Practical 3

3 Cultural transposition; compensation
Hofmannsthal, H. von. 1975. 'Das Dorf im Gebirge, II' from *Sämt-*
  liche Werke XXVIII, Erzählungen 1. Frankfurt: Fischer Verlag,
  pp. 35–6.

Practical 4

4.1 The formal properties of texts; introduction to the analysis of TTs
Ryan, L. 1962. *Friedrich Hölderlin*, 2. Auflage, Stuttgart: J. B. Metzlersche
  Verlagsbuchhandlung, pp. 53–4.

4.2 Speed translation
Translation of 250-word German newspaper article.

Practical 5

5.1 The formal properties of texts
Andersch, A. 1971. 'Mit dem Chef nach Chenonceaux' from *Gesammelte*
  Erzählungen. Zürich: Diogenes Verlag AG, pp. 101–2.

5.2 The formal properties of texts
Mann, Th. 1954. *Der Tod in Venedig*. Fischer-Bücherei, Frankfurt:
  Lizenzausgabe des S. Fischer Verlages, pp. 15–16.

Practical 6

6.1   The formal properties of texts
Brecht, B. 'Großer Dankchoral' from *Gedichte I.* Frankfurt: Suhrkamp Verlag, p. 77.

6.2   The formal properties of texts
Mann, Th. 1954. *Der Tod in Venedig.* Fischer-Bücherei, Frankfurt: Lizenzausgabe des S. Fischer Verlages, p. 55, lines 6–18.

6.3   The formal properties of texts
Liliencron, D. von. 1956. 'Der Blitzzug', (ed.) S. H. Steinberg. *Fifteen German Poets from Hölderlin to George.* London: Macmillan, pp. 165–6, stanzas 2–4.

Practical 7

7.1   Particularizing, generalizing and partially overlapping translation
Mann, Th. 1954. *Der Tod in Venedig.* Fischer-Bücherei, Frankfurt: Lizenzausgabe des S. Fischer Verlages, pp. 17–18.
Mann, Th. 1983. *Death in Venice.* H. T. Lowe-Porter (trans.), Harmondsworth: Penguin, pp. 17–18.

7.2   Speed translation
Translation of 250-word German newspaper article.

Practical 8

8.1   Connotative meaning
Brecht, B. 1958. 'Vom armen BB' from *Gedichte und Lieder.* Frankfurt: Suhrkamp Verlag, pp. 8–9.

8.2   Connotative meaning
Carossa, H. 1977. 'Alter Baum im Sonnenaufgang', (ed.) K. O. Conrady. *Das Große Deutsche Gedichtbuch* Kronberg/Ts: Athenäum-Verlag, p. 675.

Practical 9

9.1   Language variety: dialect and sociolect
'Die Linde', *Deutsche Dialekte*, Inter Nationes, Bonn (Kultureller Tonbanddienst), pp. 24–5.

9.2   Language variety: dialect and sociolect
'Tabakspflanzen', *Deutsche Dialekte*, Inter Nationes, Bonn (Kultureller Tonbanddienst), pp. 25–6.

Practical 10

10.1 Language variety: social register and tonal register
Lampe, F. 1953. *Eduard: eine kleine Formenfibel*, (ed.) L. Forster, *German Tales of our Time*, London: Harrap, pp. 107–10.

10.2 Language variety
Zuckmayer, C. 1962. *Des Teufels General*. London: Harrap, pp. 188–91.

Practical 11

11.1 Genre
'Wort der Bischöfe', *Amtsblatt des Erzbistums Köln*, 15.9.1980.

11.2 Genre: crossover between oral and written genres
Brecht, B. 1988. 'Die Seeräuberjenny' from *Gedichte I*. Frankfurt: Suhrkamp Verlag, pp. 135–6.
'Die Seeräuberjenny', sung by Lotte Lenya, music by Kurt Weill, *Die Dreigroschenoper* (conductor Wilhelm Brückner-Rüggeberg), CBS 72991 (CBS 77268), 1972, Side 2.

Practical 12

12.1 Subtitling
'Missedainen', *Deutsche Dialekte*, Inter Nationes, Bonn (Kultureller Tonbanddienst), pp. 88–90.

12.2 Speed translation
Zuckmayer, C. 1960. *Der Hauptmann von Köpenick, Gesammelte Werke*, Vol. III. Frankfurt: Fischer Verlag, pp. 302–3.

Practical 13

13.1 Technical Translation
Stackelberg, M. von. 1934. 'Die Struktur einer Reihe von Karbiden' from *Die Bauprinzipien der Karbide*, Z. Phys. Chem B., Vol. 27, p. 56.

Practical 14

14.1 Consumer-oriented texts
'Kräuterrührei' from 'Was Essen Wir Heute?', *Brigitte, Rezept-Sonderheft* (1979). Hamburg: Verlag Gruner und Jahr, p. 69.

14.2 Consumer-oriented texts
'Scheiterhaufen' from 'Was Essen Wir Heute?', *Brigitte, Rezept-Sonderheft* (1979). Hamburg: Verlag Gruner und Jahr, p. 69.

14.3   Consumer-oriented texts
'Verbundfahren mit Fahrschein', information leaflet produced by the Frankfurter Verkehrs- und Tarifverbund, 1975.

Practical 15

15.1   Stylistic editing
Musil, R. 1957. 'Grigia' from *Sämtliche Erzählungen*. Hamburg: Rowohlt, p. 225 (rough TT produced for editing purposes by course tutor).

Suggested 'contrastive topics' German–English:

Contrastive Topic 1
Problems of translating German modal particles.

Contrastive Topic 2
Translation problems related to flexible word order in German predicative clauses.

Contrastive Topic 3
Problems of translating German verbal constructions: verbs with separable and inseparable prefixes.

Contrastive Topic 4
Translation problems related to German modal verbs.

OUTLINE OF SPANISH COURSE

Practical 1

1.1   Intralingual translation
Genesis 3, vv. 1–10, *The Holy Bible*, Authorized Version.

1.2   Gist translation
500-word extract from an editorial in a Spanish newspaper.

Practical 2

2.1   Strategic decisions and decisions of detail; translation loss
Cortázar, J. 1976. 'Estación de la mano', *Los relatos: juegos*, Madrid: Alianza Editorial, pp. 57–8.

2.2   Speed translation
500-word newspaper article in Spanish to be converted into 300-word English article.

Practical 3

3   Cultural transposition; compensation
Castro, A. 1954. *La realidad histórica de España*. Mexico: Editorial Porrúa, pp. 131–4.

Practical 4

4.1   The formal properties of texts; introduction to the analysis of TTs
Aznar, J. C. 1974. 'La paradoja de la incomprensión y de la aceptación' from *Filosofía del arte*, Madrid: (Colección Austral) Espasa-Calpe, pp. 190–1.

4.2   Speed translation
Translation of 250-word Spanish newspaper article.

Practical 5

5.1   The formal properties of texts
Martín-Santos, L. 1961. *Tiempo de silencio*. Barcelona: Seix Barral, pp. 104–6.

5.2   The formal properties of texts
Fagoaga, C. y Saavedra, P. 1986. *Clara Campoamor*. Madrid: Ministerio de Cultura, pp. 108–10.

Practical 6

6.1   The formal properties of texts
Goytisolo, J. 1985. *Reivindicación del conde don Julián*. Barcelona: Seix Barral, pp. 194–5.

6.2   The formal properties of texts: graphic form
Fuertes, G. 1983. *Plumilindo (El cisne que quería ser pato)*. Madrid: (Colección infantil y juvenil) Editorial Escuela Española, p. 44.

6.3   The formal properties of texts
Huidobro, V. 1964. 'La golondrina', *Obras completas*, (ed.) B. Arenas, Santiago de Chile: Zig-Zag, p. 398.

Practical 7

7.1   Particularizing, generalizing and partially overlapping translation
Teresa de Jesús, *Libro de su vida*, in *Obras completas*, (ed.) Fr. Tomás de la Cruz, C. D. 1982. Burgos: (Archivo Silveriano Vol. 1), Editorial Monte Carmelo, 3rd rev. ed., pp. 5–7.

The Life of Saint Teresa of Avila by Herself, J. M. Cohen (trans.) 1957. Harmondsworth: Penguin, pp. 23–5.

7.2   Speed translation
Translation of 250-word Spanish newspaper article.

Practical 8

8.1   Connotative meaning
García Lorca, F. 1973. *Yerma*. Madrid: (Colección Austral) Espasa-Calpe, pp. 204–6.

8.2   Connotative meaning
García Lorca, F. 1979. 'Romance de la guardia civil española' from *Romancero gitano*. Buenos Aires: Losada, p. 91.

Practical 9

9   Language variety: dialect and sociolect
Alvar, M. 1960. *Textos hispánicos dialectales (antología histórica)*, Vol. II, Anejo 73 de la *Revista de Filología Española*. Madrid.

Practical 10

10.1   Language variety: social register and tonal register
Sastre, A. 1987. *Escuadra hacia la muerta*. Madrid: Clásicos Castalia, pp. 72–3.

10.2   Language variety
Marín, F. M. 1977. *El comentario lingüístico*. Madrid: Ediciones Cátedra, pp. 52–3.

Practical 11

11.1   Genre
Hickey, L. 1977. *Usos y estilos del español moderno*. London: Harrap, pp. 30–1.

11.2   Genre: crossover between oral and written genres
'Granada', sung by José Carreras, *Carreras, Domingo, Pavarotti in Concert* (conductor Zubin Mehta), Decca 430 433–4, 1990, Side 1.
'Granada', sung by Harry Secombe (with the Wally Stott Orchestra), *At your request No.1*, Philips BBE 12236, 1958.

'Gracias a la vida', sung by Mercedes Sosa, *Mercedes Sosa en Argentina*, Philips 7589003, 1982, Side 1.

Practical 12

12.1 Subtitling
One-minute extract from *En Español; Materiales vídeo, Guía Didáctica*, 4, Dirección General de Cooperación Cultural: Arsenio E. Lope Huerta, Ministerio de Cultura, Madrid, 1988, Bloque 3, no. 36, pp. 24–5.

12.2 Speed translation
Vallejo, A. B. 1967. *Historia de una escalera*. London: University of London Press, pp. 18–22.

Practical 13

13 Technical translation
Hickey, L. 1977. *Usos y estilos del español moderno*. London: Harrap, pp. 127–8.

Practical 14

14.1 Consumer-oriented texts
Ortega, S. 1985. 'Tortilla de patatas a la española', *1080 Recetas de Cocina*. Madrid: Alianza, p. 303.

14.2 Consumer-oriented texts
Balfour, S. 1982. *Business case studies: Spanish*. London: Longman, p. 18.

14.3 Consumer-oriented texts
Balfour, S. 1982. *Business case studies: Spanish*. London: Longman, p. 35.

Practical 15

15 Stylistic editing
Stylistic editing of Spanish tourist brochure.

Suggested 'contrastive topics' Spanish–English

Contrastive Topic 1
English passive constructions contrasted with Spanish passive reflexive.

Contrastive Topic 2
Problems of translating Spanish subjunctive in subordinate clauses.

Contrastive Topic 3
Problems of translating Spanish gerund and infinitive.

Contrastive Topic 4
Problems of translating Spanish prepositions.

1

Preliminaries to translation as a process

There are people who believe that skill in translation cannot be learned and, especially, cannot be taught. Behind this attitude is the assumption that some people are born with a gift of being good translators or interpreters, whereas others simply do not have the knack; in other words, skill in translation is a talent: either you've got it or you haven't.

To some extent, we would accept this view. It is doubtless true, for instance, that some people take to mathematics or physics, whereas others have little aptitude for such subjects, but are inclined towards the 'humanities'. There is no reason why things should be otherwise for translation; some are good at it, others find it difficult, just as some enjoy translating and others do not.

The twin assumption behind this book is that it will help its readers acquire proficiency in translation, and that we are addressing ourselves to people who do enjoy translating, even if they are not brilliant at it. Indeed, this element of enjoyment is a vital ingredient in acquiring proficiency as a translator. This, again, is normal – elements of enjoyment and job satisfaction play a vital role in any skilled activity that might be pursued as a career, from music to computer technology. Note, however, that when we talk of proficiency in translation we are no longer thinking merely of the basis of natural talent an individual may have, but of the skill and facility that require learning, technique, practice and experience. Ideally, translators should combine their natural talent with acquired skill. The answer to anyone who is sceptical about the formal teaching of translation is twofold: students with a gift for translation invariably find it useful in building their native talent into a fully-developed proficiency; students without a gift for translation invariably acquire some degree of proficiency.

Since this is a course on translation method, it introduces a number of technical terms and methodological notions bordering on the 'theoretical'.

(These are set in bold type when they are first explained in the text, and they are listed in the Glossary on pp. 247–54.) However, our aims are primarily methodological and practical rather than theoretical. In other words, we believe that methods and practices are best when underpinned by thoughtful consideration of a rationale behind them. This book is, therefore, only 'theoretical' to the extent that it encourages a thoughtful consideration of the rationale behind solutions to practical problems encountered in the process of translation or in evaluating translations as texts.

Throughout the course, our aim is to encourage students to make two sets of reasoned decisions. The first set are what we shall call **strategic decisions**. These are decisions which the translator makes before actually starting the translation, in response to such questions as 'what are the salient linguistic characteristics of this text?'; 'what are its principal effects?'; 'what genre does it belong to and what audience is it aimed at?'; 'what are the functions and intended audience of my translation?'; 'what are the implications of these factors?'; and 'which, among all such factors, are the ones that most need to be respected in translating this particular text?' The other set of decisions may be called **decisions of detail**. These are, of course, arrived at in the light of the strategic decisions, but they concern the specific problems of grammar, lexis, and so on, encountered in translating particular expressions in their particular context. We have found that students tend to start thinking about decisions of detail without realizing the crucial prior role of strategic decisions. This is why, in the practicals, students will usually be asked first to discuss the strategic problems confronting the translator of a given text, and subsequently to discuss and explain the decisions of detail they have made in translating it.

TRANSLATION AS A PROCESS

The aim of this preliminary chapter is to look at translation as a process – that is, to examine carefully what it is that a translator actually does. Before we do this, however, we should note a few basic terms that will be used throughout the course. Defining these now will clarify and simplify further discussion:

Text Any given stretch of speech or writing produced in a given language and assumed to make a coherent whole. A minimal text may consists of a single word – for example, 'Zut!' – preceded and followed by a period of silence. A maximal text may run into volumes – for example, Proust's *A la recherche du temps perdu*.

Source language (SL) The language in which the text requiring translation is couched.

Target language (TL)   The language into which the original text is to be translated.

Source text (ST)   The text requiring translation.

Target text (TT)   The text which is a translation of the ST.

With these terms in mind, the translation process can, in crude terms, be broken down into two types of activity: understanding a ST and formulating a TT. These two types of process do not occur successively, but simultaneously; in fact, one may not even realize that one has imperfectly understood the ST until one comes up against a problem in formulating or evaluating a TT. In such a case, one may need to go back to square one, so as to reinterpret and reconstrue the ST in the light of one's new understanding of it. In this way, ST interpretation and TT formulation go hand in hand. Nevertheless, for the purposes of discussion, it is useful to think of them as different, mutually separable, processes.

The component processes of translation are not qualitatively different from certain ordinary and familiar processes that all speakers perform every day. For a start, comprehension and interpretation are commonplace processes that we all perform whenever we listen to or read a piece of linguistically imparted information. The act of understanding even the simplest message potentially involves all the beliefs, suppositions, inferences and expectations that are the stuff of personal, social and cultural life. Understanding everyday messages is therefore not all that different from what a translator must do when first confronting a ST – and it is certainly no less complicated. It is, however, true that messages may be understood with varying degrees of precision. For instance, suppose that a mother asked her son to get the blue biro from the top left-hand drawer of the bureau, and he responded by giving her a black biro that happened to be handy. She would be justified in thinking that he had not understood the message fully, as he had evidently not paid attention to a number of details in it. Yet he could not be accused of total lack of comprehension, because he did register and retain the one salient fact that he had been asked for a biro.

In everyday communication, evidence that a message has been understood may come from appropriate practical response. Another indication of how precisely a message has been understood is appropriate *linguistic* response. Appropriate linguistic response includes such simple things as returning a correct greeting, giving a satisfactory answer to a question, or filling in a form. While none of these are translation-like processes, they do show that the comprehension and interpretation stage of the translation process involves what can be a perfectly ordinary, everyday activity requiring no special skill or power of intellect, only an average native command of the language used.

There is, however, another kind of ordinary, everyday linguistic response that *is* rather similar to translation proper. Here is a commonplace example:

BOY   Ask your Dad if I can take you to the disco tonight.
GIRL   O.K. (*Exit to find her father*)
GIRL   (*to father*) Dad, there's a disco on at the Y.M.C.A. tonight. Can I go?
DAD   Just a minute. Who's taking you?
GIRL   Guess who.
DAD   Oh, I see. And what time does it start?
GIRL   Eight o'clock – and it finishes at midnight.
DAD   Right. If you make sure you get your homework done by seven and
       get what's-his-name to walk you home the moment the thing finishes,
       you can go. But I want you back here by 12.15 at the latest, and no
       messing around going to friends on the way, or whatever it is you lot
       get up to in the middle of the night. And you come right in and go to
       bed when you get home, is that clear? No hanging around at the door
       saying goodnight for hours on end.
GIRL   O.K., Dad. Thanks. (*Goes back to find* BOY)
BOY   Well, what did your Dad say?
GIRL   He says we can go as long as we're back by quarter past midnight and
       you behave yourself.

In this verbal exchange, the girl gives ample evidence of having understood
very precisely what her father has said. She does so, not by appropriate
practical response, or by making the appropriate reply, but by first
interpreting her father's words (including managing to read skilfully between
the lines), and then *reporting the gist* of her father's intended message *in her
own words*.

This twofold process is strongly reminiscent of translation proper.
Extracting a message (by comprehension and interpretation) from a given
form of words, and then re-expressing (by formulation and re-creation) the
contents of that message in a different form of words is what translators do.
We can even distinguish in the example between a ST (the words used by
Dad) and a TT (the girl's reply to 'what did your Dad say?'). The only
difference between this example and translation proper is that both ST and
TT are in English. We shall follow Jakobson in referring to the reporting or
rephrasing of a text in the same language as **intralingual translation**
(Jakobson 1971, pp. 260–6).

Jakobson also talks of **inter-semiotic translation** (ibid.). This is another
commonplace, everyday process, as can be shown in a banal example:

A   What does your watch say?
B   It says 'five past three'.

Of course, the watch does not actually *say* anything. The words 'five past
three' are just a verbal rendering of a message conveyed by the position of
the hands of the watch. Verbalizing this non-linguistic message is simply a

way of *translating*, not from one language to another, but from a non-linguistic communication system to a linguistic one. The common denominator between the two is that they are both 'semiotic systems' (that is, systems for communication), and Jakobson is right to call the process inter-semiotic translation. This is another reason, then, for arguing that everybody is a translator of a sort.

Another common process of interpretation similar to translation proper is an intra-linguistic process whereby one expands on a particular text and its contents. A good example would be an explanatory commentary on the Lord's Prayer, which might expand the message contained in the single phrase 'Our Father' to read as follows:

> When we pray, we should not pray by ourselves and only ourselves; prayer should always be a corporate activity (compare 'Wherever two or three of you are gathered together . . .'). This, we may say, is the significance of the word 'our': a first person plural inclusive pronoun.
>
> In using the word 'Father' Jesus is suggesting forcefully that one should not think of God as an abstraction, but as a person, and not as a distant, unapproachable one at that, but as a person having the attributes associated with a father-figure: head of the household, strict, caring, loving, provident, and so on.

This type of expository interpretation can, as here, easily develop into a full-scale textual exegesis that tries to analyse and explain the implications of a text (perhaps with the addition of cross-references, allusions, footnotes, and so on). This process may not tally with everyone's view of translation, but it does share some common features with translation proper: there is a ST which is subjected to comprehension and interpretation, and a TT which is the result of a creative reformulation of the ST.

The first and third examples above represent two extremes on a continuum of translation-like processes. At one end, the TT expresses only the gist of the ST message; we shall call this **gist translation**. At the other end, the TT is more wordy than the ST, explaining it and elaborating on it; we shall call this **exegetic translation**.

Half-way between these two extremes there is, in principle at least, a process that adds nothing to, and omits nothing from, the message content of the ST, while couching it in terms that are radically different from those of the ST. In *form of expression* ST and TT are quite different, but in *message content* they are as close as possible to one another. We shall call this ideal process **rephrasing**. Thus, we can say that 'Stop!' is a rephrasing of 'red traffic light', and 'I consumed a small quantity of alcohol approximately 60 minutes ago' is a rephrasing of 'I had a little drink about an hour ago'.

The attainability of ideally precise rephrasing is a question that will continue to occupy us in what follows. From the examples just cited, it is clear that this is a relative matter. 'Stop!' is perhaps a successful inter-semiotic rephrasing of 'red light' (but it omits the associations of danger and the law), while 'I consumed a small quantity of alcohol' is a distinctly less exact (intralingual) rephrasing of 'I had a little drink'. These examples illustrate what is surely a fundamental maxim of translation, namely that rephrasing never allows a *precise reproduction* of the message content of the ST, because of the very fact that the two forms of expression are different. We shall return to this in Chapter 2, in discussing the concept of translation loss.

So far, then, we have suggested that there are three basic types of translation-like process, defined according to the degree in which the TT abstracts from, adds to, or tries to reproduce faithfully, the details contained in the ST message.

It should be added that there are two important respects in which these three types of process are on an equal footing with one other, as well as with translation proper. First, they all require intelligence, mental effort and linguistic skill; there can be no substitute for a close knowledge of the subject matter of the ST, and a careful examination and analysis of its contents. Second, in all three cases, mastery of the TL is a prerequisite. It is salutary to remember that the majority of English mother-tongue applicants for translation posts in the European Commission fail *because of the poor quality of their English* (McCluskey, 1987, p. 17). In a translation course, TL competence needs as close attention as SL competence. There is, after all, not much point in people who do not have the skill to rephrase texts in their native language trying their hand at translation proper. Consequently, synopsis-writing, reported speech, intralingual rephrasing and exegesis are excellent exercises for a translator, because they develop one's technique in finding, and choosing between, alternative means of expressing a given message content. That is why the first exercise in this course is a piece of intralingual translation in English.

PRACTICAL 1

1.1 Intralingual translation

Assignment
  (i) Assess the purpose of the text given below.
 (ii) Recast the story in different words, adapting it for a specific purpose and a specific type of audience (define carefully what these are).
(iii) Discuss the textual changes you found it necessary to make, and the reasons for these alterations. (Do this by inserting into your TT a superscript note-number after each point you intend to discuss, and then discussing the points in order on a fresh sheet of paper.

Whenever you annotate your own TTs, this is the system you should use.)

Text

Now the serpent was more subtil than any beast of the field which the LORD God had made. And he said unto the woman, Yea, hath God said, Ye shall not eat of every tree in the garden?

And the woman said unto the serpent, We may eat of the fruit of the trees of the garden: 5

But of the fruit of the tree which is in the midst of the garden, God hath said, Ye shall not eat of it, neither shall ye touch it, lest ye die.

And the serpent said unto the woman, Ye shall not surely die:

For God doth know that in the day ye eat thereof, then your eyes shall be opened, and ye shall be as gods, knowing good and evil.   10

And when the woman saw that the tree was good for food, and that it was pleasant to the eyes, and a tree to be desired to make one wise, she took of the fruit thereof, and did eat, and gave also unto her husband with her; and he did eat.

And the eyes of them both were opened, and they knew that they were   15
naked; and they sewed fig leaves together, and made themselves aprons.

And they heard the voice of the LORD God walking in the garden in the cool of the day: and Adam and his wife hid themselves from the presence of the LORD God amongst the trees of the garden.

And the LORD God called unto Adam, and said unto him, Where art   20
thou?

And he said, I heard thy voice in the garden, and I was afraid, because I was naked; and I hid myself.

(Genesis 3, v. 1–10)

1.2 Gist translation

Assignment

You will be asked to produce a gist translation of a passage given to you in class by your tutor. The tutor will give you any necessary contextual information, and tell you how long you should take over the translation.

2

Preliminaries to translation as a product

As we saw in Chapter 1, translation can be viewed as a process. In this chapter, we shall view it as a product. Here, too, it is useful to examine two diametric opposites, in this case two opposed degrees of translation, showing extreme SL bias on the one hand and extreme TL bias on the other.

At the extreme of SL bias is **interlineal translation**, where the TT does not necessarily respect TL grammar, but has grammatical units corresponding to every grammatical unit of the ST. Interlineal translation is rare, and is normally only used in language teaching or in descriptive linguistics. Since it is of little practical use to us, we shall not, in fact, consider it, other than to note its position as the furthest degree of SL bias. Interlineal translation is actually an extreme form of the much more common **literal translation**, where the literal meaning of words is taken as if from the dictionary (that is, out of context), but TL grammar is respected. (Literal meaning will be discussed as such in Chapter 7.) For our purposes, we shall take literal translation as the practical extreme of SL bias.

At the extreme of TL bias is completely **free translation**, where there is only a global correspondence between the textual units of the ST and those of the TT. The following example contrasts a literal and a free translation of a stock conversation in Chinese between two people who have just been introduced:

Literal TT	Free TT
A Sir, are you well?	A How do you do?
B Are you well?	B Pleased to meet you.
A Sir comes from where?	A Do you come here often?
B I come from England.	B No, this is my first visit.
A How many persons in your family?	A Nice weather for the time of year.

	Literal TT		Free TT
B	Wife and five children. And you?	B	Yes, it's been quite warm lately.

The type of extreme freedom seen in the second version is known as **communicative translation**, which is defined as follows: where, in a given situation (like introducing oneself to a stranger), the ST uses a SL expression standard for that situation, the TT uses a TL expression standard for an equivalent target culture situation. This degree of freedom is no more to be recommended as general practice than interlineal translation. Communicative translation is, however, mandatory for many culturally conventional formulae that do not allow literal translation. Public notices, proverbs and conversational clichés illustrate this particularly clearly, as in:

Objets trouvés.	Lost property.
Faute de grives, on mange des merles.	Half a loaf is better than no bread.
Je vous en prie.	Don't mention it.

For further examples, see pp. 31–3 below.

Between the two extremes of literal translation and free rendering, one may imagine an infinite number of degrees, including some sort of ideal halfway point between the two. Whether this ideal is actually attainable is the question behind our discussion of 'equivalence' and 'translation loss' below. For the moment, we simply suggest that translation can usefully be judged on a parameter between the two polarities of extreme SL bias and extreme TL bias. The points on this parameter are schematized on the following diagram adapted from Newmark (1982, p. 39):

SL bias $\longleftarrow$ $\longrightarrow$ TL bias

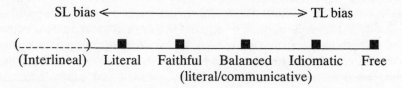

| (Interlineal) | Literal | Faithful | Balanced (literal/communicative) | Idiomatic | Free |

Between the literal and free extremes, the Chinese conversation given above might be rendered at the three intermediary points as follows:

Faithful TT	Balanced TT (literal/communicative)	Idiomatic TT
A Are you well?	A How do you do?	A How do you do?
B Are you well?	B How do you do?	B How do you do?

Faithful TT	Balanced TT (literal/communicative)	Idiomatic TT
A Where do you come from?	A Where are you from?	A Where are you from, then?
B I come from England.	B England.	B I'm English.
A How big a family do you have?	A Have you any family?	A Any family?
B A wife and five children. And yourself?	B Yes, a wife and five children. Have you?	B Wife and five kids. How about you?

EQUIVALENCE

In defining communicative translation, we used the term 'equivalent target culture situation'. Before going any further, we should make it clear what we mean – or rather, what we do not mean – by 'equivalence' and 'equivalent'.

The literature on translation studies has generated a lot of discussion of what is generally known as *the principle of equivalent effect*. In a nutshell, this principle stipulates that the TT should produce 'the same' effects on its audience as those produced by the ST on its original readers.

In so far as 'equivalence' is taken as a synonym of 'sameness', the concept runs into serious philosophical objections, which we will not go into here. The claim that ST and TT effects and features are 'equivalent' in the sense of 'the same' is in any case unhelpful and misleading for the purposes of translation methodology, for two main reasons.

First, the requirement that the TT should affect its recipients in the same way as the ST does (or did) its original audience raises the difficult problem of exactly how any one particular recipient responds to a text, and the extent to which texts have constant interpretations even for the same person on two different occasions. Before one could objectively assess textual effects, one would need to have recourse to a fairly detailed and exact theory of psychological effect, capable, among other things, of registering the aesthetic sensations that are often paramount in texts. Second, the principle of equivalent effect also presumes that the translator can know in advance what the effects of a TT will be on its intended audience. In the face of these problems, the temptation for translators is covertly to substitute their own subjective interpretation for the effects of the ST on recipients in general, and also for the effects of the TT on its intended audience.

It seems obvious, then, that if there is 'equivalence' here, it is not an *objective* equivalence, because the translator remains the final arbiter of the imagined effects of both the ST and the TT. Under these circumstances, even a relatively objective assessment of 'equivalent effect' is hard to envisage.

More fundamentally still, unlike intralingual translation, translation proper has the task of bridging the cultural gap between monolingual speakers of different languages. The backgrounds, shared knowledge, cultural assumptions and learnt responses of monolingual TL speakers are inevitably culture-bound. Given this fact, SL speakers' responses to the ST are never likely to be replicated exactly by effects on members of a different culture. Even a small cultural distance between the ST audience and the TT audience is bound to produce a *fundamental* dissimilarity between the effects of the ST and those of the TT – such effects can at best be similar in a global and limited sense; they can never be 'the same'.

To take a simple example. A translator who decides that the effect of a given ST is to make its audience laugh can replicate that effect by producing a TT that makes its audience laugh. However, claiming 'sameness' of effect here would only be at the expense of a gross reduction of the effects of a text to a single effect. In fact, of course, few texts can be attributed such a monolithic singleness of purpose, and as soon as a ST has multiple effects, it is unlikely that the TT will be able to replicate them all. (In any case, humour itself is a highly culture-bound phenomenon, which means that the cross-cultural equivalence of laughter itself is questionable.)

Another point one must query about the principle of objective equivalent effect concerns the requirement that the TT should replicate the effects of the ST on its *original* audience. This might conceivably be possible for a contemporary ST, but for a work of any appreciable age it may not be feasible, or even desirable. It may not be possible for the translator to determine how audiences responded to the ST when it was first produced. But even if one assumes that such effects can be determined, one is still faced with a dilemma: should the effects of the TT be matched to those of the ST on its *original* audience, or on a modern SL audience? The Voltaire extract set for gist translation in Practical 1 is a good example of these problems. Even if it were translated into the English of the 1730s, could one ever know if the TT produced the same effects on a twentieth-century English-speaking readership as the ST did on its eighteenth-century French readership? The choice is fraught with difficulties whatever one decides: on the one hand, the TT may be trivial without the effects it produced on its original audience; on the other, the original cultural importance of the ST may even be incomprehensible to a modern TL audience. For example, in the case of a play by Racine, most people in a seventeenth-century French audience would appreciate the rhetoric for its own sake, as well as the feelings expressed; but today, few playgoers in France – and still fewer in Britain – have enough knowledge of rhetoric to be able to appreciate it as Racine's original audiences must have done.

In short, we find the principle of equivalent effect, in so far as it implies 'sameness', too vague to be useful in a methodology of translation. At best, a TT produces a carefully fabricated approximation to some of the manifest properties of the ST. This means that a sound attitude to translation methodology should avoid an absolutist attempt to *discover sameness* in things that are crucially different (ST and TT), in favour of a relativist attempt to *minimize dissimilarities* between things that are clearly understood to be different. Once the latter approach is accepted, there is no objection to using the term 'equivalence' as a shorthand term for 'not dissimilar in relevant respects'. It is in this everyday sense of the word that we use it in this book.

TRANSLATION LOSS

Our position is best explained in terms of an analogy with engineering. All engineering is based on the admission that the transfer of energy in any mechanical device necessarily involves a certain degree of 'energy loss'. A machine that permits energy loss is not a theoretical anomaly in engineering: engineers are not puzzled as to why they have not achieved perpetual motion, and their attention is directed at trying to design machines with increased efficiency, by reducing energy loss. By analogy, believing in translation equivalence in the sense of 'sameness' encourages translators to believe in the elusive concept of a perfect translation, standing at the ideal half-way point between SL bias and TL bias. But it is much more realistic to start by admitting that the transfer of meaning from ST to TT necessarily involves a certain degree of **translation loss**; that is, a TT will always lack certain culturally relevant features that are present in the ST. Once one accepts the concept of inevitable translation loss, a TT that is not, in all important respects, a replica of its ST is not a theoretical anomaly, and the translator can concentrate on the realistic aim of cutting down on translation loss, rather than the unrealistic one of seeking *the* ultimate translation of the ST.

An important corollary of this concept of translation loss is that it embraces *any* failure to replicate a ST exactly, whether this involves *losing* features in the TT or *adding* them. For example, in rendering 'chapardeur' by 'light-fingered', an obvious translation loss is that the TT does not have the concision of the ST (even though there is a 'gain' in vividness), while rendering 'light-fingered' by 'chapardeur' entails an equally obvious translation loss, in that the TT does not have the vivid image of the ST (even though there is a 'gain' in directness and concision). Similarly, translating 'borgne' by 'blind in one eye' is an instance of translation loss, even though the TT is not only literally exact, but has 'gained' three words *and* makes explicit reference to blindness and eyes. A third example exhibits still more sorts of translation loss – the translation of 'capital transfer tax' by 'impôt sur le transfert des capitaux', and vice versa. The English is more concise, but its grammar is a potential source of ambiguities for a lay person; for instance, is this a transfer tax that is capital, or a tax that is a capital transfer, or a tax on transfers that are capital, or a tax on the transfer of capital? The grammar of the French expression eliminates all such ambiguity, but it is more cumbersome than the English. As these three examples show, translation loss, as we have defined it, is inevitable, even where the ST gains in, say, economy, vividness, or avoidance of ambiguity. The challenge to the translator is thus not to eliminate translation loss altogether, but to reduce it by deciding which of the relevant features in the ST it is most important to preserve, and which can most legitimately be sacrificed in preserving them.

Our approach assumes, then, that the translator is striving to reduce translation loss, to minimize difference rather than to maximize sameness. Once this approach is adopted, the culturally relevant features in the ST will tend to present themselves to the translator in a certain order. The most immediately obvious features which may prove impossible to preserve in a TT are 'cultural' in a very general sense, arising from the simple fact of transferring messages from one culture to another – references to the source culture's history, geography, literature, folklore, and so on. We shall, therefore, discuss such issues in the next chapter. The second step will be to analyse the objectively ostensible formal properties of the ST – syntax, lexis, and so on; we shall suggest a systematic framework for discussing these properties in Chapters 4–6. Subsequent ST features which will inevitably be lacking in any TT will have to do with nuances of literal or connotative meaning; yet others will stem from such aspects of language variety as dialect, sociolect and register. We shall be discussing literal and connotative meaning in Chapters 7 and 8 respectively, and the question of language variety in Chapters 9 and 10.

PRACTICAL 2

2.1 Strategic decisions and decisions of detail; translation loss

Assignment
  (i) Discuss the strategic problems confronting the translator of the following text, and outline your own strategy for translating it.
 (ii) Translate the text into English.
(iii) Explain the main decisions of detail you made in producing your TT, paying special attention to the question of translation loss.

Contextual information
The passage is from Jean Dutourd's *Au Bon Beurre* (1952), a satirical novel about the German Occupation of France in 1940–4. The passage begins

when the naïve Léon, a prisoner of war in Germany, having unintentionally escaped from captivity and survived for a week by stealing food and clothes, eventually finds himself in a crowded street in Hamburg.

Text

Une belle fille lui sourit. Le cœur de Lélé battit comme il n'avait pas battu dans les plus grands périls.

Elle était un peu grande, cette fille; son manteau de loutre élargissait singulièrement sa carrure. Avec ses chaussures à hauts talons, elle dépassait Lélé d'une demi-tête. Lélé pensa: 'C'est une walkyrie', et il 5
manœuvra pour s'approcher d'elle. La walkyrie sourit encore; le cœur de Lélé résonnait jusque dans ses oreilles.

– *Liebling*! murmura la walkyrie en le prenant sans façon par le bras. Léon défaillit presque quand il pénétra dans un petit studio situé au sommet d'une maison neuve de la Michaëlisstraße. Qu'allait-il 10
devenir? Léon était vierge, sans le sou, et ne parlait pas allemand. Le studio empestait le patchouli. La walkyrie enleva son manteau de fourrure et apparut dans une robe de jersey bleu. Lélé s'écria:

– Je suis Français!

Elle le regarda avec surprise et partit d'un rire un peu grave. 15

– *Man spricht französisch*! Prisonnier évadé tu es, je crois? dit-elle d'une voix de contralto extrêmement émouvante.

– *Ja wohl*! dit Lélé.

– Je devrais avoir douté, avec ton habit et barbe.

– Vous êtes très *schön*, dit Lélé en tremblant. Je n'ai jamais vu une 20
aussi belle *Fräulein*.

– Embrasse-moi, Français!

Jusqu'à ce moment, Lélé n'imaginait pas ce que c'était qu'un baiser. Celui qu'il reçut dura cent vingt secondes et lui causa les sensations les plus exaltantes. La femme qu'il serrait dans ses bras était ferme, dure, 25
bien musclée, quasi anguleuse; il ne concevait pas qu'on pût être plus séduisante. Cette bouche peinte, ces joues poudrées, ce cou de lutteur l'enflammaient. Il demanda:

– Comment vous appelez-vous?

– J'appelle Helmuth Krakenholz. 30

– Helmuth? dit Lélé, badin, ce n'est pas un nom de femme.

– Aussi femme je ne suis pas, mais *Oberleutnant* dans la Luftwaffe.

– Quoi, dit Léon, subitement glacé, vous êtes un homme?

– Oui, mais une âme tendre et mélancolique j'ai, comme une dame. J'aime militaires, même militaires français. 35

Reprinted by kind permission from Dutourd, J., *Au Bon Beurre* (Paris: Gallimard, Coll. Folio, 1972), copyright © Editions GALLIMARD.

2.2   Speed translation

Assignment
You will be asked to produce a 300-word newspaper article in English based
on a 380-word French ST given to you in class by your tutor. The tutor will
tell you how long you have for the exercise. This assignment combines an
element of gist translation with an introduction to one of the main demands
made of professional translators: working under pressure and at speed.

Valkyrie. any one of the minor goddesses who conducted the slain from the battlefield to Valhalla

3

Cultural issues in translation; compromise and compensation

The first part of this chapter brings together, under a single heading, a number of issues directly connected with the fact that translating involves not just two languages, but a transfer from one culture to another. The second part looks at two related translation techniques necessitated by the transfer from one cultural mode of expression to another: compromise and compensation.

CULTURAL TRANSPOSITION

We shall use the general term **cultural transposition** as a cover-term for the various degrees of departure from literal translation that one may resort to in the process of transferring the contents of a ST into the context of a target culture. That is to say, the various kinds of cultural transposition we are about to discuss are all alternatives to a maximally SL-biased literal translation. Any degree of cultural transposition involves the choice of features indigenous to the TL and the target culture in preference to features with their roots in the source culture. The result is to minimize 'foreign' (that is, SL-specific) features in the TT, thereby to some extent 'naturalizing' it into the TL and its cultural setting.

The various degrees of cultural transposition can be visualized as points along a scale between the extremes of *exoticism* and *cultural transplantation*:

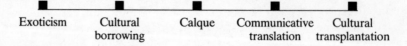

| Exoticism | Cultural borrowing | Calque | Communicative translation | Cultural transplantation |

Anvers = Antworp.

Some of the most straightforward examples of the basic issues in cultural transposition are offered by place-names and proper names. Translating names is not usually a major concern, but a brief look at the question provides a simple introduction to what are often complex problems.

Eng   French
Lyons   Lyon
Marseilles   Marseille

Translating names

In translating a name there are, in principle, at least two alternatives. Either the name can be taken over unchanged from the ST to the TT, or it can be adapted to conform to the phonic/graphic conventions of the TL. The first alternative is tantamount to literal translation, and involves no cultural transposition. It is a form of 'exoticism'. It may be impracticable if, as with Russian names, it creates problems of pronounceability and comprehension in an oral TT, or problems of spelling and memorization in a written one. The second alternative, **transliteration**, is less extreme: conversional conventions are used to alter the phonic/graphic shape of a ST name so that it comes more into line with TL patterns of pronunciation and spelling. Transliteration is the standard way of coping with, for example, Chinese names in English texts.

How a name is transliterated may be entirely up to the translator, if there is no established precedent for transcribing the name in question, or it may require following a standard transliteration created by earlier translators. Standard transliteration varies, of course, from language to language. Examples are common in the translation of place-names: 'Wien/Vienna/ Vienne'; 'Москва/Moscow/Moscou'; 'Livorno/Leghorn/Livourne', and so on.

Some names do not need transliteration, but have standard indigenous TL equivalents. For example, Flemish 'Luik' = French 'Liège' = German 'Lüttich'; French 'Saint Etienne' = English 'St Stephen' = Hungarian 'Szent István'. Where such conventional equivalents exist, the translator may feel constrained to use them. Not to do so would either display ignorance, or be interpreted as a significant stylistic choice. For example, deliberately using 'la Manche' instead of 'the Channel' in an English TT would be a form of exoticism, a stylistic device for drawing attention to the French origins of the text.

A further alternative in translating names is **cultural transplantation**. This is the extreme degree of cultural transposition. SL names are replaced by indigenous TL names that are not their literal equivalents, but have similar cultural connotations. For example, in the English translations of Hergé's Tintin books, 'Dupont et Dupond' have become 'Thompson and Thomson'. This ingenious cultural transplantation anglicizes the characters concerned, retains the connotation of commonness of the names, and reproduces the play on difference in spelling found in 'Dupont et Dupond'. Cultural transplantation of names is, however, a risky option. For example, if

Hergé's illustration showed two detectives called Thompson and Thomson having a drink at their local *brasserie*, the effect would be incongruous.

When translating names, one must, therefore, be aware of three things: first, existing options for translating a particular name; second, the implications of following a particular option (for example, if 'Sean Connery' were a character in a novel written in English, a French translator of the novel might want to alter the surname enough for it not to come across to the reader as the vulgar 'connerie'); and third, all the implications of a choice between exoticism, transliteration and cultural transplantation.

We will now look at issues raised by the various degrees of cultural transposition in more complex units than names.

Exoticism — keeping local colour

In general, the extreme options in signalling cultural foreignness in a TT fall into the category of **exoticism**. A TT translated in an exotic manner is one which constantly resorts to linguistic and cultural features imported from the ST into the TT with minimal adaptation, and which, thereby, constantly signals the exotic source culture and its cultural strangeness. Of course, this may be one of the TT's chief attractions, as with some translations of Icelandic sagas or Arabic poetry that deliberately trade on exoticism. However, such a TT has an impact on TL audiences which the ST could never have had on a SL audience, for whom the text has no features of an alien culture.

Cultural transplantation

At the opposite end of the scale from exoticism is cultural transplantation, whose extreme forms are hardly translations at all, but more like adaptations – the wholesale transplanting of the entire setting of the ST, resulting in the text being completely rewritten in an indigenous target culture setting. Examples include Craig Raine's *'1953'* (a transplantation of Racine's *Andromaque* into a Rome where Angus LeSkye, claimant to the British throne, is held captive after Britain's defeat by the Axis) and the transplantation of Rostand's *Cyrano de Bergerac* into the film *Roxanne*. As these examples show, cultural transplantation on this scale can produce successful texts, but it is not normal translation practice. However, on certain points of detail – as long as they do not have knock-on effects that make the TT incongruous – cultural transplantation may be considered as a serious option; a successful recent example is Siân Reynolds's translation of Louis Pergaud's 'L'argument décisif' which is set in the Franche-Comté, into a *Huckleberry Finn* idiom (Cross, 1988, pp. 286–7).

By and large, normal translation practice avoids both wholesale exoticism and wholesale cultural transplantation. In attempting to avoid the two

Leitmotiv – element that recurs.

extremes, the translator may have to consider the alternatives lying between them on the scale given on p. 28.

Using word this is cultural borrowing

Cultural borrowing

Bildungs Roman – protagonist learns sth about him/herself.

eg. Germinal

The first alternative is to transfer a ST expression verbatim into the TT. This is termed **cultural borrowing**. The translator will resort to it when it proves impossible to find a suitable TL expression of indigenous origins for translating the ST expression. '*Weltanschauung*' is an example: first attested in English in 1868, it is defined in the OED as 'a philosophy of life; a conception of the world'. A vital condition for cultural borrowing is that the textual context of the TT should make the meaning of the borrowed expression clear. Cultural borrowing will be most frequent in texts on history or social or political matters, where the simplest solution is to give a definition of terms like 'taille', 'département' or pre-Revolution 'parlement', and then to use the SL word in the TT.

Of course, cultural borrowing only presents translators with an open and free choice in cases where previous translation practice has not already set up a precedent for the verbatim borrowing of the ST expression. The Saussurean linguistic terms '*langue*' and '*parole*' are good examples of this issue. The option of translating 'langue' and 'parole' as 'language' and 'speaking' does exist, but the fact that English texts frequently resort to the borrowed terms '*langue*' and '*parole*' in the precise linguistic sense prejudices the issue in favour of borrowing. Furthermore, where terms with SL origins have already passed into the TL without significant change of meaning, thus constituting standard conventional equivalents of the original SL terms borrowed, the translator may not be faced with a significant decision at all. So, for example, such expressions as '*joie de vivre*', '*savoir-faire*', 'sauerkraut', 'totem', or 'taboo' can be treated as standard conventional equivalents of the corresponding foreign expressions. Unless special considerations of style can be invoked, there is little reason not to render such terms verbatim in an English TT. On occasion it may even seem perverse not to do so.

Communicative translation

chien méchant – Beware of the dog.

Idiomatic.

In contrast with cultural borrowing, the translator may opt for communicative translation. As we saw briefly in Chapter 2 (p. 21), this is often mandatory for culturally conventional formulae where a literal rendering would be inappropriate.

For example, many proverbs, idioms and clichés have readily identifiable communicative equivalents in the TL. Only special contextual reasons can justify opting against a standard communicative translation in such cases. Otherwise the result is likely to be ludicrous translationese, as in the deliberately comic rendering of the exclamation 'I say' by 'Je dis' in *Astérix chez les Bretons* (Goscinny and Uderzo, 1966, *pass*.). The translator has virtually no freedom of choice in rendering stock institutionalized phrases like the following: 'Chien méchant/Beware of the dog/Vorsicht, bissiger Hund'; 'Sens interdit/No entry/Keine Einfahrt'; 'Légitime défense/Self-defence/Notwehr'. Similarly, only for reasons of blatant exoticism, or (again) for special contextual reasons, could one avoid a communicative translation of 'une hirondelle ne fait pas le printemps' as 'one swallow doesn't make a summer', or of 'vieux comme le Pont-Neuf' as 'as old as the hills'. The very fact that the ST uses a set phrase or idiom is usually part and parcel of its stylistic effect, and if the TT does not use corresponding TL set phrases or idioms this stylistic effect will be lost.

However, it often happens that set phrases in the ST do not have identifiable communicative TL equivalents. In such cases, the translator has a genuine choice between a literal rendering and some kind of communicative translation. Assuming that a communicative translation is appropriate in the context, it can only be achieved by rendering the situational impact of the phrase in question with a TT expression that is not a cliché but is nevertheless plausible in the context defined by the TT. An example of this choice and its implications can be drawn from translating a Hungarian ST into English. (We choose Hungarian because it is unfamiliar to most readers, and therefore capable of giving a genuinely exotic impression.) Waking on the first morning of the holiday, the children are disappointed to find that it is raining heavily. Their mother comforts them with a proverb, suggesting that it will soon clear up: 'Nem baj! Reggeli vendég nem maradandó.' Compare these three translations of her words:

Literal 'Never mind! The morning guest never stays long.'

Communicative equivalent 'Never mind! Sun before seven, rain before eleven.'

Communicative paraphrase 'Never mind! It'll soon stop raining.'

The only possible advantage of the literal translation is its exoticism, but this advantage is cancelled by two things: the obscurity of the TT, and the lack of contextual plausibility. If there were good reason for preserving the exoticism, one could mitigate these disadvantages by obliquely signalling in the TT that the mother is using what is, for TL readers, an exotic proverb: 'Never mind! You know the saying: the morning guest never stays long.'

The communicative equivalent has the advantage of rendering proverb for proverb. However, in the circumstances, the communicative equivalent is incongruous – what the context requires is 'rain before seven, sun before eleven', but this is not the form of the English proverb.

The communicative paraphrase has the advantage of being idiomatic and plausible in the TT – it is the kind of thing the children's mother might plausibly say in English in the situation. It has the disadvantage of losing the stylistic flavour of 'speaking in proverbs' (which might be an important feature of the way the mother speaks).

Which solution is deemed best will naturally depend on contextual factors outside the scope of this example. Nevertheless, the example illustrates very well the alternatives in cultural transposition, including the one we have yet to discuss, namely calque.

Calque   *cultural borrowing*
to trace

'The morning guest never stays long' is an instance of **calque**, an expression that consists of TL words and respects TL syntax, but is unidiomatic in the TL because it is modelled on the structure of a SL expression. In essence, then, calque is a form of literal translation. A bad calque imitates ST structure to the point of being ungrammatical in the TL; a good calque manages to compromise between imitating a ST structure and not offending against the grammar of the TL.

Calquing may also be called a form of cultural borrowing, although, instead of verbatim borrowing of expressions, only the model of SL grammatical structures is borrowed. For example, if ST 'cherchez la femme' in a detective story is rendered in the TT as *'cherchez la femme'*, that is cultural borrowing proper, whereas TT 'look for the woman' would be calque. Like cultural borrowing proper, and for similar reasons, translation by creating calques does occur in practice. Furthermore, as also happens with cultural borrowing proper, some originally calqued expressions become standard TL cultural equivalents of their SL origins. Examples are French 'poids mouche', calqued on English 'flyweight'; English 'world-view', calqued on German 'Weltanschauung' (also existing as a borrowing, as we have seen); French 'jardin d'enfants', calqued on German 'Kinder-garten'; and French-Canadian 'bienvenue' (in response to 'merci bien'), calqued on 'you're welcome'.

Clearly, there are certain dangers in using calque as a translation device. The major one is that the meaning of calqued phrases may not be clear in the TT. In the worst cases, calques are not even recognizable for what they are, but are merely puzzling to the reader or listener. This is why, in our Hungarian example, we suggested using a device like 'you know the saying' to signal the calquing process. But, of course, it is not sufficient for the TT to make it clear that a particular phrase is an intentional calque. The meaning of the calqued phrase must also be transparent in the TT context. The most successful calques need no explanation; less successful ones may need to be explained, perhaps in a footnote or a glossary.

Like all forms of cultural borrowing, calque exhibits a certain degree of exoticism, bringing into the TT the cultural foreignness and strangeness of the source culture. Consequently, it should generally be avoided in texts where exoticism is inappropriate, such as an instruction manual, whose prime function is to give clear and explicit information. In any text, one should also definitely avoid unintentional calquing resulting from too slavish a simulation of the grammatical structures of the ST. At best, such calques will give the TT an unidiomatic flavour, as in 'the some 500 pages of this novel', calqued on 'les quelque 500 pages de ce roman'. At worst, the TT may become effectively ungrammatical, as in 'do you feel a spirit of sculptor?', calqued on 'vous sentez-vous une âme de sculpteur?'.

In brief summary of the discussion so far: where standard communicative equivalents exist for a ST expression, the translator should give these first preference, unless there are particular reasons for not doing so. Where standard communicative equivalents are lacking, and also a particular ST concept is alien to the target culture, preference should be given to cultural borrowing, *unless* there are particular reasons against it.

The emphasis in the previous paragraph on solutions being preferable *unless* certain conditions militate against them draws attention to the need to balance one set of considerations against another. This is, indeed, a general feature of the translation process, and remarking on it in the context of a choice between literal translation, communicative translation, cultural transplantation and so on brings us to discussion of compromises made necessary by this feature.

COMPROMISE AND COMPENSATION

Throughout this course, it will be obvious that translation is fraught with compromise. Compromise in translation means reconciling oneself to the fact that, while one would like to do full justice to the 'richness' of the ST, one's final TT inevitably suffers from various translation losses. Often one allows these losses unhesitatingly. For instance, a translator of prose may without qualms sacrifice the phonic and prosodic properties of the ST in order to make its literal meaning perfectly clear, while a translator of verse may equally happily sacrifice much of the ST's literal meaning in order to achieve certain desired metric and phonic effects. These are just two examples of the many kinds of compromise translators make every day.

Compromise should be the result of *deliberate* decisions taken in the light not only of what latitudes are allowed by the SL and TL respectively, but also of all the factors that can play a determining role in translation: the nature of the ST, its relationship to SL audiences, the purpose of the TT, its putative audience, and so forth. Only then can the translator have a firm grasp of which aspects of the ST can be sacrificed with the least detriment to the effectiveness of the TT, both as a rendering of the ST and as a TL text in its own right. Much of the material of this book will in fact draw attention, in both principle and practice, to the different kinds of compromise suggested – perhaps even dictated – by different types of text.

The issue of undesirable, yet apparently inevitable, translation losses raises a special problem for the translator. The problem consists in knowing that the loss of certain features sacrificed in translation does have detrimental effects on the quality of the TT, but seeing no way of avoiding these unacceptable compromises. So, for instance, 'cake' is not an exact translation of the literal meaning of 'galette', and it also lacks the connotation of 'Epiphany', which is a feature of the French word. (The 'galette des Rois' is a special cake eaten on Twelfth Night.) Nevertheless, translating 'galette' as 'cake' may be an acceptable compromise if 'Epiphany' is thematically irrelevant in the ST. However, it is less acceptable if 'les Rois' is mentioned in the ST and the author seems to be deliberately trading on the association between 'galette' and 'les Rois'. And it is a quite unacceptable compromise if 'galette' is the sole means by which an important textual allusion is made to 'Epiphany'.

It is when faced with apparently inevitable, yet unacceptable, compromises that translators may feel the need to resort to techniques referred to as **compensation** – that is, techniques of making up for the loss of important ST features through replicating ST effects approximately in the TT by means other than those used in the ST. For methodological purposes it is useful to distinguish four different aspects of compensation (while remembering that they frequently occur together).

Compensation in kind

The first aspect we shall call **compensation in kind**. This refers to making up for one type of textual effect in the ST by another type in the TT. One area where compensation in kind is often needed is in the differences between French and English narrative tenses. The contrast between past historic and imperfect is the one that causes most problems (there are examples in the texts by Jean Dutourd, in Practical 2, and Simone de Beauvoir, in Practical 7). In the following extract from a text about a schoolteacher in the French Resistance, the contrast between past historic and perfect has a powerful effect that cannot be rendered by literal translation:

> Arrêtée avec un convoi d'enfants qu'elle accompagnait en Suisse, elle fut emprisonnée à Annemasse. Refusant l'offre d'être libérée sans les enfants, elle continua de leur prodiguer ses soins en prison.
>
> Quelques jours après la Libération, on <u>retrouva</u> son corps dans un charnier. <u>Elle a été</u> fusillée le 8 juillet 1944 à l'âge de 23 ans.
>
> <u>Elle fut</u> une militante exemplaire [. . .]

(Audisio, 1945, p. 57)

The use of the perfect tense in this passage is striking, for two reasons. First, one would have expected the pluperfect – she had been shot before her body was found. Second, the perfect contrasts vividly with the predominant past historic. The effect is greatly to increase the emotional charge, as if the writer is still reeling from the impact of this monstrous episode. The final past historic then brusquely distances us again, definitively separating the girl's life from the present – she is dead and gone and nothing can bring her back, however moved we still are by her fate.

The English tense system does not in itself permit the expressive power which this ST derives from the alternation of past historic and perfect. One way of overcoming this lack might be to compensate in kind, by translating the last two sentences thus: 'This girl was shot on 8 July 1944, at the age of 23. She was an exemplary *résistante*.' In this TT, the emotional impact of the ST's play on tenses is conveyed by three things. 'This girl' and the rhetorical comma stress her youth; and the use of '*résistante*' instead of 'activist' or 'militant' is a cultural borrowing which has a distancing effect, locating the event in a specific period of the past history of another country.

Compensation in kind can be further illustrated by three of its most typical forms. First, literal meanings in the ST may be compensated for by connotative meanings in the TT. In the following example from the subtitles of the film *Tirez sur le pianiste*, ST 'tu' explicitly denotes 'familiar addressee', while TT 'old man' connotes 'familiarity'; equally ST 'tutoyer' explicitly denotes the use of familiar address, while TT 'no formalities' connotes this by implication:

Monsieur Charlie, permets-moi de te tutoyer; Monsieur Charlie, tu vas mourir.	Charlie, old man, no formalities; Charlie, old man, I'm going to kill you.

Second, connotative meanings in the ST may be compensated for by literal meanings in the ST. Here is a simple example:

[La mer] ne sort jamais de ses bornes qu'un peu, met *elle-même* un frein à la fureur de ses flots. (Ponge, 1965, p. 66; Ponge's italics)	[The sea] never oversteps its bounds by much, and needs no God to help it bridle its wild waves.

The ST contains an allusion to Racine's *Athalie*: 'Celui qui met un frein à la fureur des flots/Sait aussi des méchants arrêter les complots'. To an English-speaking reader, the implicit reference to the Almighty would be lost if '*elle-même*' were translated by 'itself'. The loss of this connotation is compensated for by inserting the explicit reference to God. (We shall discuss literal and connotative meaning as such in Chapters 7 and 8.)

Third, where, for example, the humour of the ST hinges on the mutual incomprehension of speakers of different dialects, the TT may have to derive its humour from other sources, such as puns. Successful examples of this sort of compensation in kind abound in the Astérix books; compare, for instance, *Astérix en Corse* with *Astérix in Corsica*:

ABRARACOURCIX Eh bien, vous pourrez en constater les effets! Pour fêter l'anniversaire de Gergovie, nous allons attaquer le camp romain de Babaorum avant le dîner! Ça nous ouvrira l'appétit!
PLAINTCONTRIX Ouais!
BEAUFIX Bravo!
ALAMBIX L'ARVERNE Cha ch'est caujé!
LABELDECADIX (DE MASSILIA) Vé! C'est un peu bieng organise, cette fÂIte!
ALAMBIX Chette quoi?
LABELDECADIX Cette fÂIte! Effeu – ê – té –
ALAMBIX Ah! Chette fête!

LABELDECADIX Vouaye. Cette sÔterie si vous préférez.
(Goscinny and Uderzo, 1973, p. 11)

VITALSTATISTIX You'll soon notice its effects. We're going to attack the Roman camp of Totorum before dinner. A little punch-up by way of an aperitif.

INSTANTMIX Punch-up!
JELLIBABIX I'm pleased as punch!
WINESANSPIRIX THE ARVERNIAN That's the ticket!
DRINKLIKAFIX (FROM MASSILIA) Tickety-boo, eh?

WINESANSPIRIX Tickety what?
DRINKLIKAFIX This is what makes us tick.
WINESANSPIRIX Ah, punching Romans! They're the ticket!
DRINKLIKAFIX Not a bad punchline.
(Goscinny and Uderzo, 1980, p. 11)

Compensation in place

Compensation in place consists in making up for the loss of a particular effect found at a given place in the ST by re-creating a corresponding effect at an earlier or later place in the TT. A simple form of compensation in place may be that of compensating for an untranslatable pun in the ST by using a pun on another word at a different place in the TT, as in *Astérix the Gaul*:

Ton idée de les envoyer aux *fraises* n'est pas mal non plus . . . Ça nous fait des vacances aux *frais* de César!
(Goscinny and Uderzo, 1961, p. 32; our italics)

That was a *fruitful* suggestion of yours, sending them off after *strawberries*! We're having a nice holiday at Caesar's expense!
(Goscinny and Uderzo, 1969, p. 32; our italics)

Compensation in place is also needed in translating the following ST:

> Voilà ce que veulent dire les viriles acclamations de nos villes et de nos villages, purgés enfin de l'ennemi.

Here, the rhetoric is obviously reinforced by the alliteration and assonance, and by the phonetic resemblance of 'villes' and 'villages', which mirrors their semantic resemblance. This phonetic reinforcement cannot be precisely replicated in an English TT, because the key words do not alliterate and because 'towns' and 'villages' share no sound in common save the final [z]. The following TT attempts to compensate for this by using phonetic reinforcement in different places from the ST:

> This is what the cheering means, resounding through our towns and villages cleansed at last of the enemy.

Compensation by merging

The technique of **compensation by merging** is to condense ST features carried over a relatively long stretch of text (say, a complex phrase) into a relatively short stretch of the TT (say, a single word or a simple phrase). In some cases, compensation by merging is the only way to strike a balance between doing justice to the literal meaning of a piece of ST and constructing an idiomatic TT, as in this example:

> Le péché, *cette marque infamante qui désigne* la méchante, la damnée.

An accurate literal translation of the italicized words, such as 'that ignominious stigma/brand which designates' would be implausibly pompous. The semantic contents of the ST expression are accurately, and more idiomatically, rendered through compensation by merging:

> Sin, *which brands* a woman *as* evil, wicked and damned.

Another example is furnished by the title of an article on fire-containment in mines and its English translation:

> Amélioration des moyens de *fermeture des enceintes à confiner* en cas de *feux ou incendies*.

> Improvements in *stopping-off* methods used in the event of *fire*.

Two cases of compensation by merging are to be found in this example. First, the complex noun phrase 'fermeture des enceintes à confiner' could, in principle, be rendered with an English noun phrase: 'closure of the areas to be isolated'; but this would result in a clumsy, unidiomatic collocation: 'methods of closure of the areas to be isolated'. The semantic contents of the ST noun phrase are happily condensed into the appropriate technical term, the compound word 'stopping-off'. In the second case, the meanings of 'feux' ('small fires') and 'incendies' ('big fires') are merged into the meaning of the single word 'fire'; in a technical text like this one, a translation such as 'little fires or big fires/ones', or 'fires big and small', or 'fires and conflagrations/blazes' would be comically inappropriate or unidiomatic.

Compensation by splitting

Compensation by splitting may be resorted to, if the context allows, in cases where there is no single TL word that covers the same range of meaning as a given ST word. A simple example is furnished by the title of an article on lepidoptera, 'Les papillons', which has be to translated as 'Moths and butterflies' (or 'Butterflies and moths'). The following example is more complex, but no less typical:

> La poésie ne *comble* pas mais au contraire *approfondit* toujours davantage le manque et le tourment qui la suscitent.

For both 'comble' and 'approfondit', the context mobilizes more than one of their potential meanings. Their double direct object is the pair of abstract nouns, 'manque' and 'tourment'. If 'comble' were used *on its own* with these abstract direct objects, it would probably be taken in one of its regular figurative senses: 'to fill (a gap/lack)', 'to meet/satisfy (a need)'. If 'approfondit' were used on its own with these direct objects, it would probably be taken in its figurative sense of 'to go deeper/further into, to investigate (a problem/question)'. But the fact that *both* verbs are used, in *opposition* to one another, triggers their latent opposed concrete meanings: 'to fill up (a hole)' and 'to deepen (a hole)'. This in turn triggers the (barely) latent physical connotations of 'tourment'. The result is a concentrated sentence whose message is that poetry springs from an anguished spiritual/ intellectual need experienced as some kind of painful, physical void or wound, and that, far from meeting the need and soothing the pain, it makes them ever worse by digging further into them in its effort to understand and explain them. Unfortunately, for neither 'comble' nor 'approfondit' does there seem to be an English verb that will on its own convey the multiple meaning found here. One way of translating the sentence would therefore be to use compensation by splitting:

> Poetry does not *soothe or heal* the lack and the torment that prompt it, but *opens and probes* them ever more deeply.

In this TT, 'soothe' corresponds to the figurative sense in 'comble' of 'to meet/satisfy (a need)'; 'heal' implies the closing up of a wound, and corresponds to the concrete sense of 'to fill up (a hole)'; 'opens' corresponds to the concrete sense in 'approfondit' of 'to deepen (a hole)'; 'probes' corresponds to the figurative sense of 'to investigate further'. The medical connotations of 'soothe', 'heal' and 'probes' convey the physical dimension of the spiritual/intellectual lack and torment, while this context also confers on 'opens' the connotation of an open wound. As well as illustrating compensation by splitting, then, the TT is also an example of compensation in kind. We will not analyse this any further, because what is involved is the question of literal versus connotative meaning, and these questions are not addressed until Chapters 7 and 8. Suffice it to say that the TT exhibits the substitution of connotative meaning for literal meaning, and of one kind of connotative meaning for another.

These four types of compensation can, of course, take many different forms; and, as our last example suggests, it also often happens that a single case of compensation belongs to more than one category. Good examples of multiple compensation will be found in the texts set for analysis in Practical 3.

We conclude with a word of caution: while compensation exercises the translator's ingenuity, the effort it requires should not be wasted on textually unimportant features. The aim is to reduce some of the more undesirable translation losses that necessarily result from the fundamental structural and cultural differences between SL and TL.

PRACTICAL 3

3.1 Compensation

Assignment
 (i) Discuss the strategic problems confronting the translator of the following text, and outline your own strategy for translating it.
 (ii) Translate the text into English.
(iii) Explain the main decisions of detail you made in producing your TT.

Contextual information
The text, by Michel Caste, appeared in *Le Monde* on 24.12.1980, and refers to a price-war between bakers.

Text

MA MIE

Les boulangers qui vendent le pain à un franc ont certes du pain sur la
planche, disent leurs concurrents, mais à force de proposer leur baguette
pour une bouchée de pain et de n'avoir pour tout bénéfice que des
miettes, ils risquent fort de se retrouver bientôt au pain sec.   5

Pour une fois que ce n'est pas nous que l'on roule dans la farine et que
l'on fait marcher à la baguette, nous voudrions pourtant bien que ces
boulangers, pour avoir voulu nous faire manger notre pain blanc, ne se
retrouvent pas ensuite dans le pétrin.

Quoi qu'il en soit, nous leur devrons d'avoir, au moins pendant un 10
moment, pensé que la tartine pouvait ne pas toujours tomber du côté du
beurre, et, ne serait-ce que pour cela, nous avons envie d'embrasser ces
boulangers . . . comme du bon pain.

Reprinted by kind permission from *Le Monde*, 24.12.1980.

3.2   Cultural transposition; compensation

Assignment
Working in groups, analyse the various cases of cultural transposition and of
compensation in the following TT. Give your own version where you can
improve on the TT.

Contextual information
The poem is by Marc de Larreguy de Civrieux, who was killed in action in
1916. It is one of two satirical poems written by an ugly monkey in the
trenches of Argonne to a parrot in Paris. The soldiers are seen as
dehumanized by their experiences and thereby, ironically, more truly
human than armchair strategists and patriots in Paris. The poem is a
sarcastic attack on Maurice Barrès, with allusions to two books by him: *Sous
l'œil des barbares* and *Colette Baudoche*. Colette is a patriotic French girl in
German-occupied Alsace, who refuses to marry a German. The poem's
allusion to Bayard (d. 1524), the 'chevalier sans peur et sans reproche',
further satirizes Barrès's cult of the dead and the soil, these two things being
in his view the essence of *patrie*. Barrès was a right-wing jingoist, whose
sabre-rattling Germanophobia and predictions of early victory were given
daily space in the *Echo de Paris*. From 1914 to 1918, this newspaper was the
archetype of the fervour-whipping, conscience-salving ignorance (or
avoidance) of the facts of military life which outraged as many soldiers as it
reassured civilians. 'On les aura' (line 6) was a great patriotic slogan of the
War.

L'EPITRE AU PERROQUET

As-tu lu le journal, Jacko, mon vieux Jacko?
Il me semble aujourd'hui t'entendre qui jacasse
    — De la façon la plus cocasse —
    Tous les 'en-tête' rococos   5
    De la gazette de l''Echo':
'Crr . . . Crr . . . on les aurra . . . Crr . . . Rrr . . . Victoire prroche . . .'
    Et tu rêves que tu bamboches
    Avec quelques tripes de Boches!
    Te voici donc l''alter ego'   10
    De ton grand maître, l'Hidalgo,
    (Toujours 'sans peur et sans reproche')
    Qui — 'loin de l'œil des Wisigoths' —
    Ecrit, pour tous les bons gogos,
    Au nom de Maurice . . . Baudoche!   15
    Crois-le, je suis fier de connaître
    Un perroquet aussi savant
    Qui peut répéter à son Maître:
    'Nous les tenons!' et 'En avant!'
    Car nous, les Singes des grands Bois,   20
    Dans notre Argonne, loin des Hommes,
    Nous les oublions et nous sommes
    Bien plus sauvages qu'autrefois!
  'Le hareng toujours se sent dans la caque',
    A dit un bipède écrivain: 25
Vouloir imiter l'homme est ridicule et vain
A moins que l'on ne soit perroquet ou chauvin
. . . Et j'aime mieux rester:
                Ton fidèle
                    Macaque.

Target text

THE EPISTLE TO THE PARROT

Have you read the paper, little Jacko?
I seem to hear you jabbering away
     — In the comicallest way —
     With all the military rococo   5
     Of the headlines of the *Echo*:
'Crr . . . Over by Chrristmas . . . The Hun must pay . . .'
     And planning orgies of brioches
     With flour milled from bones of Boches!
     So there you are, in parrotry   10
     Mirror to your Matamore
     (E'er the Captain of necrolatry)
     Who, far from eye of Goth and Thor,
     For simpleton lays down the law,
     And signs the column Maurice Barr . . . atry!   15
     Believe you me, I'm proud to know
     So very clever a macaw,
     Who imitates his Master's crow
     And squawks: 'Stand fast! . . . Esprrit de corps!'
     — We forest monkeys never show   20
     Ourselves to men, out in Argonne;
     We have forgotten man, and gone
     More savage than you've ever known!
'Will out in the flesh what's bred in the bone',
     Any biped hack might echo: 25
To ape a man is to disgrace your own,
Unless you are a jingoist or Jacko.
So, warts and all,
           I'm faithfully
              Macaque.

3.3 Compensation

Assignment
Working in groups:

(i) Discuss the strategic problems confronting the translator of the following ST, and say what your own strategy would be.
(ii) In the light of your findings in (i), analyse the translation of the last paragraph (see p. 44), paying particular attention to compensation. Give your own version where you can improve on the TT.

Contextual information

The text is from Francis Ponge's *Le Parti pris des choses* (1942), in which the renderings of objects, plants and animals draw the reader's attention, through the challenge presented to expression by even the simplest description, both to the qualities of the thing described and to the nature of language. One of the ways Ponge does this is to create structural analogies between the thing described and the language used to describe it: inevitably, this brings out the irreducible, and tonic, *difference* between things, language and the human mind.

Source text

LES MURES

Aux buissons typographiques constitués par le poème sur une route qui ne mène hors des choses ni à l'esprit, certains fruits sont formés d'une agglomération de sphères qu'une goutte d'encre remplit.   5

*

Noirs, roses et kakis ensemble sur la grappe, ils offrent plutôt le spectacle d'une famille rogue à ses âges divers, qu'une tentation très vive à la cueillette.

Vue la disproportion des pépins à la pulpe les oiseaux les apprécient peu, si peu de chose au fond leur reste quand du bec à   10
l'anus ils en sont traversés.

*

Mais le poète au cours de sa promenade professionnelle, en prend de la graine à raison: 'Ainsi donc, se dit-il, réussissent en grand nombre les efforts patients d'une fleur très fragile quoique par un rébarbatif enchevêtrement de ronces défendue. Sans beaucoup 15
d'autres qualités — *mûres*, parfaitement elles sont mûres — comme aussi ce poème est fait.'

Target text

BLACKBERRIES (last paragraph)

But the poet, on his professional ramble, rightly picks an example and lets it bear seed in his mind: 'So it is,' he says to himself, 'that the patient efforts of a flower which, while defended by a rebarbative tangle of brambles, is very fragile, in great numbers succeed. Without many other qualities – black blackberries are ripe: exactly ripe blackberries are black – just as this poem is now exact.'

4

The formal properties of texts: intertextual, inter-sentential and sentential issues in translating

---

If one takes translation as a challenge, not to replicate a ST in the TL, but to reduce translation loss, the immediate problem that arises after the general cultural issues have been assessed is that of its objectively ostensible formal properties. There are, doubtless, problems in establishing what the ostensible properties of a text are, but it can at least be said that whatever effects, meanings and reactions are triggered by a text must originate from features objectively *present in it*. It is, therefore, necessary for the translator to look at the text as a linguistic object.

THE FORMAL PROPERTIES OF TEXTS

In trying to assess the formal properties of texts, one can usefully turn to some fundamental notions in linguistics. There is no need for a detailed incursion into linguistic theory, but linguistics does offer a hierarchically ordered series of systematically isolated and complementary *levels* on which the formal properties of texts can be discussed in a methodical way.

It is true of any text that there are various points on which it could have been otherwise. For instance, where there is an allusion to the Bible, there might have been a quotation from Shakespeare; or where there is a question mark there might have been an exclamation mark (compare 'Was he drinking?' and 'Was he drinking!'); or where the text has a letter 'c' there might have been a letter 'r' (compare 'It's cutting time for tea roses' and 'It's rutting time for tea-cosies'). All these points of detail where a text could have been different (that is, where it could have been *another* text) can be designated **textual variables**. It is these textual variables that the series of levels defined in linguistics makes it possible to identify.

Taking the linguistic levels one at a time has two main advantages. First, looking at textual variables on a series of isolated levels enables one to see which textual variables are important in the ST and which are less important. As we have seen, some ST features will inevitably fall prey to translation loss. It is, therefore, excellent strategy to decide which of the textual variables are indispensable, and which can be ignored, for the purpose of formulating a good TT. (In general, as we shall see, the more obvious a role a particular textual variable plays in triggering the effects and meanings of a text, the more important it is.)

Second, one can assess a TT, whether one's own or somebody else's, by isolating and comparing the formal variables of both ST and TT. This enables the translator to see precisely what textual variables of the ST are absent from the TT, and vice versa. That is, it is possible to make a precise accounting of translation loss on each level. This also permits a more self-aware and methodical way of reducing details of translation loss.

We propose six levels of textual variables, hierarchically arranged, in the sense that each level is, as it were, built on top of the following one. Naturally, other schemes could have been offered, but arguing about alternative frameworks would involve a deeper plunge into linguistic theory than is useful for our purposes. In this chapter and the next two, we shall work our way down through the levels, showing what kinds of textual variable can be found on each, and how they may function in a text. Together, the six levels constitute a kind of 'filter' through which the translator can pass a text to determine what levels and formal properties are important in it and most need to be respected in the TT. Surprising as it may seem at this early stage, this method does not imply a plodding or piecemeal approach to texts: applying this filter (and others) quickly becomes automatic and very effective. (A schematic representation of all the filters we are suggesting can be found on p. 246.)

THE INTERTEXTUAL LEVEL

The topmost level of textual variables is the **intertextual level**. On this level are considered the external relations a particular text bears to other texts within a given culture. No text exists in total isolation from other texts. Even an extremely innovative text cannot fail to form part of an overall body of literature by which the impact and originality of individual texts is coloured and defined. The originality of Joyce's *Ulysses*, for instance, is measured and defined by reference to a whole body of literature from Homer onwards, including the most unoriginal of works.

The inevitable relationship any text bears to its neighbours in the SL culture can cause translators notable problems. If the ST is an utterly 'average' specimen of an established SL genre, the translator may be obliged to produce a similarly unoriginal TT. Formulating a TT that is as unoriginal in the TL as the ST is in the SL has its own difficulties, obliging the translator to identify a TL genre that closely corresponds to the genre of the ST. Such correspondences are, at best, approximative, and may sometimes be non-existent. The same is true, *a fortiori*, of STs that are predominantly original. For instance, in terms of classical tragedy, Dryden may be as close an English counterpart to Racine as any, but in terms of prestige and common knowledge, a better counterpart would be Shakespeare. Similarly, there may be poetic and musical counterparts of Brassens and Brel in English – Jake Thackray? Neil Innes? Richard Stilgoe? – but there are none that enjoy the same popularity.

If the ST is stylistically innovative, it may be appropriate, where circumstances permit, to formulate a TT that is equally innovative in the SL. Alternatively, it may be necessary to allow the originality of the ST to be lost in translation, for example in the case of technical or scientific texts, where the subject matter and thematic content outweigh considerations of style. There are, however, academic texts (Jacques Lacan's writings, for instance) where the style and the thematic content together form an indissoluble whole. In such cases, translation cannot do justice to the ST without trying to re-create the innovative nature of the ST. Whatever the text, these are all matters for strategic evaluation and decision by the translator.

Texts are also in significant relationship with other texts if they directly invoke, by allusion or quotation, parts of other texts, such as Racine or the Bible. The quotation from Ponge on p. 36 is an example. The translator must always be on the look-out for such echoes. What to do with them depends on the circumstances. Some will simply necessitate finding the appropriate TL passages and invoking them in the TT (although in the case of the Bible or ancient classics, thought will have to be given to which version to choose). In other cases, allusion or quotation in the TT will have to refer explicitly to the SL passage invoked in the ST (rather as we added 'you know the saying' in the Hungarian example on p. 32). In yet other cases, the echoes are too abstruse or unimportant from the point of view of a TL audience to be worth building into the TT.

We shall return to the problem of allusion, with examples, on pp. 107–9.

Another significant mode of intertextuality is imitation. An entire text may be designed specifically as an imitation of another text or texts, as in pastiche or parody. Alternatively, sections of a text may deliberately imitate different texts or genres – an example is David Lodge's *The British Museum is Falling Down*, in which each chapter parodies a different author. Here, the overall effect is of a text contrived as a mixture of styles that recall the various genres from which they are copied. (We shall return to this question in Chapter 11.) This aspect of intertextuality has to be borne in mind, because there are STs that can only be fully appreciated if one is aware that they use the device of imitating other texts or genres. Furthermore, to re-create this device in the TT, the translator must be familiar with target culture genres, and have the skill to imitate them.

THE DISCOURSE LEVEL

We now move down a step, to the **discourse level**. The textual variables considered here are the features that distinguish a cohesive and coherent textual flow from a random sequence of unrelated sentences. This level is concerned both with relations between sentences and with relations between larger units: paragraphs, stanzas, chapters, volumes and so on.

To take the larger units first, there are some very basic and obvious textual variables whose function is to form parts of a text into clearly recognizable units, and to indicate something about how they relate to one another. Devices like titles, paragraphs, sub-sections, cross-references, and so on are typical examples.

Looking next at individual sentences in discourse reveals that there are also 'markers' whose main role is to give a text a transparent inter-sentential organization. Compare, for instance, these two texts:

> I was getting hungry. *So* I went downstairs. *Well* . . . I knew the kitchen was on the ground floor. *I mean*, I suspected *it* must be *there*. *Actually*, I don't know why I was so sure, but I was. *However*, I didn't expect to find *it* so easily. *Anyway*, I made myself a sandwich.

> I was getting hungry. *So* I went downstairs. *Well* . . . I knew the kitchen was on the ground floor. *I mean*, I suspected it must be *there*. *Actually*, I don't know why I was so sure, but I was. *However*, I didn't expect to find it so easily. *Anyway*, I made myself a sandwich.

The first text is so devoid of inter-sentential connectives that, if it hangs together at all – that is, if it is *cogent* at all – this is only thanks to the underlying chronological narrative structure. In the second text, however, a rational 'train of thought' is restored by filling in the discourse-connectives (in italics) missing from the first text, which act as markers of a transparent inter-sentential structure. Some of the markers are rather like illocutionary particles, while others are instances of **anaphora** – that is, the replacement of previously-used words and phrases by elements such as pronouns or adverbs that refer back to them; here, the anaphoric elements are 'it' (replacing 'the kitchen') and 'there' (replacing 'on the ground floor'). The place of these markers is in individual sentences, but their function would seem to be *outside* them – an inter-sentential function relating sentences to one another.

Cogency

The degree to which a text hangs together is known as its **cogency**. The considerable recent research into what it is that makes texts cogent suggests that there may be tacit, yet conventional, strategies and constraints that regulate cogency. If such strategies and constraints can indeed be isolated and found to vary from culture to culture (as they have been in the case of ritual greeting formulae), then this suggests that rational discourse is not a universal concept identical for all language-users in all communities, but a culture-specific concept. If this is the case, translators must be aware of two things.

First, the SL may have different standards of cogency from the TL. Second, what counts for normal, rational cogency in texts in one culture may give the appearance of lack of rational cogency or excessive fussiness to members of another culture, so that a TT that reproduced the discourse-structure of the ST, and did not reorganize it in the light of the TL, might appear stilted, poorly organized or over-marked to a TL audience. So, for instance, it is more common in French than in English for texts to be explicitly structured by the use of connectives ('or', 'donc', 'ainsi', 'en effet', and so on) that signpost the logical relationships between sentences. Consequently, an English TT that uses explicit connectives to reproduce all those found in a French TT is likely to seem tediously over-marked in discourse structure, and therefore stilted, pedantic or patronizing. This piece of dialogue is a simple example:

– On remarque ces qualités chez Hugo.
– C'est bien à Hugo que je pensais.

In an oral TT, this 'bien' would probably be rendered not with a connective, but by voice stress and intonation:

'You find these qualities in Hugo.'
'I was *thinking* of Hugo.'

In a *written* TT, one might well render 'bien' with a connective: 'I was indeed thinking of Hugo.' The decision will be heavily influenced by the genre of the ST – in a play or a novel, italics would probably be used rather than the connective; but in an academic text, or if the character in the play or novel were a pompous type, the connective would be more likely than the italics. As this example shows, one cannot lay down a rigid rule for translating connectives. Nevertheless, in the case of emphasis, one can say that English readily uses voice stress or italics where French tends to use some syntactic device, as in the sentence 'Ce n'est pas moi qui vais le ramasser': this would most likely be translated as '*I'm* not picking it up', not 'It's not me who's picking it up'. (Conversely, '*Je* ne vais pas le ramasser' would be very odd in French.) In respect of emphasis, this difference between French and English is observable even in quite formal written texts.

Cohesion and coherence

Halliday and Hasan (1976) offer a useful way of distinguishing two aspects of cogency in discourse: cohesion and coherence.

Cohesion refers to the transparent linking of sentences (and larger sections of text) by the use of explicit discourse connectives like 'then', 'so', 'however', and so on. If correctly used, these act as 'signposts' in following the thread of discourse running through the text. Discourse connectives need careful attention in translating, not just because they are more commonly used in some languages than in others, but because they can be *faux amis*. For instance, it is tempting to render 'en effet' by 'in effect', or by 'in fact' (usually a contrastive connective), whereas 'en effet' is usually a confirmatory connective, such as 'and indeed'. Here is an example:

– Vous n'étiez pas là hier?
– En effet, j'étais souffrant.

Here, 'En effet' would be well translated as 'that's right'.

As the example of going down to the kitchen suggested, another common way of signalling explicit cohesion is to use anaphora. It is clear from that example that not using anaphora can make for an absurdly stilted text. However, rules of anaphora differ from language to language. This implies that translators should follow the anaphoric norms of the TL, rather than slavishly reproducing ST anaphora. Translating from French, this is vividly illustrated by the anaphoric element 'dont'. For example, 'Le taxi était une vieille Renault dont le chauffeur était à moitié sourd' is better rendered as 'The taxi was an old Renault with a driver who was half deaf' than as 'The taxi was an old Renault whose driver was half deaf'; and 'ces ouvrages exigeants dont ils savent qu'ils ne les vendront pas' is better rendered as 'these demanding works which they know they will not sell' than as 'these demanding works about which they know they will not sell them'. Preserving the ST anaphora in such cases simply produces unidiomatic calques.

Coherence is a more difficult matter than cohesion, because it is, by definition, not explicitly marked in a text, but is rather a question of tacit, yet discernible, thematic development running through the text. Coherence is best illustrated by contrast with cohesion. Here, first, is an example of a *cohesive* text (units responsible for the explicit cohesion are italicized):

The oneness of the human species does not demand the arbitrary reduction of diversity to unity; *it* only *demands* that it should be possible to pass from one particularity to another, *and that* no effort should be spared in order to elaborate a common language in which each *particularity* can be adequately described.

If we systematically strip this text of all the units on which its explicitly marked cohesion rests, the resultant text, while no longer explicitly cohesive, nevertheless remains *coherent* in terms of its thematic development:

The oneness of the human species does not demand the arbitrary reduction of diversity to unity. All that is necessary is that it should be possible to pass from one particularity to another. No effort should be spared in order to elaborate a common language in which each individual experience can be adequately described.

While coherence is clearly culture-specific in some respects, it may also vary significantly according to subject matter or textual genre. The coherence of a TT has, by and large, to be judged in TL terms, and must not be ignored by the translator.

THE SENTENTIAL LEVEL

The third level of textual variables is the **sentential level**, on which sentences are considered. By 'sentence' we mean a particular type of linguistic unit that is a complete, self-contained and ready-made vehicle for actual communication: nothing more needs to be added to it before it can be uttered in concrete situations. So, for example, the starter's one-word command 'Go!' is a sentence. Words and phrases are mere abstractions from sentences, abstractions stripped of practical communicative purpose, intonation, and other features that make sentences genuine vehicles of linguistic utterance.

For the nature of the textual variables on the sentential level to be grasped, a distinction must be drawn between spoken and written texts, for spoken languages and written languages differ sharply on this level.

A spoken text counts on the sentential level as a sequence of sentences, each with a built-in communicative purpose conveyed by one or more such features as *intonation* (for example the rising pitch that signals a question in English and French); *sequential focus* (for example the word-order of 'Him I don't like', which shifts the emphasis onto the object of the sentence); or *illocutionary particles* (for example, the question-forming particle 'n'est-ce pas', or the particle 'hélas', which has the force of qualifying a statement as an expression of regret – in other words, an illocutionary particle tells the listener how to take an utterance). These features do not fit into syntax proper; their function, and 'meaning', consists in marking sentences for particular communicative purposes.

Thus a number of different sentences, marked for different purposes, can be created purely through intonation:

'The salt' (with falling intonation: *statement*)
'The salt' (with rising intonation: *question*)
'The salt' (with fall–rise intonation: *demand*)
'The salt' (with high, level intonation: *command*)

Similar effects can be achieved by a combination of intonation and other features of sentential function:

'That's the salt' (falling intonation: *statement*)
'Surely that's the salt' (illocutionary particle + fall–rise intonation: *question*)
'Is that the salt' (fall–rise intonation + inverted sequence: *question*)
'That's the salt, isn't it' (fall–rise intonation + illocutionary particle: *question*)
'The salt, please' (falling intonation + illocutionary particle: *request*)
'The salt, damn it' (fall–rise intonation + illocutionary particle: *peremptory command*)

The breakdown of a spoken text to its constituent sentences, as indicated by intonation contours, can be very significant in determining its impact in terms of practical communication. Compare, for instance:

'Yes, please pass the salt.' (with a single-sentence intonation)
'Yes. Please pass the salt.' (with a fall and a pause after 'yes')
'Yes, please. Pass the salt.' (with a rise on 'please' followed by a pause)
'Yes. Please. Pass the salt.' (uttered as three sentences)

As these examples suggest, the sentential level of oral languages is extremely rich, with fine shades of intonation distinguishing sentences with subtly different nuances. A lot of these refinements tend to disappear in written texts, as a result of the relatively impoverished sentential level in writing systems. Most notably, the only ways of conveying intonation in writing are punctuation and typography, which offer far fewer alternatives than the rich nuances of speech. Failing that, the writer has to fall back on explicit information about how the sentences are spoken, as in 'she exclaimed in surprise', 'she said angrily', and so on.

In translating both oral and written texts, then, the sentential level of language demands particular care. Fortunately, sequential focus and illocutionary particles can be represented in written texts, but they are often problematic all the same. For instance, the impact of 'bien' as an illocutionary particle in 'Je t'avais bien dit de rester chez toi' is not easily rendered in a written English TT; the translator must choose from various alternatives including 'I did *tell* you to stay at home', 'I *told* you to stay at home', and 'Didn't I *tell* you to stay at home?'. Even more difficult is how to convey the intonational nuancing of a TT sentence like 'I'm not picking it up', depending on which of the following STs it is meant to render:

'Je ne le ramasse pas' (with gradually falling intonation: *statement*).
'Je ne le ramasse pas' (with rising intonation: *question*).
'Ce n'est pas moi qui vais le ramasser' (with emphasis on 'moi': *belligerent statement*).
'Je ne le ramasse donc pas' (with emphasis on 'pas': *firm statement of intent*).
'Je ne vais tout de même pas le ramasser' (with emphasis on 'ramasser': *indignant statement of intent*).

Languages vary significantly in the sentence-marking features they possess and the way they use them. For example, there are no exact English counterparts to the French illocutionary particles 'n'est-ce pas' and 'donc', or the German illocutionary particle 'doch'; and there are differences between English, French and German punctuation.

Sentence markers are capable of self-conscious, patterned uses as devices contributing to the thematic development of the overall text in which they are distributed. For instance, a dialogue containing insistent recurrences of sentential 'Well . . . um . . .' may highlight the tentativeness and uncertainty typical of a particular character in a novel or play. Recurrences of 'innit, eh?' may have a similar function in the characterization of another protagonist. Or a philosophical argument may be constructed by the regular alternation of question and answer. (A famous example using a related device is the 'Controverse des MAIS' in Voltaire's *Histoire de Jenni* (see Voltaire, 1960, pp. 65–71), an argument between Freind and a theologian, in which all the latter's ridiculous contributions begin with 'mais'.) In less obvious cases than these, the progression of a textual theme may be supported or underlined by a patterned progression between sentence types. This can be an effective dramatic device in an introspective monologue or soliloquy. An example is Titus's monologue in *Bérénice*, Act IV, 4, in which the many questions and answers have a variety of affective and dramatic functions (see Racine, 1960, pp. 334–6).

Clearly, where the translator finds a clear correlation in the ST between thematic motifs and patterned use of sentential features, the features are most likely not accidental and incidental to the meaning, but devices instrumental in creating it. In such cases, it is more or less incumbent on the translator to use appropriate sentential features of the TL as devices enhancing the theme in the TT. Not to do so would probably incur unacceptable translation loss.

PRACTICAL 4

4.1   The formal properties of texts; introduction to the analysis of TTs

Assignment
Working in groups:

(i)   Discuss the strategic problems confronting the translator of the ST on p. 56; pay special attention to its salient formal properties, concentrating on the *discourse* and *sentential* levels of textual variables; say what strategy you would use for translating the text.

(ii) In the light of your findings in (i), analyse the TT printed opposite the ST. Where you think the translation can be improved, give your own edited TT and explain your decisions of detail.

Contextual information
This is the first part of a radio speech broadcast to the nation by General de Gaulle four days after the Liberation of Paris in August 1944. The 'vaillants combattants' (line 12) are the *Forces françaises de l'intérieur*, the combined armed units of the Resistance. The translation is by H. Erskine and J. Murchie.

N.B. Since this is the first time you have been asked systematically to evaluate a TT, here are some guidelines to be borne in mind whenever you do this kind of work. Part (i) of the exercise is not different from any other discussion of strategic decisions, except in so far as you are asked here to single out certain types of feature for special discussion. In part (ii), work your way through the ST and the TT, picking out the most relevant points one by one. Identify each extract you discuss with a brief reference to the ST line number(s), and give your edited TT (that is, your own version) at the end of your comments on the extract. Here is an example of how to lay out your material under (ii):

ST 1–2: 'Il y a . . . libéré'
  1   The two most notable features here are the rhetorical repetition of 'il y a quatre jours que' at the start of each sentence, and the difference in

length between the two sentences. The repetition is an example of a characteristic source of cogency in the ST as a whole. [*You will have discussed this as a strategic factor under (i)*.] It also combines with the contrast in length between the two sentences to emphasize the message: because the two sentences begin in the same way, one expects the parallel between them to extend further; consequently, when the second sentence ends sooner than expected, the crucial word 'libéré' is highlighted. The TT preserves these two important features.

2 However, 'four days ago' is, in both cases, strictly speaking inaccurate. The literal meaning of 'Il y a quatre jours *que* les Allemands [. . .] *ont* capitulé' is 'It is four days since the Germans capitulated'; and the literal meaning of 'Il y a quatre jours *que* Paris *est* libéré' is 'For four days Paris has been free(d)'. Unfortunately, translating literally loses the rhetorical repetition: 'It is four days/For four days'. The published TT is, therefore, defensible, because the entire ST is so self-consciously rhetorical that an equally rhetorical TT is indicated. However, in view of the second paragraph of the ST, I would choose literal accuracy and compensate for the consequent loss of symmetry with an additional 'now' as a rhetorical reinforcement.

Ed TT: It is four days now since the Germans holding Paris surrendered to French troops. For four days now, Paris has been free.

ST 3: 'Une joie . . . Nation'
(and so on)

Note that, *for this exercise*, other translation choices ('holding' versus 'who held'; 'surrendered' versus 'capitulated'; 'French troops' versus 'the French') are not discussed. In global terms, these are just as relevant as the ones we have indicated, but they are more appropriately examined on the *grammatical* level of textual variables (see Chapter 5). However, you will be asked from time to time to analyse in a given text *all* the relevant features introduced in the course. In such cases, you will need to review the whole gamut of translation choice, and select whichever features you think most deserve discussion in the TT in question.

Source text

Il y a quatre jours que les Allemands qui tenaient Paris ont capitulé devant les Français. Il y a quatre jours que Paris est libéré.

Une joie immense, une puissante fierté ont déferlé sur la Nation. Bien plus, le monde entier a tressailli quand il a su que Paris émergeait de l'abîme et que sa lumière allait, de nouveau, briller.   5

La France rend témoignage à tous ceux dont les services ont contribué à la victoire de Paris; au peuple parisien d'abord qui, dans le secret des âmes, n'a jamais, non jamais, accepté la défaite et l'humiliation; aux braves gens, hommes et femmes, qui ont longuement et activement mené ici la résistance à l'oppresseur avant d'aider à sa déroute; aux soldats de   10 France qui l'ont battu et réduit sur place, guerriers venus d'Afrique après cent combats, vaillants combattants groupés à l'improviste dans les unités de l'intérieur; par-dessus tout et par-dessus tous, à ceux et celles qui ont donné leur vie pour la Patrie sur les champs de bataille ou aux poteaux d'exécution.   15

Mais la France rend également hommage aux braves et bonnes armées alliées et à leurs chefs dont l'offensive irrésistible a permis la libération de Paris et rend certaine celle de tout le territoire en écrasant avec nous la force allemande.

A mesure que reflue l'abominable marée, la Nation respire avec délices   20 l'air de la victoire et de la liberté. Une merveilleuse unité se révèle dans ses profondeurs. La Nation sent que l'avenir lui offre désormais, non plus seulement l'espoir, mais la certitude d'être bel et bien une nation victorieuse, la perspective d'un ardent renouveau, la possibilité de reparaître dans le monde, au rang où elle fut toujours, c'est-à-dire au rang   25 des plus grands.

Mais la Nation sent aussi quelle distance sépare encore le point où elle en est de celui qu'elle veut et peut atteindre. Elle mesure la nécessité de faire en sorte que l'ennemi soit complètement, irrémédiablement battu et que la part française dans le triomphe final soit la plus large possible. Elle   30 mesure l'étendue des ravages qu'elle a subis dans sa terre et dans sa chair. Elle mesure les difficultés extrêmes de ravitaillement, de transports, d'armement, d'équipement, où elle se trouve, et qui contrarient l'effort de combat et l'effort de production de ses territoires libérés.

Reprinted by kind permission from de Gaulle, Ch., *Discours de Guerre*, Vol. 3 (Paris: Egloff, 1945), copyright © Librairie Plon.

Target Text

Four days ago the Germans who held Paris capitulated to the French.
Four days ago Paris was liberated.

An immense joy and a powerful pride spread through the nation. More,
a tremor shook the whole world when they heard that Paris was rising
from ruin and that her light was going to shine again.   5

France is grateful to all who contributed to the victory of Paris; to the
people of Paris first of all who in their secret hearts never, never accepted
defeat and humiliation; to the brave people, men and women, who
opposed and resisted the oppressor long and actively before helping to
rout him; to the soldiers of France who beat and defeated him here,   10
warriors from Africa with a hundred battles behind them or warriors
organized on the spur of the moment into units of the French Forces of the
Interior; and, above all, to those who gave their lives for their country on
the battlefield or who were executed.

France equally pays homage to the good and courageous Allied armies 15
and their leaders whose irresistible offensive made the liberation of Paris
possible: and which make the liberation of all the territory and the
crushing of German strength a certainty.

As the abominable tide recedes, the nation sniffs the air of victory and
freedom with delight. A marvellous unity is visible. The nation feels that 20
the future offers, not merely the hope but the certainty of being, at last, a
victorious nation; the prospect of an ardent regeneration and gives France
the chance of reappearing in the world in her old place, that is to say
amongst the greatest.

But the nation also knows that a great distance still separates it from the 25
point it is at and the point which it wants to, and can, reach. It appreciates
the necessity of seeing that the enemy is completely and irremediably
beaten and that the French rôle in the final triumph should be as great as
possible. It knows what ravages it has suffered both materially and in
human terms. It appreciates the extreme difficulty of feeding the 30
population, arranging transport, arms and equipment; difficulties which
hamper the war effort and the productivity of the liberated territory.

Reprinted by kind permission from de Gaulle, Ch., *War memoirs. Unity: 1942–4.*
Documents edited and translated by Erskine, H. and Murchie, J. (London:
Weidenfeld & Nicolson, 1959), U.K. and Commonwealth copyright © George
Weidenfeld & Nicolson Ltd 1959; U.S.A. and world rights © Librairie Plon.

4.2 Speed translation

Assignment

You will be asked to produce an accurate and stylistically appropriate
translation of a French ST given to you in class by your tutor. The tutor will
tell you how long you have for the exercise. There is no element of gist translation in this assignment – the whole text needs to be translated as it stands.

5

The formal properties of texts: grammatical and lexical issues in translation

The level of textual variables considered in this chapter is the **grammatical level**. It is useful to divide the contents of this level into two areas: first, grammatical arrangement of meaningful linguistic units into structured constructions (such as syntactic structure); second, the actual meaningful linguistic units that figure in constructions (in particular, words).

A great deal of the explicit literal meaning of a text is carried by the configuration of words and phrases. Therefore part of interpreting any text consists in construing the literal meaning conveyed by its grammatical structure. (Literal meaning as such will be discussed in Chapter 7.) Furthermore, a TT has normally to be constructed by putting words into grammatical configurations according to the conventions and structures of the TL, and using the lexical means available in the TL. Consequently, translators can never ignore the level of grammatical variables in either the ST or the TT. Let us look at the question of grammatical arrangement first.

GRAMMATICAL ARRANGEMENT

Under this heading we subsume two main types of grammatical structure: first, the patterns by which complex or compound words are formed – that is, affixation/inflection, compounding and word-derivation; second, the successive patterns whereby words are linked to form phrases, and phrases can be linked to form yet more complex phrases.

It is important to remember that these structural patterns differ from language to language. Even where apparent cross-linguistic similarities occur, they are often misleading, the structural equivalent of *faux amis*. The following pairs illustrate this point:

habité	inhabited, lived in
inhabité	uninhabited
il est mal coordonné	he's uncoordinated
incoordination	lack of coordination
[*Answering a question*] je n'en ai pas la moindre idée	I haven't the slightest idea (*not* I haven't the slightest idea of it)
tasse à café	coffee-cup (*not* cup for coffee)

In fact, much of what one might be tempted to call the 'ethos' of a typical French, German, or classical Chinese text is simply a reflection of preponderant grammatical structures specific to these languages. Thus, to take an obvious example, the potential for complex word-formations such as 'Donaudampfschiffskapitän' is typical of German, and is often not found in other languages. This implies that, for example, a translator into English cannot in principle replicate 'Donaudampfschiffskapitän' as a compound word, but must resort to syntactic means, probably using the complex phrase 'captain of a steam ship on the Danube'. (Another obvious example from German is its characteristic word order, which we have already seen Jean Dutourd exploiting in French for comic purposes, in Practical 2.)

The extent to which grammatical differences between languages can cause major translation loss is dramatically illustrated from 'exotic' languages, for instance from a comparison of English with Chinese. In a normal predicative phrase in Chinese, there are three particularly troublesome grammatical features. First, for neither subject nor object does it have to be specified whether it is singular or plural. Second, there is no definite or indefinite article for either subject or object. Third, there may be no indication of a tense or mood for the predicate. Since all these features are obligatorily present in predicative phrases in English, the Chinese phrase 'rén mǎi shū' (interlineally rendered as 'man buy book') has no exact literal counterpart in English, but has to be rendered, according to what is most plausible in the context, as one of the following combinations:

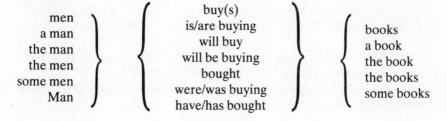

men a man the man the men some men Man	buy(s) is/are buying will buy will be buying bought were/was buying have/has bought	books a book the book the books some books

Because English syntax is so different from Chinese the phrase 'rén mǎi shū' can only be translated if one specifies in the TT certain details not expressed in the ST – that is, at the cost of considerable, but inevitable, translation loss (as defined in Chapter 2).

Wherever the grammatical structures of the ST cannot be matched by analogous structures in the TT, the translator is faced with the prospect of major translation losses. The problems that may be caused by this are not necessarily serious, but they are complex and many, which means that we can only touch on them briefly here. (Such problems are illustrated in more detail in Chapters 16–19.)

The need for circumlocution in the TT is one of the commonest of these problems. For example, the simple and ordinary word 'kolkhoz' in Russian may have to be rendered in English by the circumlocution 'state-owned cooperative farm'. This is an obvious source of translation loss, a neat and simple piece of ST corresponding to a relatively complex and long-winded TT. What may be less obvious is that the converse case of rendering a complex ST phrase by a single word in the TT is just as much a translation loss, because the grammatical proportions of the ST are not adhered to in the TT. For example, translating English 'member of parliament' by French 'député' entails a translation loss in terms of grammatical structure. These examples show how, as a rule, *semantic* considerations override considerations of *grammatical* translation loss, priority being given to the *mot juste* and to constructing grammatically well-formed TL sentences.

Nevertheless, translators should be aware of grammatical differences between SL and TL, and aware of them as potential sources of translation loss, for there are exceptions to this 'rule', namely STs with salient textual properties manifestly resulting from the manipulation of grammatical structure. Take, for example, this opening sentence from a business letter in English:

We acknowledge receipt of the consignment sent by you on 6 April.

This is a more likely formula than 'We have received the consignment you sent on 6 April' or 'Thank you for the consignment you sent on 6 April'. In putting the sentence into French, the translator should not aim at the simplest, most everyday grammatical structure capable of rendering the literal message of the ST, but should take into consideration the respective effects of 'formality' required in English and French business letters:

Nous vous accusons réception de votre expédition du 6 avril.

This is more likely in French business letters than, say, 'Nous vous accusons réception des marchandises que vous nous aviez expédiées le 6 avril'. A related example is this sentence from a French business letter, which *thanks* the sender as well as acknowledging receipt:

Nous vous accusons réception de votre commande du 6 avril et nous vous en remercions.

The corresponding English letter would take receiving the order for granted and say simply:

Thank you for your order of 6 April.

As these examples show, a great deal depends on nuances of convention within the particular TL genre, an issue to which we shall return in Chapters 11–14.

Grammatical structure may assume particular importance in literary translation. A prestigious author's hallmark may partly consist in characteristic grammatical structuring. For example, Kafka's style can be recognized by the extreme streamlining of his syntax, Proust's by its extreme syntactic complexity. By way of example, here is a relatively short Proustian construction from *A la recherche du temps perdu*:

Je poursuivais jusque sur le talus qui, derrière la haie, montait en pente raide vers les champs, quelque coquelicot perdu, quelques bluets restés paresseusement en arrière, qui le décoraient çà et là de leurs fleurs comme la bordure d'une tapisserie où apparaît clairsemé le motif agreste qui triomphera sur le panneau [. . .]

(Proust, 1987, p. 137)

Proust's intricate elaboration of syntactic structure typically contains numerous layers of phrases embedded in phrases. To reduce it to a series of small, easily digestible English sentences would be inappropriate, because it would fail to give TL speakers a TT from which they could appreciate something of Proust's writing. The following version is just such a failure:

The slope rose steeply behind the hedge towards the fields. I would climb it in pursuit of a lonely poppy or a few lingering cornflowers. The scattered flowers were an adornment to the bank, like the border round a tapestry hinting at the pastoral motif that dominates the panel itself.

A more suitable TT would need to be fairly complex and elaborate syntactically, and that is no easy problem. Here, for discussion in class, is the original Scott Moncrieff translation:

My eyes followed up the slope which, outside the hedge, rose steeply to the fields, a poppy that had strayed and been lost by its fellows, or a few cornflowers that had fallen lazily behind, and decorated the ground here and there with their flowers like the border of a tapestry, in which may be seen at intervals hints of the rustic theme which appears triumphant in the panel itself [. . .]

(Proust, 1966, p. 189)

There is another reason why translators must keep a close eye on grammatical structure – contrasts and recurrences in syntactic patterning can be used as devices creating special textual effects. A simple example is seen in the well-known children's rhyme about magpies:

> One for sorrow
> Two for joy
> Three for a girl
> Four for a boy,
> Five for silver,
> Six for gold,
> Seven for a secret that's never been told.

The grammatical patterns underlying this rhyme can be schematized as follows:

	number	preposition	abstract noun ⎫ (antonyms)
	number	preposition	abstract noun ⎭
(part of an	number	preposition	article + common noun ⎫ (antonyms)
ascending	number	preposition	article + common noun ⎭
series)	number	preposition	mass noun ⎫ (part of an ascending series)
	number	preposition	mass noun ⎭
	number	preposition	article + abstract noun + relative phrase

To translate this rhyme into another language, one would have to give careful consideration to the grammatical patterning as schematized above, because the loss of these effects would deprive the text of much of its point – in effect, the structural scheme would be the basis for formulating a TT.

Much less playful texts, such as rhetorical speeches, may make similar use of devices based on syntactic patterns of contrast and recurrence. In such cases, it would be a serious error not to recognize the textual importance of these grammatical devices, and a potentially serious translation loss not to try to reconstruct them in the TT. This was a major consideration in translating the speech by General de Gaulle in Practical 4.

WORDS

For reasons of educational bias (for instance, the paramount use of dictionaries and lexically arranged encyclopedias), people are far more directly aware of individual *words* than of other units and structures of language. In particular, mentioning 'meaning' or the semantic properties of languages (and therefore also of texts) tends to evoke first and foremost the level of individual words. Yet meanings are not exclusively concentrated in the dictionary containing words individually listed in isolation. Any text shows that the combination of words creates meanings that they do not possess in isolation, and even meanings that are not wholly predictable from the literal senses of the words combined.

As our multi-level approach to textual variables indicates, lexical translation losses (such as the inability to find an exact translation for a particular word) are just one kind of translation loss among many. There is no *a priori* reason, as long as the overall sense of the ST is successfully conveyed by the TT, why they should be given a heavier weighting than other kinds of translation loss. In fact, as we saw in Chapter 3, communicative translation is often more important than word-for-word correspondences. For instance, 'on dirait qu'elle est contente' can be plausibly translated as 'she looks happy', not as 'one would say that she is happy'; even then, the choice of 'looks' rather than 'sounds' or 'seems' would be entirely a matter of context.

Lexical translation losses, then, are no more avoidable than other kinds of translation loss. Exact synonymy between SL and TL words is the exception rather than the rule, and problems arising from this should be neither maximized nor minimized, but treated on a par with other translation losses that affect the overall meaning of the TT.

Comparing the lexical meanings of words across languages underlines the fact that lexical translation losses are as likely to result from 'particularization' (where the TT word has a narrower meaning than the ST word) as from 'generalization' (where the TT has a wider meaning than the ST word). So, for example, translating French 'conscience' as 'conscience', rather than 'consciousness', is an inevitable particularization, because one has to choose one of these two TL words, but each has a narrower range of reference than French 'conscience'. Conversely, translating 'il a un revolver!' as 'he's got a gun!' is a case of generalization, because 'gun' can also mean 'pistolet', 'fusil' and 'canon' – that is, it has a wider range of reference than 'revolver'. The translation problems arising from particularization and generalization are very common, and we shall return to them in Chapter 7.

Another reason why no TL word is ever likely to replicate precisely the 'meaning' of a given SL word is that, in each language, words form idiosyncratic associations with sets of other words. Such associations may hold by virtue of the *forms* of words, as in the homonymic association between 'crane' (bird) and 'crane' (machine); or by virtue of the literal meanings of the words, as with the associations of relative value in 'gold', 'silver' and 'bronze'; or by virtue of culture-bound prejudices and assumptions, as in the association of 'law' and 'order' (or 'brutality') with 'police'.

The exact associative overtones of words in the overall context of the ST are often difficult enough to pinpoint, but it is even more difficult, if not impossible, to find TL words that will, over and above conveying an appropriate literal meaning, also produce appropriate associative overtones in the context of the TT. This is another source of lexical translation loss, and another potential dilemma between choosing literal meaning at the expense of associative overtones, or vice versa. We shall return to these questions in Chapter 8.

Series of words can be distributed in contrastive and recurrent patterns that create or reinforce the thematic development of the text. In the rhyme about magpies on p. 62, there are a number of examples of the patterned use of lexical sets over an entire text. In Aphek and Tobin (1988), the term **word system** is used to denote this phenomenon. A word system is a pattern (within a text) of words having an associative common denominator and which 'nurtures the theme and message of the text with a greater intensity' (Aphek and Tobin, 1988, p. 3). Aphek and Tobin illustrate their concept of theme-reinforcing word systems from texts in Hebrew. In Hebrew, words consist of consonantal roots with variable vocalic fillers. Thus, for instance, the word 'XaZiR' ('pig') has the basic consonantal root 'X–Z–R'. All words with the same consonantal root are perceived in Hebrew as belonging to a single associative set. (This is mainly because of the system of writing, in which vocalic fillers may be omitted.) There is therefore an associative lexical set based on the 'X–Z–R' root, members of which may form a word system if distributed over a text in a way that reinforces the theme and message of the text. Aphek and Tobin discern an 'X–Z–R' word system in a Hebrew short story entitled 'The Lady and the Pedlar', in which 'X–Z–R' words are systematically placed at various key points of the narrative:

A Jewish pedlar *makes his rounds* (meXaZeR al ptaxim) in villages.

He meets a gentile woman and he *bows before her repeatedly* (XoZeRet vehishtaxava).

He takes out and *replaces* (maXZiR) his merchandise, but she *goes back* (XoZeRet) indoors.

He *returns* to the woods (XoZeR), but then is invited into her house to work.

The man begins to *court* (meXaZeR) the woman and becomes her lover. He forgets to live according to Jewish customs (for example, he eats pork).

Eventually it transpires that the woman is a vampire, and, in a climactic argument, she laughs at him and calls him a *pig* (XaZiR).

As a turning-point in the story, the man *returns* (XoZeR) to the forest, *returns* (laXZoR) to his religion and *repents* (XoZeR betshuva).

Returning (XoZeR) to the house, he finds that the woman has stabbed herself with his knife. She dies.

The pedlar *resumes his rounds* (XiZeR ve-XiZeR) *crying* (maXRiZ) his wares *repeatedly* (XoZeR ve-maXRiZ; n.b. the inversion of X–Z–R to X–R–Z).

The example speaks for itself. The pattern of 'X–Z–R' (and 'X–R–Z') words coincides with salient points of the narrative, thus marking and reinforcing them. It also highlights the important thematic points in the interplay between abandoning Jewish religious observance, eating pork, being a metaphorical pig in the eyes of the vampire woman, and eventual repentance. These points are more tightly bound together by the 'X–Z–R' word system than they would be by the mere narrative sequence of the text alone.

This example shows that it is worth scanning certain types of text for theme-reinforcing word systems (such as a series of thematic key-words, or phonetic patterns, or an extended metaphor), because such things may be important textual devices. Where a word system is found in the ST, the construction of some analogous word system in the TT may be desirable; if so, this will be a strong factor influencing the translator's lexical choice. Indeed, in translating a text like the Hebrew example, one of the first strategic decisions will be whether to give this type of pattern priority over other levels of textual variables.

PRACTICAL 5

5.1   The formal properties of texts

Assignment
Working in groups:

  (i)   With particular reference to its salient formal properties – especially those on the *grammatical* level – discuss the strategic problems confronting the translator of the following text, and outline your own strategy for translating it.
 (ii)   Translate the second paragraph of the text into English.
(iii)   Explain the main decisions of detail you made in producing your TT.
 (iv)   After discussion of the translations, your tutor may give you a published TT for analysis and discussion in class.

Contextual information
The passage is taken from André Gide's *L'Immoraliste* (1902). Michel, the narrator, has grown up surrounded by books, learned six ancient languages, and made an early reputation as an ancient historian. He marries at the age of 25, as he says, 'n'ayant presque rien regardé que des ruines ou des livres,

et ne connaissant rien de la vie'. He nearly dies of tuberculosis, and develops an overwhelming urge to 'live', henceforth scorning scholarship, books and the past, and pursuing physical pleasures. At the point where this passage comes, he is living on his well-farmed estate in Normandy, his wife Marceline is pregnant, and he has taken to riding through his admirably productive fields in the mornings, with a friend. He is writing a course of lectures on the Goths of the fourth century, in whose barbarism he sees the very opposite of all that Greece and Rome represent. Michel thinks – clearly mistakenly – that this choice of subject is tantamount to a rejection of his bookish past, which was characterized, as he puts it, by 'la culture tuant la vie'.

Text

Je rentrais ivre d'air, étourdi de vitesse, les membres engourdis un peu d'une voluptueuse lassitude, l'esprit plein de santé, d'appétit, de fraîcheur. Marceline approuvait, encourageait ma fantaisie. En rentrant, encore tout guêtré, j'apportais vers le lit où elle s'attardait à m'attendre, une odeur de feuilles mouillées qui lui plaisait, me disait-elle. Et elle 5
m'écoutait raconter notre course, l'éveil des champs, le recommencement du travail . . . Elle prenait autant de joie, semblait-il, à me sentir vivre, qu'à vivre. — Bientôt de cette joie aussi j'abusai; nos promenades s'allongèrent, et parfois je ne rentrais plus que vers midi.

Cependant je réservais de mon mieux la fin du jour et la soirée à la 10
préparation de mon cours. Mon travail avançait; j'en étais satisfait et ne considérais pas comme impossible qu'il valût la peine plus tard de réunir mes leçons en volume. Par une sorte de réaction naturelle, tandis que ma vie s'ordonnait, se réglait et que je me plaisais autour de moi à régler et à ordonner toutes choses, je m'éprenais de plus en plus de l'éthique fruste 15
des Goths, et, tandis qu'au long de mon cours je m'occupais, avec une hardiesse que l'on me reprocha suffisamment dans la suite, d'exalter l'inculture et d'en dresser l'apologie, je m'ingéniais laborieusement à dominer sinon à supprimer tout ce qui la pouvait rappeler autour de moi comme en moi-même. 20

5.2 The formal properties of texts

Assignment
Working in groups:

(i) With particular reference to its salient formal properties, discuss the strategic problems confronting the translator of the following text, and outline your own strategy for translating it.

(ii)   Translate the text into English.
(iii) Explain the main decisions of detail you made in producing your TT.

Contextual information

The text is from Beaumarchais's play *Le Barbier de Séville* (1775), II. viii. Bartholo is Rosine's guardian, but intends to marry her. He is in conversation with Dom Bazile, her music teacher. Bartholo wants to be rid of Count Almaviva, who is in love with Rosine, and he thinks of murdering him. Bazile is shocked at the risk entailed, and suggests that *la calomnie* would be a much better method. Bartholo is unconvinced.

Text

BAZILE   La calomnie, monsieur! Vous ne savez guère ce que vous dédaignez; j'ai vu les plus honnêtes gens près d'en être accablés. Croyez qu'il n'y a pas de plate méchanceté, pas d'horreurs, pas de conte absurde, qu'on ne fasse adopter aux oisifs d'une grande ville en s'y prenant bien: et nous avons ici des gens d'une adresse! . . . D'abord un léger bruit, rasant ‑ 5
le sol comme hirondelle avant l'orage, *pianissimo* murmure et file, et sème en courant le trait empoisonné. Telle bouche le recueille, et *piano*, *piano*, vous le glisse en l'oreille adroitement. Le mal est fait; il germe, il rampe, il chemine et *rinforzando* de bouche en bouche il va le diable; puis tout à coup, ne sais comment, vous voyez calomnie se dresser, siffler, 10
s'enfler, grandir à vue d'œil. Elle s'élance, étend son vol, tourbillonne, enveloppe, arrache, entraîne, éclate et tonne, et devient, grâce au ciel, un cri général, un *crescendo* public, un *chorus* universel de haine et de proscription. Qui diable y résisterait?

6

The formal properties of texts: prosodic and phonic/graphic problems in translation

We come now to the last two levels of textual variables, the prosodic level and the phonic/graphic level. We should say at the outset that, although they are the 'lowest' in the hierarchy, these levels demand the translator's attention just as much as the others – even if, after due consideration, the decision is that they are not important enough in a given ST to be allowed to influence translation choice.

THE PROSODIC LEVEL

On the **prosodic level**, utterances count as 'metrically' structured stretches, within which syllables have varying degrees of prominence according to accent, stress and emphasis, varying melodic qualities in terms of pitch modulation, and varying qualities of rhythm, length and tempo. Groups of syllables may, on this level, form *contrastive* prosodic patterns (for example, the alternation of a short, staccato, fast section with a long, slow, smooth one), or *recurrent* ones, or both.

In texts not designed to be read aloud, such prosodic patterns, if they are discernible at all, are unlikely to have any textual importance. However, in texts intended for oral performance, such as plays, speeches, poetry or songs, prosodic features can have a considerable theme-reinforcing and mood-creating function. In texts where prosodic special effects play a vital role, the translator may have to pay special attention to the prosodic level. A humorous example is found in Goscinny and Uderzo (1965), where an

Alexandrian says 'Je suis, mon cher ami, très heureux de te voir', and this flowery greeting, which has the metric properties of an alexandrine, is explained by someone else with the observation 'C'est un Alexandrin'. (For notes on the alexandrine as a verse form, see below, pp. 70–2.)

In most cases, it is not possible to construct a TT that both sounds natural in the TL and reproduces in detail the metric structure of the ST. This is because languages often function in fundamentally different ways from one another on the prosodic level, just as they do on the phonic/graphic level. In English, for instance, patterns of accent are distributed idiosyncratically over the syllables of words, with each polysyllabic word having one maximally prominent, and a number of less prominent, syllables in a certain configuration – for example, '^{1}un^{2}na^{1}tu^{1}ral^{0}ly' (the numbers denoting a greater or lesser degree of stress). Only by knowing the word can one be sure what its prosodic pattern is; that is, accent patterns in a group of words are tied to the identity of the individual words. This is known as *free word-accent*, and is characteristic of English.

French, however, differs radically from English in two ways. First, the main accent in any polysyllabic word spoken in isolation is always on the final syllable (this is known as *fixed word-accent*). Second, phrase-accent overrides word-accent. So, for example, in the word '^{0}é^{0}mi^{2}nence' spoken in isolation, the stress is on the last syllable (with the optional possibility of a slight secondary stress on the first: '^{1}é^{0}mi^{2}nence'); but in the phrase '^{1}é^{0}mi^{0}nence ^{2}grise' the main stress is on 'grise', because it is the last syllable of the phrase, with a slight secondary stress on the first syllable of 'éminence'. Similarly, compare '^{1}com^{2}ment', '^{1}vous ^{0}al^{2}lez' and '^{1}com^{0}ment ^{1}al^{0}lez-^{2}vous?' This mobility of accent, dependent on the sense-group in which the words occur, explains the fundamental difference between French and English versification, namely that French verse is *syllabic* and English verse *metrical*.

RUDIMENTS OF FRENCH AND ENGLISH VERSIFICATION

The difference between French and English versification is a major problem facing the translator of verse. We deal here in elementary terms with the basics of the two systems, so that they can be compared. Such metrical structure is a main feature of the patterned use of recurrences on the prosodic level. (It does not, however, exhaust the entire field of prosody, since it ignores tempo and melodic pitch, which may also constitute vital textual variables.) We do not deal here with free verse, which would need too detailed a study for the purposes of this course. However, in so far as free verse is defined by its difference from fixed-form verse, our analysis will help translators isolate the relevant features of STs in free verse.

Our examination of prosody provides a basic system of notation. For English, there is a well-tried system, which we adopt here. For French, we suggest a simple numerical notation of main and secondary stresses and pauses. This notation brings out clearly the rhythmic patterns, and the variations in them, which are so fertile a source of special textual effects. Only when these patterns have been identified in a ST, and their effects defined, can the translator begin to decide what – if any – TL prosodic patterns will be appropriate in the TT. That there will need to be prosodic patterns in the TT is virtually certain; that they will hardly ever replicate those of the ST is even more certain. The challenge to the translator is to find appropriate counterparts.

French

French verse is *syllabic*. That is, the writer does not have to choose among conventional combinations of stressed and unstressed syllables, as is the case in traditional English or German verse. The line of verse in French is defined in terms of the *number* of syllables it contains, and the pattern of stresses may vary greatly within that framework.

The commonest lines in traditional verse have an even number of syllables: they are the *alexandrine* (twelve syllables), *decasyllable* (ten) and *octosyllable* (eight).

Ever since the sixteenth century, the alexandrine has been the staple of French verse. It is the line of the great playwrights and lyric poets, and is still commonly used today. Until the mid-nineteenth century, it nearly always had a natural pause, or *caesura*, after the sixth syllable; since then, the caesura or caesuras in the alexandrine are very often positioned more flexibly.

The decasyllable was the line used in epic. Now it is much less common than the alexandrine. It has never had a fixed caesura, though it has tended to divide either 4/6, 6/4 or 5/5. The 5/5 division lends the decasyllable to light, song-like use.

The octosyllable is the second most common traditional line. It has no fixed caesura. It is found in odes and lyrical verse of all kinds, including folk songs, ballads and humorous verse.

Lines with an odd number of syllables are less common. They are more fluid, since it is impossible to divide them equally. They lend themselves to light, playful or popular verse, but they can also be very loaded emotionally. The commonest is the *heptasyllable* (seven syllables).

The mute e, or *e atone* ([ ]) is pronounced in the interior of a line of verse, but only if it is *immediately preceded and followed* by a pronounced consonant. This is illustrated in the following examples (the italicized letters represent pronounced consonants immediately adjacent to a mute e):

```
 1   2 3  4
```
l'homme vaincu   = 4 syllables
```
1 2 3
```
elle hait   = 3 syllables   (note that the aspirate h counts as a pronounced consonant, and is in any case often sounded as [h] in verse)

```
1     2
```
ell(e) est   = 2 syllables
```
1  2       3
```
tu jou(e)ras   = 3 syllables
```
1   2
```
ils voi(e)nt   = 2 syllables
```
1   2 3   4    5  6
```
ils travaillent souvent   = 6 syllables
```
1   2  3 4   5  6
```
ils travaillent en vain   = 6 syllables   (note that liaison is more strictly observed in verse)

```
1  2       3  4
```
ils voi(e)nt en vain   = 4 syllables

The rigorous application of this rule in traditional verse explains why the texts of songs so often contain apostrophes to show where the singer must *break* the rule in order to fit the words to the music. Note also that *sung* verse is different from spoken verse in that a mute e *at the end of the line* is also pronounced unless otherwise indicated. These features are illustrated in this anonymous song, sung after the French defeat at Sedan in 1870 ('Badinguet' was a derogatory nickname for Napoleon III):

> V'là le sir' de Fisch-Ton-Kan   = 7
> Qui s'en va-t-en guerre,   = 6
> En deux temps et trois mouv'ments,   = 7
> Badinguet, fich' ton camp.   = 6
> L'pèr', la mèr' Badingue,   = 6
> A deux sous tout l'paquet,   = 6
> L'pèr', la mèr' Badingue,   = 6
> Et le p'tit Badinguet!   = 6

For practical purposes, the following simple system is an adequate way of notating stress in French verse:

Lă nătur(e) ĕst ŭn templ(e) / où dĕ vĭvănts pĭliĕrs / = 3+3/4+2/

Lăissĕnt părfois sŏrtir / dĕ cŏnfusĕs părŏl(e)s; / = 1+3+2/3+3/

L'hŏmm(e) y̆ păss(e) / ă trăvĕrs dĕs forêts dĕ sy̆mbŏl(e)s / = 1+2/3+3+3/

Quĭ l'ŏbse/rvĕnt ăvĕc dĕs rĕgărds fămĭliĕrs. / = 3/6+3/

In this notation, the following symbols are used:

[˘] denotes an unstressed syllable, ['] a stressed one;
[/] denotes a caesura;
a digit immediately before [/] denotes a group containing that number of
syllables and ending with a main stress;
a digit immediately before [+] denotes a group containing that number of
syllables and ending with a secondary stress.

Occasionally, a group ends with a mute e, which is always unstressed. This
exceptional feature usually has expressive effect, the nature of which
depends on the context. Such cases can be notated thus:

Măis părlĕ: / dĕ sŏn sort / quĭ t'ă rĕndŭ l'ărbĭtre? / = 2(+1)/3/1+5/

Rhyme. Absence of rhyme is relatively rare in French verse, whereas blank
verse is common in English. The degree of rhyme, whether minimal (as in
'**donner/allé**') or maximal (as in '**table/lamentable**' or '**amorti/sorti**'), may
play an important part in the effect of a French text.

Reading. In French verse, there are no fixed metrical patterns into which
one has to force one's reading. There is no *a priori* reason for, say, a /˘/˘/ or
a ˘˘/˘˘/ reading, or for any other. Naturally, in some texts certain rhythms
will emerge as predominant, but the only prosodic constraint is to sound the
mute e where required. That apart, one's reading should be guided purely
by the meaning, just as for prose.

English

Whereas the French line is defined in terms of syllables, the English line is
defined in terms of *feet*. A foot is a conventional group of stressed and/or
unstressed syllables in a specific order, and a line of traditional verse consists
of a fixed (conventional) number of particular feet. For example:

Thĕ cūr | fĕw tōlls | thĕ knēll | ŏf pār | tĭng dāy

This line is a *pentameter*; that is, it is divided into five feet. In this particular
case, the feet consist of one unstressed followed by one stressed syllable:

|˘ ¯ |. This is an *iamb*, or iambic foot. A line consisting of five iambs is an iambic pentameter. It is the most common English line, found in the work of the great playwrights and lyric poets.

A line consisting of three iambs is an iambic *trimeter*; one consisting of four iambs is an iambic *tetrameter*; one consisting of six iambs is an iambic *hexameter*. The shorter lines are more usual than the pentameter in songs, ballads and light verse. The commonest other sorts of foot are:

the trochee : |¯˘ |

the spondee : |¯ ¯|

the anapest : |˘ ˘ ¯|

the dactyl : |¯ ˘ ˘ |

the pyrrhic : |˘ ˘ |

Most are exemplified in this mnemonic by Coleridge:

Trochee | trips from | long to | short.   (trochaic tetrameter – as usual in a trochaic line, the last syllable is missing)

From long to long in solemn sort

Slow Spon | dee stalks; | strong foot! | yet ill able (spondaic trimeter – plus a bit)

Ever to | come up with | Dactyl tri | syllable. | (dactylic tetrameter)

Iam | bics march | from short | to long; | (iambic tetrameter)

With a leap | and a bound | the swift A | napests throng. | (anapestic tetrameter)

Most poems do not, of course, have a regular beat throughout. For example, lines one and six of Wordsworth's 'Composed upon Westminster Bridge' will be described as iambic pentameters, because they do have five feet, they are predominantly iambic, and the rest of the poem also has these qualities:

line 1. Earth has | not a | nything | to show | more fair |

line 6. Ships, tow | ers, domes, | theatres, | and temp | les lie |

One other sort of English metre is worth mentioning, *strong-stress metre*. This is different from the syllable-and-stress metre described above. Only the stresses count in the scanning, the number of weak syllables being variable. There are usually, but not necessarily, four stresses in a line. Much modern verse uses this metre, often in combination with syllable-and-stress metre.

THE PHONIC/GRAPHIC LEVEL

The most basic level of textual variables is the **phonic/graphic level**. Taking a text on this level means looking at it as a sequence of sound-segments (or *phonemes*) if it is an oral text, or as a sequence of letters (or *graphemes*) if it is a written one. Although phonemes and graphemes are different things, they are on the same level of textual variables: phonemes are to oral texts as graphemes are to written ones. To help keep this in mind, we shall refer to the 'phonic/graphic level' regardless of whether the text in question is an oral one or a written one.

Every text is a unique configuration of phonemes/graphemes, these configurations being restricted by the conventions of a particular language. This is why, in general, no text in a given language can reproduce exactly the same sequence of sound-segments/letters as any text in another language – occasional coincidences apart, ST and TT will always consist of markedly different sequences. This always and automatically constitutes a source of translation loss. The real question for the translator, however, is whether this loss matters at all. Could we not simply put it down as a necessary consequence of the transition from one language to another, and forget about it?

The suggestion that the translator should not bother with the sound/ letter sequences in texts echoes the slogan found in Lewis Carroll: 'Take care of the sense and the sounds will take care of themselves.' We may give two initial answers to this slogan. First, some translators have been known to pay special attention to re-creating phonic/graphic effects of the ST, at times even to the detriment of the sense. Second, some texts would lose much of their point if deprived of their special phonic/graphic properties.

As a matter of fact, even in the most ordinary, prosaic text one may come across problems that have to do specifically with the phonic/graphic level. The transcription of names is a prime example. When looking, in Chapter 3, at the possibilities for cultural transposition of names we noted that it is a matter of conventional cultural transposition that accounts for the trans- lation equivalence between German 'Wien' and English 'Vienna', Russian 'Москва' and English 'Moscow', and so on. Equally conventional is the standard English transliteration 'Mao Tse tung'. This transliteration in fact occasions a phonic distortion (from [mɑwdzduŋ] to [mɑwtsit'uŋ]), which does not much matter even to the few people who are aware of it. On the other hand, for word-associative reasons, one might well be reluctant to use the transliteration 'Low dung fang' for the name of the Chinese politician.

As these examples show, a measure of phonic/graphic ingenuity and decision-making may be involved in the process of translation. These resources are, of course, called upon to a much greater degree in translating a ST that makes important use of phonic/graphic variables for *special effects*. We mean by such special effects the use of phonic/graphic features in order to create or – more usually – reinforce a thematic motif or mood within a text.

The simplest example of such special effects is onomatopoeia. Onomato-poeia is either directly *iconic* – that is, the phonic form of a word impressionistically imitates a sound which is the referent of the word – or *iconically motivated* – that is, the phonic form of the word imitates a sound associated with the referent of the word (for example, 'cuckoo'). If it has a thematically important function, onomatopoeia may require care in trans-lation. Some examples are straightforward, of course, as in translating French 'ploc!' by 'plop!', which presents little difficulty or translation loss. Others, while still straightforward, are potentially more problematic, as in the conventional translation of French 'pan!' ([pɑ̃]) into English 'bang!' ([bæŋ]), where there is slightly more phonic translation loss and that loss could conceivably be significant in certain contexts.

Cross-cultural variations in onomatopoeia are common – compare, for example, French 'plouf!' with English 'splash!'. Furthermore, many SL onomatopoeic words do not have one-to-one TL counterparts. For instance, 'squeak' may be rendered in French as 'couic' (if a mouse is making the noise) or as 'cric-crac' (if it is a floorboard); French 'siffler' may be rendered as 'hiss' or 'whistle' or 'wheeze', depending on who or what is making the noise and in what circumstances; similarly, French 'floc!' may translate as 'plop!' or 'splosh!' or 'splash!'. In these and many other cases the range of reference of the SL word does not coincide exactly with that of its nearest TL counterpart. These types of cross-cultural difference are phonic in nature, and are in themselves potential sources of translation problems.

Onomatopoeia may cause more of a translation problem where the nearest semantic equivalents to an onomatopoeic SL word in the TL are not onomatopoeic. For instance, English 'peewit' is clearly onomatopoeic (when referring to the bird), but its French rendering as 'vanneau huppé' cannot plausibly be regarded as onomatopoeic. To the extent that the very fact of onomatopoeia is an effect contributing to textual meaning, its loss in the TT is a translation loss that the translator may regret.

Other translation difficulties may be caused by onomatopoeia where cross-cultural differences arise on the grammatical as well as the phonic/ graphic level. Words like 'floc!', 'pan!' and 'plouf!' are onomatopoeia at its most basic: sound-imitative interjections, not onomatopoeic nouns. 'Coucou' is a noun, but it is still onomatopoeic; translating it as 'cuckoo' involves little translation loss. Translating French 'cri-cri' as 'cricket', on the other hand, involves more translation loss, which could be significant in certain contexts. Some onomatopoeic words, however, can be used both as interjections and as nouns or verbs; for example, French 'plouf' and 'cric-crac' double as nouns, and their English counterparts, 'splash' and 'creak' (or 'squeak') are even more grammatically versatile (nouns or verbs). Where such onomatopoeic counterparts exist, translation loss is limited to the phonic/graphic level. Take, however, a case from Vinay and Darbelnet (1958, p. 298), who translate 'a crack like a revolver-shot' as 'un craquement sec comme un coup de revolver'. The onomatopoeic ST 'crack' is a noun which can also act as an interjection; but French 'crac!' can only occur as an interjection. Consequently, the option of translating the ST as 'un *crac!* comme un coup de revolver', which would involve minimum translation loss on the phonic/graphic level, creates considerably more loss on the grammatical level. In fact, here the TT does not both denote and imitate the noise, but only imitates it: that is, the TT is more directly iconic, and resembles a vivid oral text more than a written one. It is, presumably, to avoid this loss of register that the translators have used the noun 'craquement' – but this choice brings problems of its own, for 'craquement' (while still onomatopoeic) has a much wider range of reference than ST 'crack', embracing English 'crackle', 'creak', and even 'squeak' as well. This, no doubt, is why the translators chose to add 'sec', which specifies the kind of 'craquement', while adding its own phonic effect (consisting in a recurrence of [k] sounds) that helps to underline the sharp crispness of the noise. (This is incidentally a good example of compensation, as discussed in Chapter 3.) This recurrence of [k], however, has its own disadvantages – it may interfere with the literal meaning by phonically suggesting a multiple crackling rather than a single crack. This typifies a common translation problem: a single thematic clue combining with onomatopoeia or the recurrence of phonic/graphic variables to give unwanted connotative force to a TT expression.

Even something as simple as onomatopoeia, then, may need attention in translating. (The same is true, in fact, of any type of word play that hinges on phonic/graphic similarities between expressions with different meanings. For example, the more obviously a pun or a spoonerism is not accidental or incidental in the ST, the more it is in need of translating. A major strategic decision will then be whether to seek appropriate puns or spoonerisms for the TT, or whether to resort to some form of compensation. Typical problems of this kind will be found in Practicals 6 and 8.)

A more frequently encountered area of phonic/graphic special effects is alliteration and assonance. We define **alliteration** as the recurrence of the same sound/letter or sound/letter cluster at the beginning of words (for example, '**m**any **m**ighty **m**idgets'), and **assonance** as the recurrence, within words, of the same sound/letter or sound/letter cluster (for example, 'my **craft**y hi**st**ory-ma**st**er's ba**t**htub'). It is important to remember a vital difference between alliteration/assonance and onomatopoeia. Alliteration and assonance do not involve an imitation of sounds (unless they happen to coincide with onomatopoeia, as was the case in 'un craquement sec comme un coup de revolver'). We have already seen something of how alliteration and assonance work, in the Hebrew text discussed in Chapter 5. The crucial associative feature in the 'word system' in that text is the X–Z–R phonic/graphic pattern (involving a combination of alliteration and assonance). Every time this pattern recurs, it coincides with a vital moment in the narrative, so that it very soon acquires emphatic force, underlining crucial narrative and thematic points. A major strategic decision for the translator of this story arises, then, on the phonic/graphic level, but affecting also the grammatical level: whether to create a word system in the TT and, if so, whether to make systematic phonic/graphic recurrences the hub of the TT word system.

This example makes clear why the problems raised by phonic/graphic special effects can be so intractable. It is common to find that the literal sense and the mood of a text are reinforced by some of the phonic qualities of the text (so-called 'sound symbolism'). This makes it all the easier to forget the contribution of the reader/listener's subjectivity to the textual effect. This subjective input is relatively minor in the case of onomatopoeia, but it is greater in texts like the Hebrew story, and greater still where alliteration and assonance are more varied and objectively less obtrusive. The important thing to keep in mind is that, onomatopoeia aside, the sound-symbolic effect of words is not intrinsic to them, but operates in conjunction with their literal and connotative meanings in the context.

For example, the sound [s] does not, in and of itself, suggest the horrifying menace of snakes, or misty dreaminess, or death by choking and suffocation. Yet it may be said to suggest the first of these things at the end of Racine's *Andromaque*, where Oreste in his hallucination sees the Furies advancing on him and cries: 'Pour qui sont ces serpents qui sifflent sur vos têtes?' (Racine, 1960, p. 171). And it may be said to carry the other connotations in Baudelaire's 'Harmonie du soir': the first, at the very start of the poem:

> Voici venir les temps où vibrant sur sa tige
> Chaque fleur s'évapore ainsi qu'un encensoir;

the second, at a turning-point in the text, where the mood momentarily changes to one of anguish and fear:

> Le soleil s'est noyé dans son sang qui se fige.
> (Baudelaire, 1961, p. 52)

In each case, [s] draws suggestive power from four things in particular: first, the lexical meaning of the words in which it occurs; second, the lexical meanings of the words associated with those in which it occurs; third, other phonetic qualities of both those groups of words; and fourth, the many other types of connotative meaning at work in these texts, as in any other. (We shall discuss connotative meaning as such in Chapter 8.)

In these three examples, sound-symbolism clearly has such an important role that translating the texts without producing appropriate sound-symbolic effects in the TT would incur severe translation loss. The more a text depends for its very existence on the interplay of onomatopoeia, alliteration and assonance, the more true this is – and the more difficult the translator's task becomes, because, as our examples show, sound-symbolism is not only largely language-specific, but a very subjective matter as well.

By far the most widespread textual effects arising from the use of phonic/ graphic variables involve the exploitation of *recurrences*. Apart from alliteration and assonance, rhyme is the most obvious example. When such recurrences are organized into recognizable patterns on a large scale, for example in a regularly repeated rhyme scheme, they are clearly not accidental or incidental. At this point, the translator is forced to take the resulting phonic/graphic special effects into serious consideration. However, this does not mean that one is obliged, or even well-advised, to reproduce the patterns of recurrence found in the ST. In fact, opinions are divided among translators of verse about the extent to which even such obvious devices as rhyme scheme should be reproduced in the TT. In English, for example, blank verse is a widespread genre with at least as high a prestige as rhyming verse, so that there is often a case for translating STs from other languages into blank verse. In the end, this is a decision for individual translators to make in individual cases; often the genre of the ST and the availability of TL genres will be a crucial factor in the decision. (We shall consider the importance of genre as a factor in translation in Chapter 11.)

We can conclude so far that the phonic/graphic level of textual variables *may* merit the translator's attention, and that translation losses on this level *may* be serious. There is no suggestion here that attention to sounds should be to the detriment of sense; on the contrary, it is where ignoring phonic/ graphic features would damage the sense of the text that they are considered important.

There is, however, a style of translation that actually more or less reverses the dictum found in Lewis Carroll; that is, it concentrates on taking care of the sounds and allows the sense to emerge as a kind of vaguely suggested impression. This technique is generally known as **phonemic translation**. An extraordinary example, whose authors seem to take it perfectly seriously, is a translation of Catullus's poetry by Celia and Louis Zukovsky. Here is part of one poem, followed by (i) the phonemic translation and (ii) a literal prose translation:

Ille mi par esse deo videtur,
Ille, si fas est, superare divos,
qui sedens adversus identidem te
    spectat et audit
dulce ridentem, misero quod omnis
eripit sensus mihi; [. . .]

(i)   He'll hie me, par *is* he? the God divide her,
    he'll hie, see fastest, superior deity,
    quiz – sitting adverse identity – mate, in-
       spect it and audit –
    you'll care ridden then, misery hold omens,
    air rip the senses from me; [. . .]
                     (Zukovsky, 1969, poem 51)

(ii) He seems to me to be equal to a god, he seems to me,
    if it is lawful, to surpass the gods, who, sitting
    opposite to you, keeps looking at you and hearing you
    sweetly laugh; but this tears away all my senses,
    wretch that I am.

We shall not dwell on this example, beyond saying that it perfectly illustrates the technique of phonemic translation: to imitate as closely as possible the actual phonic sequence of the ST, while suggesting in a vague and impressionistic way something of its literal content.

As a matter of fact, it is difficult, if not impossible, for a TT to retain a close similarity to the actual phonic sequences of the ST and still retain anything more than a tenuous connection with the meaning of the ST. This difficulty is ensured by the classic 'arbitrariness' of languages, not to mention the language-specific and contextual factors which, as we have seen in discussing onomatopoeia, alliteration and assonance, make phonic effect such a relative and subjective matter.

An entertaining illustration of the way phonic imitation in a TT renders the sense of the ST unrecognizable is *Mots d'heures: gousses, rames* (*Mother Goose Rhymes!*), which consists in a playful phonic imitation of English nursery rhymes. So, for example, 'Humpty-Dumpty sat on a wall' is reproduced as 'Un petit d'un petit / S'étonne aux Halles' (Van Rooten, 1968, poem 1). However, while providing an entertaining pastiche, *Mots d'heures: gousses, rames* does not really count as phonemic translation proper: there is no attempt in it at all to render anything of the literal meaning of the ST.

A form of pastiche which consists in intralingual phonic imitation of a well-known text is sometimes used for satirical purposes. Translating such a text presents considerable difficulties. Here, by way of example, is a piece of satirical phonic imitation by Robert Desnos:

Donnez-nous aux joues réduites,
notre pain quotidien.
Part, donnez-nous, de nos œufs foncés
Comme nous part donnons
à ceux qui nous ont offensés.
Nounou laissez-nous succomber à la tentation
et d'aile ivrez-nous du mal.

(Desnos, 1968, p. 52)

And here is the ST that (with slight adjustments) Desnos was imitating:

Donnez-nous aujourd'hui
notre pain quotidien.
Pardonnez-nous nos offenses
comme nous pardonnons
à ceux qui nous ont offensés.
Ne nous laissez pas succomber à la tentation,
mais délivrez-nous du mal.

If one wanted to translate Desnos's text, or any similar pastiche, into English, the strategic decision would be whether to translate literally, or attempt a phonemic translation, or produce an English phonic imitation of an English version of the Lord's Prayer that tried to retain some of the ST's satirical effect.

Although phonemic translation cannot be recommended as a technique for serious translation of sensible texts, there are texts that are not intended to be sensible in the original and which qualify as suitable objects for phonemic translation. Nonsense rhymes, like 'Jabberwocky', are a good example.

Finally, though they are less common than sound-symbolism, special effects may also be contrived through the spatial layout of written texts. Such cases illustrate the potential importance of specifically *graphic* textual variables. An obvious example is the acrostic, a text in which, say, reading the first letter of each line spells out, vertically, a hidden word. Another is concrete poetry, where the visual form of the text is used to convey meaning. The Apollinaire text in Practical 6 is a good example; just as onomatopoeia is iconic phonically, this text – like much concrete poetry – is iconic graphically, imitating visually what it represents.

PRACTICAL 6

6.1 The formal properties of texts

Assignment
  (i)   With particular reference to its salient formal properties, discuss the
        strategic problems confronting the translator of the following text,
        and outline your own strategy for translating it.
 (ii)   Translate the text into English.
(iii)   Explain the main decisions of detail you made in producing your TT.

Contextual information
The passage is from Patrick Grainville's *Les Flamboyants* (1976). The mad
Tokor, king of an African country, has taken his European guest, William,
to visit Le Mourmako. They drive to the top of a hill, from which they look
down onto the town, described as a 'chancre ignoble et sublime'. William is
gripped by its vastness, and recoils at the stench that rises from the town.
(Note that, although the passage is narrated from William's point of view, he
is not the narrator.)

Text
  Le Mourmako était un bidonville unique au monde de par ses dimensions.
Il s'étendait sur plusieurs kilomètres en long et en large. Ses pittoresques
frappaient, ses complications ténébreuses, ses dédales illimités, ses
invisibles recoins. Il couvrait une surface énorme, irrégulière, composée
de buttes et de grandes cuves. L'ensemble offrait à l'œil l'ondulation d'une   5
souillure sombre et vaste de gadoue et de matières amalgamées. Le sol du
Mourmako au lieu d'être rouge ou jaune comme la plupart des paysages
du royaume était noir et gluant. Une humidité poisse baignait l'entasse-
ment des constructions disparates qui semblaient avoir poussé au hasard,
en vrac, dans des postures anarchiques et biscornues à même les   10
renflements de sombre mélasse. Les abris misérables et saugrenus se
collaient dans la boue un peu comme ces coquillages ou ces grandes algues
endeuillés qu'incrustent les enfants aux flancs de leurs châteaux de sable.
Le Mourmako était planté, roulé dans la prédominance de la fange.

6.2 The formal properties of texts

Assignment
Working in groups:

  (i)   With particular reference to its salient formal properties – especially
        on the *phonic/graphic* and *prosodic* levels of textual variables –

discuss the strategic problems confronting the translator of the ST on p. 84, and outline your own strategy for translating it.

(ii)   In the light of your findings in (i), analyse the TT printed opposite the ST. Where you think the translation can be improved, give your own edited TT and explain your decisions of detail.

Contextual information

The text was written in late 1914, and is from Guillaume Apollinaire's *Calligrammes*. It is an example of what Apollinaire called 'idéogrammes lyriques', in which the words are arranged in either figurative or abstract designs, or both. Many of these poems are, like this one, inspired by the Great War. The 'colombe poignardée', or 'bleeding-heart dove', has on its breast a large brilliant red patch and a splash of smaller ones. The translation is by Ann Hyde Greet.

Turn to p. 84

LA COLOMBE POIGNARDEE ET LE JET D'EAU

THE BLEEDING-HEART DOVE AND THE FOUNTAIN

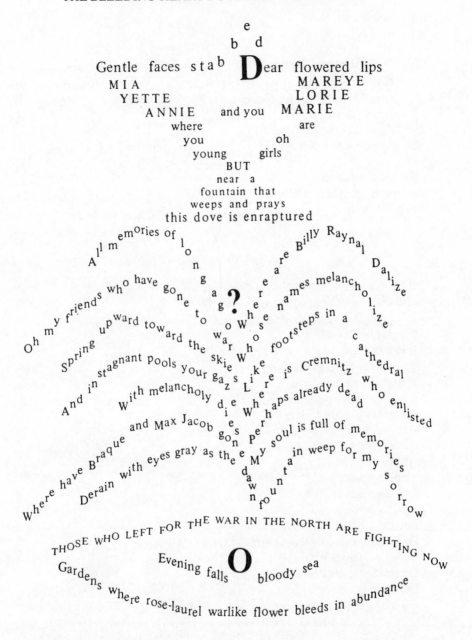

Reprinted by kind permission from Apollinaire, G., *Calligrammes: Poems of Peace and War*, translated by Anne Hyde Greet (Berkeley: University of California Press, 1980), copyright © The Regents of the University of California.

6.3 The formal properties of texts

Assignment
Working in groups:

(i) With particular reference to the *phonic/graphic* and *prosodic* levels of textual variables, discuss the strategic problems confronting the translator of the following text, and outline your own strategy for translating it.
(ii) Translate the text into English.
(iii) Explain the main decisions of detail you made in producing your TT.

Contextual information
The text is from Henri Michaux's *Qui je fus* (1927), and is one of several in which Michaux experiments with made-up words.

Text

LE GRAND COMBAT

Il l'emparouille et l'endosque contre terre;
Il le rague et le roupète jusqu'à son drâle;
Il le pratèle et le libucque et lui barufle
    les ouillais;
Il le tocarde et le marmine,   5
Le manage rape à ri et ripe à ra.
Enfin il l'écorcobalisse.
L'autre hésite, s'espudrine, se défaisse, se torse et se ruine.
C'en sera bientôt fini de lui;
Il se reprise et s'emmargine . . . mais en vain.   10
Le cerceau tombe qui a tant roulé.
Abrah! Abrah! Abrah!
Le pied a failli!
Le bras a cassé!
Le sang a coulé!   15
Fouille, fouille, fouille,
Dans la marmite de son ventre est un grand secret,
Mégères alentour qui pleurez dans vos mouchoirs;
On s'étonne, on s'étonne, on s'étonne
Et vous regarde.   20
On cherche aussi, nous autres, le Grand Secret.

7

Literal meaning and translation problems

In Chapter 2 we raised objections to using the term 'equivalence' in assessing the relationship between a ST and a corresponding TT. This was because it does not seem helpful to say that good translation produces a TT that has 'the same meaning' as the corresponding ST, when such a claim rests on the comparison of two virtually imponderable and indeterminate qualities. The term 'meaning' is especially elastic and indeterminate when applied to an entire text. At one end of the scale, the 'meaning' of a text might designate its putative socio-cultural significance, importance and impact – a historian might define the meaning of *Mein Kampf* in such terms. At the other end of the scale, the 'meaning' might designate the personal, private and emotional impact the text has on a unique individual at a unique point in time – say, the impact of *Mein Kampf* on a German bride presented with a copy of it at her wedding in 1938. Between these two extremes lie many shades of shared conventional meaning intrinsic to the text because of its internal structure and explicit contents, and the relation these bear to the semantic convention and tendencies of the SL in its ordinary, everyday usage.

Meanings in a text that are fully supported by ordinary semantic conventions (such as the lexical convention that 'window' refers to a particular kind of aperture in a wall) are normally known as **literal** (or 'cognitive') **meanings**. In the case of words, it is this basic literal meaning that is given in dictionary definitions. However, even the dictionary definition of a word, which is supposed to crystallize precisely that range of 'things' that a particular word can denote in everyday usage, is not without its problems. This is because the intuitive understanding that native language-users have of the literal meanings of individual words does itself tend to be rather fluid. That is, a dictionary definition imposes, by abstraction and crystallization of a 'core' meaning, a rigidity of meaning that words do not often show in reality. In addition, once words are put into a context, their literal meanings become even more flexible. These two facts make it infinitely difficult to pin down the precise literal meaning of any text of any complexity. This difficulty is still further compounded by the fact that literal meanings supported by a consensus of semantic conventions are not the only types of meaning that can function in a text and nuance its interpretations. As we shall see in Chapter 8, there are various connotative tendencies – not sufficiently cut and dried to qualify as conventional meanings accepted by consensus – which can play an important role in how a text is to be interpreted and translated.

SYNONYMY

Although the apparent fixity of literal meaning is something of an illusion, the concept of 'semantic equivalence' is still useful as a measure of correspondence between the literal meanings of isolated linguistic expressions (words or phrases) figuring in texts. If one is prepared to isolate such expressions, one can talk about semantic equivalence as a possible, and fairly objective, relationship between linguistic items that have identical literal meanings (such as 'viper' and 'adder', or 'bachelor' and 'unmarried man'). In what follows, we shall discuss ways of comparing degrees of correspondence in literal meaning between STs and TTs, and our discussion will presuppose the type of semantic equivalence defined here.

Our discussion will be based on one other supposition: that literal meaning is a matter of *categories* into which, through a complex interplay of inclusion and exclusion, a language divides the totality of communicable experience. So, for example, the literal meaning of the word 'page' does not consist in the fact that one can use the word to denote the object you are staring at at this moment. It consists rather in the fact that all over the world (in past, present and future) one may find 'similar' objects that are *included in* the category of 'pages', as well, of course, as all sorts of other objects that are *excluded from* it. To define a literal meaning, then, is to specify the 'range' covered by a word or phrase in such a way that one knows what items are included in that range or category and what items are excluded from it. The most useful way to visualize literal meanings is by thinking of circles, because they can be used to represent *intersections* between classes, and thus reflect overlaps in literal meaning between different expressions. In exploring correspondence in literal meaning, it is particularly the intersections between categories (represented as circles) that are significant; they provide, as it were, the measure of semantic equivalence.

The comparisons of literal meaning made possible by considering overlaps between categories, and represented by intersections between circles, are usually drawn between linguistic expressions in the same language. They allow, in the semantic description of a language, for an assessment of types and degrees of semantic correspondence between items (for example, lexical items). There is, however, no reason why analogous comparisons may not be made between expressions from two or more different languages, as a way of assessing and representing types and degrees of cross-linguistic semantic correspondence.

Thus, for instance, the expressions 'my mother's father' and 'my maternal grandfather' may be represented as two separate circles. The two ranges of literal meaning coincide perfectly. This can be visualized as moving the two circles on top of each other and finding that they cover one another exactly, as in Figure 7.1:

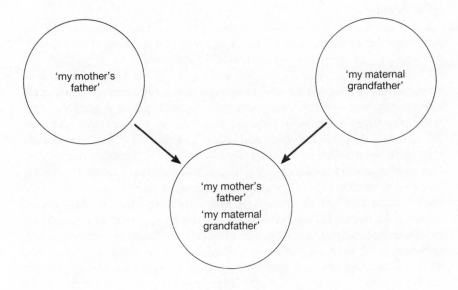

Figure 7.1

Both in general and in every specific instance of use, 'my mother's father' and 'my maternal grandfather' include and exclude exactly the same referents; that is, their literal meanings are identical in range. This exemplifies full **synonymy**, which is the strongest form of semantic equivalence.

Just as alternative expressions in the same language may be full synonyms, so, in principle at least, there may be full synonymy across two different languages. As one might expect, the closer the SL and the TL are in the way they process and categorize speakers' experience of the world, the more likely it is that there will be full cross-linguistic synonyms between the two languages. Thus, one can fairly confidently say that 'L'enfant ouvrira la fenêtre' and 'The child will open the window' cover exactly the same range of situations, and are, therefore, fully synonymous in their literal meanings: as is seen in Figure 7.2:

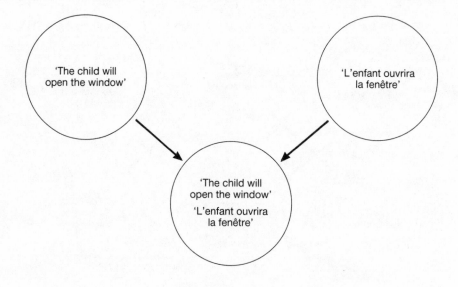

Figure 7.2

HYPERONYMY–HYPONYMY

Unfortunately, full cross-linguistic synonymy is the exception, not the rule, even between historically and culturally related languages. More often than not, the so-called 'nearest equivalent' for translating the literal meaning of a ST expression falls short of being a full TL synonym. Compare, for example, 'L'enfant ouvre la fenêtre' with 'The child opens the window'. It is at least possible that the French phrase refers to a progressive event reported by the speaker. This would have to be expressed in English by 'The child *is opening* the window'. That is, 'L'enfant ouvre la fenêtre' and 'The child opens the window' are not full synonyms, but have non-identical ranges of literal meaning. There is a common element between the two phrases, but the French covers a wider range of situations, a range that is covered by at least two different expressions in English. This can be shown diagrammatically, as in Figure 7.3:

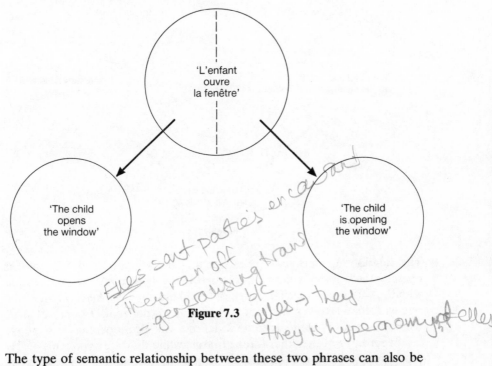

Figure 7.3

The type of semantic relationship between these two phrases can also be instanced within a single language. For example, 'He is opening the window' and 'The boy is opening the window' have a common element of literal meaning, but show a discrepancy in the fact that 'He is opening the window' covers a wider range of situations, including in its literal meaning situations that are excluded from 'The boy is opening the window' – such as 'The janitor is opening the window', 'The father is opening the window', and so on. This is seen diagrammatically in Figure 7.4 on p. 92:

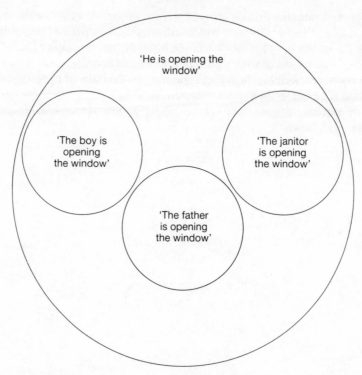

Figure 7.4

The relationship between 'He is opening the window' and 'The boy is opening the window' is known as **hyperonymy–hyponymy**. The expression with the wider, less specific, range of literal meaning is a *hyperonym* of the one with the narrower and more specific literal meaning. Conversely, the narrower one is a *hyponym* of the wider one. So 'He is opening the window' is a hyperonym of the other three phrases, while they are hyponyms of 'He is opening the window'. Similarly, 'L'enfant ouvre la fenêtre' is a hyperonym of both 'The child opens the window' and 'The child is opening the window', and they are hyponyms of the French expression.

Hyperonymy–hyponymy is so widespread in any given language that one can say that the entire fabric of linguistic reference is built up on such relationships. Take, for example, some of the alternative ways in which one can refer to an object – say, a particular biro. If there is a need to particularize, one can use a phrase with a fairly narrow and specific meaning, such as 'the black biro in my hand'. If such detail is unnecessary and one wants to generalize, one can call it 'an implement', 'an object', or, even more vaguely, just 'something'. The many expressions falling in between in range include 'a biro', 'a writing implement', and so on.

It is in the very essence of the richness of all languages that they offer a whole set of different expressions, each with a different range of inclusiveness, for designating any object, any situation, anything whatsoever. Thus the series, 'the black biro in my hand', 'a biro', 'a writing implement', 'an implement', 'an object', 'something' is a series organized on the basis of successively larger, wider inclusiveness – that is, on the basis of hyperonymy–hyponymy. The series can be visualized as a set of increasingly large concentric circles, larger circles representing hyperonyms, smaller ones hyponyms, as follows:

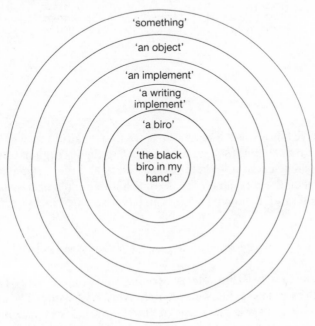

'something'
'an object'
'an implement'
'a writing implement'
'a biro'
'the black biro in my hand'

Figure 7.5

As this example shows, the same message content can be rephrased in an indefinite number of ways, depending on how precise or vague one wants to be.

By its very nature, translation is concerned with rephrasing, and in particular with rephrasing so as to preserve maximally the integrity of a ST message, including its degree of precision or vagueness. Therefore, the fact that both a hyperonym and a hyponym can serve for conveying a given message is of great importance to translation practice. It means that, as soon as one acknowledges that there is no full TL synonym for a particular ST expression, one must start looking for an appropriate TL hyperonym or hyponym. In fact, translators do this automatically (and therefore not always carefully or successfully). For example, in most contexts the phrase 'my daughters' is effectively translated into French as 'mes filles'. Yet the

French phrase is wider and less specific in literal meaning than the English one, since 'filles' could also mean 'girls'. In other words, a SL hyponym is unhesitatingly translated by a TL hyperonym as its 'nearest semantic equivalent', shown diagrammatically as follows:

Figure 7.6

Conversely, 'They are tall' necessarily translates into French either as 'Ils sont grands' or as 'Elles sont grandes'. Each of the French phrases excludes people of one sex, and is therefore narrower and more specific in literal meaning than the English phrase. Either is an example of translating a SL hyperonym by a TL hyponym. This can be represented thus:

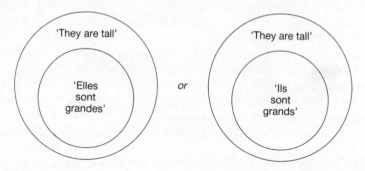

Figure 7.7

In the absence of plausible synonyms, translating by a hyperonym or a hyponym is standard practice and entirely unremarkable. Indeed, choosing a hyperonym or hyponym where a synonym does exist may actually be the mark of a good translation. For instance, even racy French narratives of battle often use 'fusant' or 'percutant' instead of the generic word 'obus', but in English, specifying 'time-shell' or 'percussion-fuse shell' would usually be clumsily unidiomatic; in all but the most technical contexts, the hyperonym 'shell' is the appropriate translation. It is, then, only when using a TL hyperonym or hyponym is unnecessary, or unnecessarily extreme, or misleading, that a TT can be criticized on this basis.

PARTICULARIZING TRANSLATION AND
GENERALIZING TRANSLATION

Translating by a hyponym implies that the TT expression has a narrower and more specific literal meaning than the ST expression. That is, the TT gives *particulars* that are not given by the ST. We shall therefore call this **particularizing translation**, or **particularization** for short. Thus, in our earlier example, 'Elles sont grandes' is a particularizing translation of 'They are tall'.

Conversely, translating by a hyperonym implies that the TT expression has a wider and less specific literal meaning than the ST expression. That is, the TT is more *general*, omitting details that are given by the ST. We shall call this **generalizing translation**, or **generalization** for short. Our earlier example of translating 'My daughters' as 'Mes filles' is a case of generalizing translation.

Particularization and generalization both naturally imply a degree of translation loss as we defined it in Chapter 2 – detail is either added to, or omitted from, the ST message. However, neither the addition nor the omission of detail is necessarily a matter for criticism, or even comment, in evaluating a TT. We outline here a set of criteria under which particularizing and generalizing translation is acceptable or unacceptable.

Particularizing translation is *acceptable* on two conditions: first, that the TL offers no suitable alternative; second, that the added detail is implicit in the ST and fits in with the overall context of the ST. For example, translating Molière's title '*L'Ecole des femmes*' as '*The School for Wives*', rather than as '*The School for Women*', accords better with the content of the play.

Particularizing translation is *not* acceptable when one or more of the following three conditions hold: first, if the TL does offer suitable alternatives to the addition of detail; second, if the added detail creates discrepancies in the TT; third, if the added detail constitutes a misinterpretation of the overall context of the ST. As an example, one may take Gide's dictum 'L'art suprême est celui qui ne se laisse d'abord reconnaître'; rendering 'd'abord' as 'first and foremost' instead of 'at first' or 'immediately' would be unacceptable for all three reasons.

Generalizing translation is acceptable on two conditions: first, that the TL offers no suitable alternative; second, that the omitted detail is clear and can be recovered from the overall context of the TT, or is unimportant to the ST. For example, on p. 100, translating feminine 'étudiante' by neutral 'student' occasions insignificant translation loss in the context.

Generalizing translation is not acceptable when one or more of the following three conditions hold: first, if the omitted details are important to the ST; second, if the TL does offer suitable alternatives to the omission of this detail; third, if the omitted detail is not compensated for elsewhere in the TT, and cannot be recovered from the overall context of the TT. Thus, to return to an earlier example, translating 'fusant' simply by 'shell' in a bomb-disposal manual, as distinct from a novel, occasions potentially lethal translation loss.

PARTIALLY OVERLAPPING TRANSLATION

As well as particularizing and generalizing translation, there is another type of semantic near-equivalence. This is more easily illustrated in phrases than in single words. Take the phrase 'my mother-in-law's soup'. 'La soupe de ma belle-mère' is as close a literal rendering into French as possible. Yet in the English phrase it is not actually specified what kind of soup it is, whereas the French TT specifies that it contains unsieved pieces of vegetable or meat. By specifying unsieved 'soupe' rather than sieved 'potage', the French TT *particularizes* (just as it would have done in specifying 'potage'). Conversely, in the English phrase, the relationship between the speaker and the woman is specified unambiguously, whereas the French TT leaves it ambiguous: the French TT *generalizes* here, because 'belle-mère' can mean either 'step-mother' or 'mother-in-law'.

In other words, this TT combines particularization and generalization, *adding* a detail not found in the ST and *omitting* a detail that is given in the ST. This is best visualized as two partially overlapping circles:

Figure 7.8

This type of case is a further category of degree in the translation of literal meaning: along with synonymic, particularizing and generalizing translation, there is **partially overlapping translation**, or **overlapping translation** for short. The concept of overlapping translation applies less obviously, but more importantly, in the case of individual words (as distinct from phrases). For example, rendering 'repousser' as 'push aside' is a case of overlapping translation: the English keeps the element of 'pushing', but it *loses* the detail of 'backwards' movement expressed in the French prefix 're-', and *adds* the detail of 'sideways' movement which is not expressed in the French.

Once again, overlapping translation may or may not invite comment when one is evaluating a TT. The conditions under which it is acceptable and the criteria for criticizing it are similar to those for particularization and generalization. Overlapping translation is acceptable on two conditions: first, if the TL offers no suitable alternatives; second, if the *omitted* detail is either unimportant or can be recovered from the overall TT context, and if the *added* detail is implicit in, or at least not contradictory to, the overall ST context. For example, in most contexts, 'she shook her head' is the accurate and idiomatic rendering of 'elle dit non de la tête', but it does *add* (in that it makes explicit) the physical movement in the ST, and *lose* (in that it makes implicit) the negation explicit in the ST.

Overlapping translation is *not* acceptable when one or more of the following three conditions hold: first, if the omitted detail is important to the ST but cannot be recovered from the overall context of the TT; second, if the added detail creates discrepancies in the TT; third, if the TL does offer suitable alternatives avoiding either the omissions or the additions or both. For an example, see the translation of 'je m'émer-veillais' by 'I was astonished' on pp. 100–1, and our comments on p. 99.

PRACTICAL 7

7.1 Particularizing, generalizing and partially overlapping translation

Assignment
  (i) Starting at line 5 ('Le matin . . .') of the ST printed on p. 100, make a detailed analysis of particularizing, generalizing and overlapping translation in the TT printed opposite the ST.
 (ii) Where possible, give an edited TT that is a more exact translation, and explain your decisions.

Contextual information
This is the beginning of *La Force de l'âge* (1960), the second volume of Simone de Beauvoir's autobiography. The first volume covered her childhood, adolescence and undergraduate career. The second begins with her renting a flat from her grandmother. The translation, by Peter Green, was published in 1962.

N.B. Here is an example of how to lay your material out for this exercise:

ST 1–2: 'Ce qui me grisa . . . liberté'

1 'most' is a slightly misleading particularizing translation (literally,
   'd'abord' covers 'first', 'at first' and 'first and foremost'): in context,
   'd'abord' means 'first in *time*', so that 'first' is a more accurate rendering
   of the ST expression.
2 'intoxicate' is a synonymous rendering of 'griser' (the only objection
   to it might be that it is stylistically too formal – perhaps 'go to one's
   head' is better in the context); however, translating 'ce qui me grisa'
   as 'intoxicating aspect' is an unnecessary and misleading particularization: first, it is unnecessary because the closest rendering
   of 'ce qui me grisa [. . .] d'abord' is 'what first intoxicated me'; and
   second, it is misleading because the ST refers to the moment after
   her return, not the *whole process* of returning (the ST has 'rentrai',
   not 'rentrais').
3 'my return' is a generalizing translation which is unnecessary, since
   'when I returned' would be a closer rendering.
4 'the freedom I now possessed' is a case of overlapping translation: ST
   and TT share the common element of freedom, but the TT *adds* the
   notion that she henceforth had her freedom, while it *loses* the ST focus
   (in the past historics and 'd'abord') on the *moment of discovering* her
   freedom. ('Now' in the TT is probably an attempt to compensate for the
   inevitable generalizing translation in the English past tense 'possessed',
   which loses the specificity of the French past historic (it can also render
   the French imperfect tense). For a similar example, see p. 26, where
   'celui qu'il reçut' would be appropriately translated as 'the one he
   got now'. In the edited TT below, 'new-found' has the same kind of
   compensatory function.)

Ed TT: What first went to my head when I returned to Paris, in
September 1929, was my new-found freedom.

ST 3–4: 'Etudiante, . . . appelai'

1 'recorded elsewhere' is a particularization, and doubly so: both the idea
   of 'setting down in writing' and that of 'elsewhere' are merely implicit in
   the ST. If the TT used a closer rendering, the reader would doubtless still
   be able to grasp the reference to Vol. 1 of the memoirs.
2 'my passionate longing' is a slight generalization: the ST explicitly refers
   to the *extent* or *degree* of the emotion, the TT only to the emotion in
   general.
3 'as a' is an inevitable generalization, demanded of English idiom by the
   context (in other contexts, alternatives would be 'when I was a', 'if I were
   a', etc.; see the material on 'absolute constructions' in Chapter 18 for
   further discussion of this sort of case).

4 'student' is a typical case of an inevitable generalization (omitting reference to gender); it is anodine in this case, because the lost information is easily recoverable from the context.

Ed TT: I have already said how passionately I longed for it as a student.

ST 4–5: 'à chacun . . . légèreté'

1 'movements' is a slight, but inevitable and anodine, generalizing translation of 'gestes', for which there is no single English synonym; 'gestures' covers a much narrower field than 'gestes', and, while in some contexts it would be the accurate rendering, it would be a misleading particularization here.
2 either 'effortlessness' or 'buoyancy' on its own would be a particularization, but 'effortless buoyancy' is very close to rendering 'légèreté' in this context (a good example of compensation by splitting – see p. 39).
3 'astonished' is an unnecessary and misleading overlapping translation: it *makes explicit* the element of surprise implied in 'm'émerveillais', but it *loses* the element of wonderment explicit in it – indeed, the 'wonderment' in 's'émerveiller' is so important that the TT amounts to a mistranslation.
4 'astonished to find' is also an overlapping translation; it *adds* the notion that she *discovered* her lightness (almost as if she had been inspecting how she moved), and it *loses* the notion that she *simply delighted* in it.

Ed TT: I marvelled at how light my every movement was.

Ce qui me grisa lorsque je rentrai à Paris, en septembre 1929, ce fut
d'abord ma liberté. J'y avais rêvé dès l'enfance, quand je jouais avec ma
sœur à 'la grande jeune fille'. Etudiante, j'ai dit avec quelle passion je
l'appelai. Soudain, je l'avais; à chacun de mes gestes je m'émerveillais de
ma légèreté. Le matin, dès que j'ouvrais les yeux, je m'ébrouais, je   5
jubilais. Aux environs de mes douze ans, j'avais souffert de ne pas
posséder à la maison un coin à moi. Lisant dans *Mon journal* l'histoire
d'une collégienne anglaise, j'avais contemplé avec nostalgie le chromo qui
représentait sa chambre: un pupitre, un divan, des rayons couverts de
livres; entre ces murs aux couleurs vives, elle travaillait, lisait, buvait du   10
thé, sans témoin: comme je l'enviai! J'avais entrevu pour la première fois
une existence plus favorisée que la mienne. Voilà qu'enfin moi aussi
j'étais chez moi! Ma grand-mère avait débarrassé son salon de tous ses
fauteuils, guéridons, bibelots.

Target text

The most intoxicating aspect of my return to Paris in September 1929 was
the freedom I now possessed. I had dreamed of it since childhood, when I
played with my sister at being a 'grown-up' girl. I have recorded elsewhere
my passionate longing for it as a student. Now, suddenly, it was mine. I
was astonished to find an effortless buoyancy in all my movements. From   5
the moment I opened my eyes every morning I was lost in a transport of
delight. When I was about twelve I had suffered through not having a
private retreat of my own at home. Leafing through *Mon Journal* I had
found a story about an English schoolgirl, and gazed enviously at the
coloured illustration portraying her room. There was a desk, and a divan,   10
and shelves filled with books. Here, within these gaily painted walls, she
read and worked and drank tea, with no one watching her – how envious I
felt! For the first time ever I had glimpsed a more fortunate way of life than
my own. And now, at long last, I too had a room to myself. My
grandmother had stripped her drawing room of all its armchairs,   15
occasional tables and knick-knacks.

7.2 Speed translation

Assignment

Your tutor will give you a text to be translated in class within a certain time
limit. You should try to apply the lessons learned so far, while meeting the
demands of speed and accuracy.

8

Connotative meaning and translation problems

As was pointed out in Chapter 7, literal meaning is only one aspect of verbal meaning. To deal with meaning in terms of the literal reference conventionally attached to verbal signs is a necessary part of unravelling a complex message, but it is not, in itself, enough. In actual fact, the meaning of a text comprises a number of different layers: referential content, emotional colouring, cultural associations, social and personal connotations, and so on. The many-layered nature of meaning is something translators must never forget.

Even within a single language, so-called referential synonyms are as a rule different in their overall semantic effects. For instance, 'the police' and 'the fuzz' must be rated as synonyms in terms of referential content, but they may be said to have different overall meanings. This is because, while 'the police' is a neutral expression, 'the fuzz' usually carries pejorative overtones. These overtones are not part of the literal meaning of the expressions, but it is clear that a reference to 'the fuzz' could be taken as disrespectful or hostile, whereas no disrespect is intended by references to 'the police'. It is impossible to ignore such overtones in responding to messages in one's own language, and one certainly cannot afford to overlook them when it comes to translating. For example, a speaker who refers to 'la flicaille' not only designates members of a particular organization, but also conveys a certain attitude to them. Consequently, while translating 'la flicaille' as 'the police' would accurately render the literal meaning of the ST, it would fail to render the disrespectful or hostile attitude connoted by 'la flicaille' (better translated as 'the fuzz' or 'the pigs').

We shall call such overtones **connotative meanings** – that is, associations which, over and above the literal meaning of an expression, form part of its overall meaning. In fact, of course, connotative meanings are many and varied, and it is common for a single piece of text to combine several kinds into a single overall effect. Nevertheless, there are six major types of commonly recognized connotative meaning, which we will review in turn. We should perhaps add that, by definition, we are only concerned here with socially widespread connotations, not private ones – as long as private connotations are recognized for what they are, and not allowed to influence the production of a TT that does justice to the ST, they are the translator's own affair.

ATTITUDINAL MEANING

Attitudinal meaning is that part of the overall meaning of an expression which consists of some widespread *attitude to the referent*. That is, the expression does not merely denote the referent in a neutral way, but, in addition, hints at some attitude to it.

Our examples of 'la flicaille' and 'the fuzz' versus 'la police' and 'the police' are clear cases of attitudinal connotations. As these examples show, attitudinal meanings can be hard to pin down. (For instance, just how hostile is the expression 'the fuzz'? Is it simply familiar, or perhaps even affectionately derogatory? This will vary from context to context.) There are two main reasons why attitudinal meanings are sometimes hard to define. First, being connotations, they are by definition meant to be suggestive – the moment they cease to be suggestive, and become fixed by convention, they cease to be connotations and become part of literal meaning. Second, being controlled by the vagaries of usage, they can change very rapidly. Both these factors are illustrated by the evolution of the word 'Tory', originally a term of abuse imported from Irish ('tóraidhe', meaning 'outlaw'), but later proudly adopted by the parties so labelled.

ASSOCIATIVE MEANING

Associative meaning is that part of the overall meaning of an expression which consists of stereotypical *expectations* rightly or wrongly *associated with the referent* of the expression.

The word 'nurse' is a good example. Most people automatically associate 'nurse' with the idea of female gender, as if 'nurse' were synonymous with 'female who looks after the sick'. This unconscious association is so widespread and automatic that the term 'male nurse' has had to be coined in order to counteract its effect. Even so, the female connotations of 'nurse' continue to persist, witness the fact that 'he is a nurse' still feels semantically odd.

Any area of reference where prejudices and stereotypes, however innocuous, operate is likely to give examples of associative meaning. Even something as banal as a date may trigger an associative meaning, for example July 14 or November 5. Similarly, in France and England – though not in Scotland – 'golf' will automatically trigger associations of an 'upper- or middle-class' milieu.

The appreciation of associative meanings requires cultural knowledge, and the translator must constantly be on the lookout for them. Take, for instance, Pierre Emmanuel's article 'Le pain et le livre', on a price-war between bakers (Emmanuel, 1981, pp. 199–203). Associatively, the expression 'le pain' evokes the usual shape of the French loaf, so that the meaning of 'le pain' is responded to as if it were synonymous with 'la baguette'. Thus, connotatively (but not literally), 'un pain' is a stick-like, baton-shaped object. This enables Emmanuel to create a word-play between the expressions 'la guerre du pain' and 'une campagne si bien menée à la baguette'. In English, 'bread' and 'loaf' do not evoke the shape of a baton, which makes 'menée à la baguette' difficult to translate effectively into English ('mener à la baguette' normally translates as 'to rule with an iron hand/a rod of iron'). This difficulty is a direct consequence of associative meaning. (Depending on the context, a possible solution might be 'the people behind this campaign are no loafers', or 'this is no half-baked price war'; alternatively, one might compensate by putting some such pun into a neighbouring sentence.)

AFFECTIVE MEANING

Affective meaning is an *emotive effect worked on the addressee by* the choice of expression, and which forms part of its overall meaning. The expression does not merely denote its referent, but also hints at some attitude of the speaker/writer to the addressee.

Features of linguistic politeness, flattery, rudeness or insult are typical examples of expressions carrying affective meanings. Compare, for instance, 'Would you mind not talking' with 'Will you belt up'. These expressions share the same literal meaning of 'Be quiet', but their overall impact in terms of affective meaning is quite different: polite and deferential in the first case, impolite and insulting in the other. That is, the speaker's tacit or implied attitude to the listener produces a different emotive effect in each case.

Not only imperative forms, but also statements and questions, can have alternative forms identical in basic literal meaning yet totally different in affective meaning, as in 'Excuse me, Madam, I think that's my seat' versus 'Oy, Ducky, that's my seat'; or 'Where are the toilets?' versus 'Where's the bog?'.

Clearly, translators must be able to recognize affective meanings in the ST. But they must also be sure not to introduce unwanted affective meanings into the TT. Take, for example, someone lending a book to a friend and saying 'Tu me le rendras mardi'. This would sound rude and peremptory if translated literally as 'You'll give it me back on Tuesday', whereas the ST does not have that affective meaning at all. A better TT would cushion what sounds to the English-speaker's ear like the brutal assertiveness of the French: '(So) you'll give it me back on Tuesday, then?'

REFLECTED MEANING

Reflected meaning is the meaning given to an expression over and above its literal meaning by the fact that its *form* is reminiscent of the completely different meaning of a *homonymic or near-homonymic expression* (that is, one that sounds or is spelled the same, or nearly the same).

An often-cited example of reflected meaning compares the connotative difference between the two synonyms 'Holy Spirit' and 'Holy Ghost' (see Leech, 1974, p. 19). Through homonymic association, the 'Ghost' part of 'Holy Ghost' is reminiscent of the reflected meaning of 'ghost' ('spook' or 'spectre'). Although such an association is not part of the literal meaning of 'Holy Ghost', it has a tendency to form part of the overall meaning of the expression, and therefore often actually interferes with its literal meaning. By another, near-homonymic, association, the 'Spirit' part of 'Holy Spirit' may call to mind the reflected meaning of 'spirits' ('alcoholic drinks'); here again, the association tends to interfere with the literal meaning. Clearly, then, while 'Holy Spirit' and 'Holy Ghost' are referential synonyms, their total semantic effects cannot be called identical, in so far as they evoke different images through different reflected meanings.

When a term is taken in isolation, its reflected meaning is usually merely latent – it is the textual *context* that triggers or reinforces latent reflected meanings. In the case of 'Holy Ghost' and 'Holy Spirit', if there is anything in the context that predisposes the hearer to think about 'spooks' or 'alcoholic drinks', reflected meaning may come across as a *double entendre*. If one were translating 'Saint-Esprit' (which does not have the reflected meanings of its English synonyms), one would have to make sure that the TT context did not trigger the latent reflected meaning of whichever English expression was selected for the TT. Otherwise the TT could be marred by infelicitous innuendo, as for example if one wrote 'Holy Spirit' just after a reference to Communion wine.

Conversely, the ST may deliberately trade on innuendo, using an expression primarily for its literal meaning, but implicitly expecting the addressee to perceive a connotation echoing the meaning of some similar expression. A good example is Pierre Emmanuel's use of 'menée à la baguette', which we have already discussed as an example of associative meaning. (It very often happens that an expression combines more than one type of connotative meaning, as here.) In such cases, a fully successful TT would be one which deliberately traded on an innuendo similar to that in the ST. This problem is exemplified in 'planté' and 'roulé' in the last sentence of the extract from *Les Flamboyants* in Practical 6.

COLLOCATIVE MEANING

Collocative meaning is given to an expression over and above its literal meaning by *the meaning of some other expression with which it collocates to form a commonly-used phrase*.

Words that frequently occur side by side – especially in clichéd phrases – will tend to form strong associative bonds, by which they can evoke one another. Thus, in the clichéd expression 'a resounding crash', the word 'resounding' collocates regularly with the word 'crash', forming such a strong stereotyped association that 'resounding' is capable of evoking the meaning of its collocative partner. This is doubtless why a collocation like 'resounding tinkle' feels incongruous – there is nothing in the literal meaning of 'resounding' to prevent its qualifying 'tinkle', but the combination it has through collocative association with 'crash' is carried over and clashes with the literal meaning of 'tinkle'. Similarly, the gender-specific connotations of 'pretty' and 'handsome' can be said to be collocative meanings, deriving from the tendency of 'pretty' to collocate with 'girl' and the tendency of 'handsome' to collocate with 'man'.

Some collocative meanings are so strong that they require very little triggering by context. For example, the word 'intercourse' (literally, 'mutual dealings') can hardly be used at all without evoking its collocative partner 'sexual', and is on the way to becoming a synonym of 'sexual intercourse'. Other collocative meanings need to be activated by the context, as with the humorous innuendo in 'I rode shotgun on the way to the wedding', based on activating the collocative echo of 'shotgun wedding'.

For the translator, collocative meanings are important, not only because they can contribute significantly to the overall meaning of a ST, but also because of the need to avoid unwanted collocative clashes in a TT. For example, translating 'il faut humecter le linge' as 'you've got to moisten the clothes [before ironing them]' produces a collocative clash – one moistens one's skin, or a dough, but one *dampens* the ironing. (An analogous collocative clash is produced by translating 'il s'humecta les lèvres' as 'he dampened his lips' instead of 'he moistened his lips'.)

Collocative clashes are always a threat when the TL offers an expression closely resembling the ST one. Compare, for example, 'a damp cellar' with 'a humid cellar' as translations of 'une cave humide'; or 'a resounding slap' with 'a sonorous slap' as translations of 'une gifle sonore'. Collocative clashes are also often produced by failure to spot the need for a communicative translation, as in rendering 'joli comme un cœur' by 'pretty as a heart' instead of 'pretty as a picture'. Worse still, translating 'il est joli garçon' as 'he's a pretty boy' produces a collocative clash which distorts the meaning of the ST (better rendered as 'he's a good-looking/nice-looking lad').

ALLUSIVE MEANING

Allusive meaning is present when an expression evokes some *associated saying or quotation* in such a way that the meaning of that saying or quotation becomes part of the overall meaning of the expression.

Allusive meaning hinges on indirectly evoking sayings or quotations that an informed hearer can recognize, even though they are not spelt out. The evoked meaning of the quotation alluded to creates an added innuendo that modifies the literal meaning of what has explicitly been said. For example, saying that 'there are rather a lot of cooks involved' in organizing a meeting evokes the proverb 'too many cooks spoil the broth', and by this allusive meaning creates the innuendo that the meeting risks being spoilt by over-organization.

In the case of allusive meaning in STs, the translator's first problem is to recognize that the ST does contain an allusive innuendo. The second problem is to understand the allusive meaning by reference to the meaning of the saying or quotation evoked. The third problem is to convey the force of the innuendo in the TT, ideally by using an appropriate allusive meaning based on a saying or quotation in the TL.

There is a simple example in Georges Brassens's 'Le testament', where the speaker envisages his widow marrying again:

> Qu'il boiv' mon vin qu'il aim' ma femme
> Qu'il fum' ma pipe et mon tabac
> Mais que jamais – mort de mon âme! –
> Jamais il ne fouette mes chats . . .
> Quoique je n'ai' pas un atome,
> Une ombre de méchanceté,
> S'il fouett' mes chats, y a un fantôme
> Qui viendra le persécuter.
> (Brassens, 1973, p. 94)

The literal meaning is clear: the widow's new husband can do what he likes, as long as he does not harm the dead man's cats. However, there is also a humorous allusion to the expression 'avoir d'autres chats à fouetter', which means 'to have more important things to attend to'. (There is also a secondary allusion to another expression – 'il n'y a pas de quoi fouetter un chat', which means 'there's nothing to fuss about'.) The innuendo is that loving the widow, drinking the wine and smoking the pipe are nothing to worry about, but attempting to duplicate the dead man's life and appropriate his memory would definitely warrant a good haunting. Fortunately, most of this allusive meaning can be rendered with an allusion to the English expression 'to have other fish to fry', which is the standard communicative translation of 'avoir d'autres chats à fouetter': 'Let him never fry my fish.' Note, however, that this solution would probably not work if the ST expression were one of a number of references to cats, or if there were already ST references to fish or frying with which the TT expression combined to introduce unwanted connotations.

Even this relatively simple example, then, is potentially problematic, but really drastic difficulties can arise if an apparent allusive meaning in the ST is obscure. Considerable research may be necessary to identify the allusion; and even when it has been tracked down and understood, the translator faces another challenge if there is no parallel to it in the TL culture. The solution is usually to compensate by some other means for the absence of a suitable allusion.

Take the following example: 'elle avait donné son amour au Grand Pourfendeur de Carthage!' (Céline, 1976, p. 269). The man in question is J. Hérold-Paquis, a collaborationist broadcaster during the German occupation of France in 1940–4, who concluded his daily bulletin with the words 'pour que la France vive, l'Angleterre, comme Carthage, doit être détruite'. After the Liberation, he was executed for his pro-German activities. When Céline's text was published, in 1957, the reader will have instantly recognized the allusion to Hérold-Paquis's bellicose watchword, and will also have been aware of his fate. The ironic allusive meaning is clear, but the translator can only render it through compensation, perhaps keeping some allusion to the Punic Wars, but making explicit who the broadcaster was and what his stance was, as in 'she'd given her love to Hérold-Paquis, broadcaster and self-styled Scipio to Churchill's Hannibal!'

A different sort of example of the same common problem is afforded by the title of Morvan Lebesque's polemical book defending Breton identity against French centralism: *Comment peut-on être Breton?*. The French reader immediately picks up the allusion to Letter XXX of Montesquieu's *Lettres persanes*, where a Persian living in Paris writes, of a social gathering:

Mais, si quelqu'un, par hasard, apprenait à la compagnie que j'étais Persan, j'entendais aussitôt autour de moi un bourdonnement: Ah! ah! Monsieur est Persan? C'est une chose bien extraordinaire! Comment peut-on être Persan?'

(Montesquieu, 1960, p. 69)

'Comment peut-on être Persan?' has acquired proverbial status as the expression of patronizing, uncomprehending insularity, and this is the allusive meaning in Lebesque's title. Perhaps recourse to tonal register and affective meaning would compensate for the absence of a suitable English allusion – something like *'Breton? Gosh, What's That?'* or *'So You're Breton? How Quaint!'* (For yet another way of translating allusive meaning by compensation, see the example from Ponge on p. 36.)

PRACTICAL 8

8.1 Connotative meaning

Assignment

Taking the expressions printed in bold type in the ST printed on pp. 110 and 112:

(i) Categorize and discuss those in which connotative meaning plays a part, and discuss the translation of them in the TT printed opposite the ST. Where necessary, give an edited TT rendering the ST connotations more successfully into English.

(ii) Identify and discuss expressions where unwanted connotative meanings have been introduced into the printed TT, give an edited TT in each case, and explain your decisions.

Contextual information

The text is from Act III of Ionesco's play *Rhinocéros* (1959). The play can be interpreted in a number of ways, but it certainly draws attention to, and perhaps attacks, conformism, racism and totalitarianism. It was inspired, in part, by Ionesco's horror at the rise of Nazism in Germany and Fascism in his native Romania, and by his experience of the German occupation of France. At this point in the play, all the characters but these three have turned into rhinoceroses, just as more and more people – even rigid conformists – were swept along by Fascism in the 1930s. Even Botard, who had long remained sceptical about this so-called 'rhinoceritis', has suddenly succumbed to it. Dudard, too, will shortly join the blindly destructive herd. The TT, by Derek Prouse, was published in 1960.

Source text

BERENGER   Eh bien, réflexion faite, le coup de tête de Botard ne
           m'étonne pas. Sa **fermeté** n'était qu'apparente. Ce qui ne
           l'empêche pas, bien sûr, d'être ou d'avoir été un brave
           homme. Les braves hommes font les braves rhinocéros.
           Hélas! C'est parce qu'ils sont de bonne foi, on peut les   5
           duper.

DAISY   Permettez-moi de mettre ce panier sur la table. (*Elle met le
           panier sur la table.*)

BERENGER   Mais c'était un brave homme qui avait des ressentiments . . .

DUDARD   (*à Daisy, s'empressant de l'aider à déposer son panier*)   10
           Excusez-moi, excusez-nous, on aurait dû vous débarrasser
           plus tôt.

BERENGER   (*continuant*) . . . Il a été **déformé** par la haine de ses chefs, un
           complexe d'infériorité . . .

DUDARD   (*à Bérenger*) Votre raisonnement est faux puisqu'il a suivi   15
           son chef justement, l'instrument même de ses exploitants,
           c'était son expression. Au contraire, chez lui, il me semble
           que c'est l'esprit communautaire qui l'a **emporté** sur ses
           impulsions anarchiques.

BERENGER   Ce sont les rhinocéros qui sont anarchiques puisqu'ils sont en 20
           minorité.

DUDARD   Ils le sont encore, pour le moment.

DAISY   C'est une minorité déjà nombreuse qui va croissant. Mon
           cousin est devenu rhinocéros, et sa femme. Sans compter **les
           personnalités**: le cardinal de Retz . . .   25

DUDARD   **Un prélat!**

DAISY   Mazarin.

DUDARD   Vous allez voir que ça va s'étendre dans d'autres pays.

BERENGER   **Dire que le mal vient de chez nous!**

DAISY   . . . Et des aristocrates: le duc de Saint-Simon.   30

BERENGER   (*bras au ciel*) **Nos classiques!**

DAISY   Et d'autres encore. Beaucoup d'autres. Peut-être un quart
           des habitants de la ville.

BERENGER   Nous sommes encore les plus nombreux. Il faut en profiter.
           Il faut faire quelque chose avant d'être submergés.   35

DUDARD   **Ils sont très efficaces, très efficaces.**

DAISY   Pour le moment, on devrait déjeuner. J'ai apporté de quoi
           manger.

BERENGER   Vous êtes très gentille, mademoiselle Daisy.

DUDARD   (*à part*) Oui, très gentille.   40

BERENGER   (*à Daisy*) Je ne sais comment vous remercier.

DAISY   (*à Dudard*) Voulez-vous rester avec nous?

DUDARD   Je ne voudrais pas être importun.

Target text

BERENGER	But now I come to think it over, Botard's behaviour doesn't surprise me. His firmness was only a pose. Which doesn't stop him from being a good man, of course. Good men make good rhinoceroses, unfortunately. It's because they are so good that they get taken in.
DAISY	Do you mind if I put this basket on the table? (*She does so.*)
BERENGER	But he was a good man with a lot of resentment . . .
DUDARD	(*to Daisy, and hastening to help her with the basket*) Excuse me, excuse us both, we should have given you a hand before.
BERENGER	(*continues*) . . . He was riddled with hatred for his superiors, and he'd got an inferiority complex . . .
DUDARD	(*to Berenger*) Your argument doesn't hold water, because the example he followed was the Chief's, the very instrument of the people who exploited him, as he used to say. No, it seems to me that with him it was a case of community spirit triumphing over his anarchic impulses.
BERENGER	It's the rhinoceroses which are anarchic, because they're in the minority.
DUDARD	They are, it's true – for the moment.
DAISY	They're a pretty big minority and getting bigger all the time. My cousin's a rhinoceros now, and his wife. Not to mention leading personalities like the Cardinal of Retz . . .
DUDARD	A prelate!
DAISY	Mazarin.
DUDARD	This is going to spread to other countries, you'll see.
BERENGER	And to think it all started with us!
DAISY	. . . and some of the aristocracy. The Duke of St Simon.
BERENGER	(*with uplifted arms*) All our great names!
DAISY	And others, too. Lots of others. Maybe a quarter of the whole town.
BERENGER	We're still in the majority. We must take advantage of that. We must do something before we're inundated.
DUDARD	They're very potent, very.
DAISY	Well for the moment, let's eat. I've brought some food.
BERENGER	You're very kind, Miss Daisy.
DUDARD	(*aside*) Very kind indeed.
BERENGER	I don't know how to thank you.
DAISY	(*to Dudard*) Would you care to stay with us?
DUDARD	I don't want to be a nuisance.

Line numbers: 5, 10, 15, 20, 25, 30, 35

DAISY   (*à Dudard*) Que dites-vous là, monsieur Dudard? Vous
            savez bien que vous nous feriez plaisir.   45

DUDARD   Vous savez bien que je ne veux pas gêner . . .

BERENGER   (*à Dudard*) Mais bien sûr, Dudard, bien sûr. Votre présence
            est toujours un plaisir.

DUDARD   C'est que je suis un peu pressé. J'ai un rendez-vous.

BERENGER   Tout à l'heure, vous disiez que vous aviez tout votre temps. 50

DAISY   (*sortant les provisions du panier*) Vous savez, j'ai eu du mal à
            trouver de quoi manger. Les magasins sont **ravagés**: ils
            dévorent tout. Une quantité d'autres boutiques sont
            fermées: **'Pour cause de transformation'**, est-il écrit sur les
            écriteaux.   55

BERENGER   **On devrait les parquer dans de vastes enclos, leur imposer des
            résidences surveillées.**

DUDARD   La mise en pratique de ce projet ne me semble pas possible.
            La société protectrice des animaux serait la première à s'y
            opposer.   60

DAISY   D'autre part, chacun a parmi les rhinocéros un parent
            proche, un ami, ce qui complique encore les choses.

BERENGER   Tout le monde est dans le coup, alors!

DUDARD   **Tout le monde est solidaire.**

BERENGER   **Mais comment peut-on être rhinocéros?** C'est impensable, 65
            impensable!

DAISY   Whatever do you mean, Mr Dudard? You know very well 40
           we'd love you to stay.
DUDARD   Well, you know, I'd hate to be in the way . . .
BERENGER   Of course, stay, Dudard. It's always a pleasure to talk
           to you.
DUDARD   As a matter of fact I'm in a bit of a hurry. I have an 45
           appointment.
BERENGER   Just now you said you'd got nothing to do.
DAISY   (*unpacking her basket*) You know, I had a lot of trouble
           finding food. The shops have been plundered; they just
           devour everything. A lot of shops are closed. It's written up 50
           outside: 'Closed on account of transformation'.
BERENGER   They should all be rounded up in a big enclosure, and kept
           under strict supervision.
DUDARD   That's easier said than done. The animals' protection league
           would be the first to object.   55
DAISY   And besides, everyone has a close relative or a friend among
           them, and that would make it even more difficult.
BERENGER   So everybody's mixed up in it!
DUDARD   Everybody's in the same boat!
BERENGER   But how can people be rhinoceroses? It doesn't bear 60
           thinking about!

8.2 Connotative meaning

Assignment
Working in four groups, each group taking three lines:

 (i) Discuss the strategic problems confronting the translator of the
      following text, paying particular attention to connotation.
      Outline your own strategy for translating the text.
 (ii) Translate the text into English.
(iii) Explain the main decisions of detail you made in producing your TT.
 (iv) After discussion of the translations, your tutor may give you a
      published TT for analysis and discussion in class.

Contextual information
Robert Desnos was one of the first Surrealists. This extract is the first part of
a text from *Langage cuit* (now collected in *Corps et biens* (1926)), in which
Desnos systematically distorts normal usage in a number of different ways.
(Compare the homonymic experiments of *L'aumonyme*, from which the

example on p. 80 is taken.) For this exercise, it would be useful to call on your imagination, as well as your knowledge of Catholicism, Homer and the clichés of popular culture.

Text

CŒUR EN BOUCHE

Son manteau traînait comme un soleil couchant
et les perles de son collier étaient belles comme des dents.
Une neige de seins qu'entourait la maison
et dans l'âtre un feu de baisers.   5
Et les diamants de ses bagues étaient plus brillants que des yeux.
'Nocturne visiteuse, Dieu croit en moi!
— Je vous salue, gracieuse de plénitude,
les entrailles de votre fruit sont bénies.
Dehors se courbent les roseaux fines tailles.   10
Les chats grincent mieux que les girouettes.
Demain à la première heure, respirer des roses aux doigts d'aurore
et la nue éclatante transformera en astre le duvet.'

9

Language variety in texts: dialect, sociolect, code-switching

In this chapter and Chapter 10, we discuss the question of language variety and translation. By way of introduction to the notion of language variety, here is a text from Marcel Pagnol's *Jean de Florette*. It is a letter from one Provençal *paysan* to another; the writer of the letter (supposedly written in the 1920s) has a Piedmontese father. We shall illustrate both chapters with points from this text (among others); if possible, it should be used as a point of reference in Practicals 9 and 10:

Collègue,
Je t'ai pas répondu de suite pourquoi ma sœur s'est marié avec Egidio, celui qui la chaspait tout le temps. Mintenant, s'est son droit. Pour les boutures, naturèlement que je t'en fais cadot. Mon père Monsieur Tornabua est d'acort. Je lui ai pas dit que tu m'a demandé le prix. Cà lui aurait fait pêne. Elles seront prête pour le mois d'April. Prépare le champ, et surtout l'eau. Mon père Monsieur Tornabua dit que pour dix mille plante il te faut une réserve d'au moins quatre cents mètres cubes. Si tu les as pas sur sur sur, c'est pas la peine de comencer pour pas finir. Tu as bien compris? Quatre cent mètres. Et pas des mètres de longueur. C'est des cube, les mêmes qu'au certificat d'études: qu'à cause de ces mètres j'ai jamais pu le passer, et mintenant je m'en sers pour gagner des sous bien plus que l'essituteur! C'est çà la vie! Ecrit moi encore, mais fais un peu entention à ton ortografe! On ni comprend rien, il faut toultan deviner! Je dis pas sa pour te vexer. Moi aussi, samarive de pas bien connaître un mot comment ca s'écrie: alors, à la place, j'en met un autre!

5
10
15

Ton ami Attilio.
(Pagnol, 1971, pp. 57–8)

Discussing this text and how to translate it will immediately highlight certain features: the regionalisms, the colloquialisms, the grammar and spelling, and the cheery tone. It is, in fact, an excellent example of one the most difficult aspects of 'meaning', namely the appreciation not of referential messages, but of characteristics *in the way the message is expressed* that voluntarily or involuntarily reveal information about the speaker or writer. These stylistically conveyed meanings are connotations: they share with the types of connotation discussed in Chapter 8 the character of meanings 'read between the lines' on the basis of associations that are widespread, although not enshrined in the dictionary.

Sorting out significant information carried by stylistic features can be a daunting practical problem – details have to be separated out as one comes to them. However, this is no reason for not trying to discuss the problem in general terms. There are two essential questions that arise. The first is: what are the *objective textual characteristics* from which stylistic information about the speaker or writer can be inferred? The simple answer must be: the way the message is expressed as compared with other possible ways it might have been expressed (whether by the same person or by somebody else). That is, the *manner in which the message is formulated* is the basic carrier of information about the speaker/writer.

The second question that arises is: what *kind of information* can be carried through the manner in which the message is formulated? The answer is two-fold: first, the manner, or style, reveals things about speakers/writers that they do not necessarily intend to reveal, notably regional affiliations, class affiliations, and the social stereotype they appear to belong to; second, it reveals things that they do intend to reveal, notably the effect they want their utterance to have on the listener/reader. Naturally, any or all of these features can occur together or overlap. The last two, in particular, are sometimes so closely associated that they cannot easily be distinguished; we shall discuss them, as different aspects of 'register', in the next chapter. In the present chapter, we look at translation issues raised by dialect, sociolect and code-switching.

DIALECT

To speak a particular **dialect**, with its phonological, lexical, syntactic and sentential features, is to give away information about one's association with a particular region. A simple phonological example in the Pagnol text is 'essituteur' ('instituteur'), and a lexical one is 'Collègue' (used in Provence in the sense of 'camarade', 'ami'). It is also possible to infer the *degree* of speakers' regional affiliations from the proportion of dialectal features in their speech; for instance, whether they are natives of the region and have little experience of other regions, or whether they are originally from the region, but retain only traces of that origin overlaid by speech habits acquired elsewhere; or whether they are incomers who have merely acquired a veneer of local speech habits. Furthermore, some speakers are notable for having a repertoire of several dialects between which they can alternate (that is, they are capable of 'code-switching'), or on which they can draw to produce a mixture of dialects. All these aspects of dialectal usage are stylistic carriers of information about a speaker, and no sensitive translator can afford to ignore them. Four main problems arise.

The first problem is easily defined: it is that of recognizing the peculiarities from which dialectal affiliation can be inferred in a ST. Clearly, the more familiar the translator is with SL dialects, the better.

The second is that of deciding how important the dialectal features in a ST are to its overall effect. The translator has always the option of rendering the ST into a bland, neutral version of the TL, with no notable dialectal traces. This may be appropriate if the dialectal style of the ST can be regarded as incidental, at least for the specific purposes of the TT. For example, in translating an eyewitness account of a murder for Interpol, one might want to ignore all dialectal features and concentrate on getting the facts clear. However, if the dialectal nature of the ST cannot be regarded as incidental – for example, in a novel where plot or characterization actually depend to some extent on dialect – the translator has to find means for indicating that the ST contains dialectal features. This creates some tricky questions.

For instance, suppose that the ST is so full of broad dialectal features as to be virtually incomprehensible to a SL speaker from a different region. The translator's first strategic decision is whether to produce a TT that is only mildly dialectal, and totally comprehensible to any TL speaker. Arguments against this solution might be similar to those against 'improving' a ST that is badly written. However, there can be circumstances where it is the best alternative; as in making any strategic decision, the translator has to consider such factors as the nature and purpose of the ST, the purpose of the TT, its intended audience, the requirements of the person paying for the translation, and so on. One may decide to inject a mere handful of TL dialectal features into the TT, just to show the audience that it is based on a ST in dialect. On the other hand, the very obscurity of a piece of ST dialect may serve important textual purposes which would be vitiated in the TT if the piece were not rendered in an equally obscure TL dialect. In such a case – and probably *only* in such a case – it may be necessary for the translator to go all the way in the use of a TL dialect.

The third problem arises if the translator does opt for a broad TL dialect: just what dialect should the TT be in? Supposing that the ST is in Marseilles dialect, is there any dialect of English that in some way corresponds to Marseilles dialect, having similar status and cultural associations among

English dialects to those held by Marseilles dialect among French dialects? There is no obvious objective answer to this question – after all, what *is* the exact position of Marseilles dialect among French dialects?

Of course, there may be certain stereotypical assumptions associated with the ST dialect which might be helpful in choosing a TT dialect (for instance, 'people from Marseilles tell tall stories', or 'the Irish have the blarney'). When a dialect is used in the ST specifically for its popular connotations (in terms of stock assumptions), it could conceivably be appropriate to select a TL dialect with similar connotations. In other cases, the choice of TL dialect may be influenced by geographical considerations. For instance, a northern dialect of French, in a ST containing references to 'northerners', might be most plausibly rendered in a northern dialect of English.

A final difficulty, if one decides to adopt a TL dialect, is of course the problem of familiarity with all the characteristics of TL dialects. If the translator does not have an accurate knowledge of the salient features of the TL dialect chosen, the TT will become as ludicrous as all the texts which, through ignorance, have Scots running around saying 'hoots mon' and 'och aye the noo'.

It will be clear by now that rendering ST dialect with TL dialect is a form of cultural transplantation. Like all cultural transplantation, it runs the risk of incongruity in the TT. For instance, having broad Norfolk on the lips of peasants from the Auvergne could have disastrous effects on the plausibility of the whole TT. The safest way of avoiding this would be to transplant the entire work – setting, characters and all – into Norfolk; but, of course, this might be quite inappropriate. Short of this extreme solution, the safest decision may after all be to make (relatively sparing) use of TL features that are recognizably dialectal, but not clearly recognizable as belonging to a specific dialect. Even safer, with a ST containing direct speech, would be to translate into fairly neutral English, and, if necessary, to add after an appropriate piece of direct speech some such phrase as 'she said, in a broad Lille accent', rather than have a Lilloise speaking Scouse or Glaswegian.

SOCIOLECT – class dialects

In modern sociolinguistics, a distinction is made between regional dialects (dialects proper) and language varieties that are, as it were, 'class dialects'. The latter are referred to by the term **sociolect**. Sociolects are language varieties typical of the broad groupings that together constitute the 'class structure' of a given society. Examples of the major sociolects in British culture are those designated as 'lower class', 'urban working class', 'white-collar', 'public school' and so on. It is noticeable, and typical, that these designations are relatively vague in reference. This vagueness is due partly to the fact that sociolects are intended as broad, sociologically convenient labels, and partly to the lack of rigid class structure in British society. In more rigidly stratified societies, where there is a strict division into formally recognized 'castes', the concept of sociolect is more obviously applicable.

A further possible reservation as to the usefulness of purely sociolectal labels is that, very often, a social classification is virtually meaningless without mention of regional affiliations. For example, the term 'urban working-class sociolect' cannot designate a particular language variety in English unless it is qualified by geographical reference. While 'upper class' and 'public school' sociolects are characteristically neutral to regional variations, the further 'down' one goes on the social scale, the more necessary it is to take social and regional considerations together, thus creating concepts of mixed regional and sociolectal language varieties such as 'Norwich urban working class', 'Edinburgh "Morningside" urban middle class', and so on. Such mixed sociolectal/regional designations are often more meaningful labels for recognizable language variants than purely sociological ones.

Whatever reservations one has about the notion of sociolect, it remains true that sociolectal features can, like a dialect, convey important information about a speaker or writer. If they are obtrusive in the ST (phonically, grammatically, lexically or sententially), the translator cannot afford to ignore them. In the Pagnol text on p. 115, the very first sentence yields two examples: 'pourquoi' (instead of 'parce que'), and 'qui la chaspait' (instead of 'qui lui jaspait', a colloquialism meaning 'who was yattering to her'); even here, the question arises of how far the letter-writer's sociolect is influenced by his having a Piedmontese father.

In the Pagnol text, the sociolect is a central feature, and requires attention from the translator. However, the fact that the ST contains marked sociolectal features does not always mean that the TT should be just as heavily sociolectally marked. As with translating dialects, there may be considerations militating against this, such as whether the sociolect has a textual role in the ST, or the purposes for which the ST is being translated. In such cases, the translator may include just enough devices in the TT to remind the audience of the sociolectal character of the ST. Alternatively, there may be good reasons for producing a TT that is in a bland 'educated middle-class' sociolect of the TL – this also is a sociolect but, for texts intended for general consumption, it is the least obtrusive one.

Once the translator has decided on a TT containing marked sociolectal features, the problems that arise are similar to those created by dialect. The class structures of different societies, countries and nations never replicate one another. Consequently, there can be no exact parallels between sociolectal varieties of one language and those of another. At best, something of the prestige or the stigma attached to the ST sociolect can be conveyed in the TT by a judicious choice of TL sociolect. The translator may therefore decide that a valid strategy would be to render, say, an 'urban working-class' SL sociolect by an 'urban working-class' TL sociolect. But this does not solve the question of *which* 'urban working-class' sociolect. The decision remains difficult, especially as the wrong choice of TL sociolect could make the TT narrative implausible for sociological reasons. This question of the socio-cultural plausibility of the TT is one of the translator's major considerations (assuming, of course, that the ST is not itself deliberately implausible). Finally, as with dialect, it goes without saying that the translator must actually be familiar enough with the chosen TL sociolect(s) to be able to use them accurately and convincingly.

CODE-SWITCHING

Passing mention was made above of **code-switching**. This well-known phenomenon occurs in the language-use of speakers whose active repertoire includes several language varieties – dialects, sociolects, even distinct languages. It consists of a rapid alternation from one moment to another between using different language varieties. Code-switching is used, by ordinary speakers and by writers, for two strategic reasons: first, to fit style of speech to the social circumstances of the speech situation; and second, to impose a certain definition on the speech situation by the choice of a style of speech. A good example of someone doing this for story-telling purposes will be seen in Practical 10.

Since code-switching is a definite strategic device, and since its social-interactional function in a text cannot be denied, the translator of a ST containing code-switching should convey in the TT the effects it has in the ST. For written dialogue, the possibility of explaining the code-switch without reproducing it in the TT does exist, as in 'he said, suddenly relapsing into the local patois'. It does not, of course, exist for the text of a play or a film, except as an instruction in a stage direction. At all events, it would be more effective, if possible, to reproduce ST code-switching by code-switching in the TT. Such cases place even greater demands on the translator's mastery of the TL, two or more noticeably different varieties of the TL needing to be used in the TT.

There is no code-switching in the Pagnol text, but it is found in the following extract from Georges Michel's play *L'Agression*. This should be prepared for discussion and translation in class.

(*Contextual information*. Set in a big city, the play shows the violent tensions between penniless, rebellious youth and comfortably-off middle-class adults in a consumer society. The adults are often represented, as here, by a 'chorus' of anonymous voices.)

AUTRE VOIX	Que dire de la dégradante et ignominieuse saleté de leurs cheveux.
	[. . .]
UNE VOIX	Ils ont le regard dur et haineux . . .
AUTRE VOIX	La sournoiserie collée au visage . . . 5
AUTRE VOIX	Le sourire amer . . .
AUTRE VOIX	L'injure aux lèvres . . .
AUTRE VOIX	La parole aigre . . .
AUTRE VOIX	La fourberie au cœur . . .
	[. . .] 10
AUTRE VOIX	On les voit flâner dans le quartier . . .
AUTRE VOIX	Avec des allures équivoques . . .
AUTRE VOIX	Demandant à l'alcool la consolation de leurs déboires . . .
AUTRE VOIX	L'oubli de leur turpitude et de leur souillure morale . . .
	[. . .] 15
DANY	T'as raison, leur société, une vraie saloperie! . . . tous des enfoirés!
JEANNOT	Un peu, ouhai, c'est à dégueuler dessus . . .
	(*Le chœur effrayé sort à reculons, quatre de chaque côté.*)
JACQUOT	Tu dis ça parce que t'as pas besoin de bosser . . . T'aurais 20 pas ta frangine qui te glisse un fafiot par-ci par-là . . .
DANY	Et alors, pourquoi que tu veux que je les refuse? . . . J'suis pas con comme toi à marner pour une mobylette . . .

(Michel, 1968, pp. 33–7)

PRACTICAL 9

9.1 Language variety: dialect and sociolect

Assignment

You will be played a sound recording of an extract from a television interview. The interviewee is explaining how he catches thrushes, which he will keep and train as decoys for the next season's shooting. After brief discussion of the salient features of the text, you will be given a transcript of it. Working in groups, each group taking half the text:

(i)   Identify and discuss the dialectal and sociolectal features in the text.
(ii) Discuss the strategic problems involved in translating the text (a) for voice-over in a television documentary and (b) for a speech in a play, and produce a translation for (a) for discussion in class.

9.2   Language variety: sociolect and code-switching

Assignment
Working in groups, take the extract from *L'Agression* given on p. 121 and:

  (i)   Discuss the strategic problems it poses for the translator. Outline your
       strategy for translating it, bearing in mind that it is part of a play.
  (ii) Translate it into English.
 (iii) Explain the main decisions of detail you made in producing your TT.

10

Language variety in texts: social register and tonal register

From dialect and sociolect, we move on to conclude our survey of language variety by looking at the other two sorts of information about speakers/writers that can often be inferred from the way the message is formulated. Both are often referred to as 'register', and they do often occur together, but they are different in kind. We shall distinguish them as 'social register' and 'tonal register'.

SOCIAL REGISTER

A **social register** is a particular style from which the listener reasonably confidently infers what kind of person is speaking, in the sense of what social stereotype the speaker belongs to. To explain this concept, we can start by taking two extremes between which social registers fall.

It is possible to imagine, at one extreme, a way of formulating messages that is so individually peculiar that it instantly identifies the author, narrowing down the possibilities to just one particular speaker or writer. Writers with virtually inimitable styles, such as Racine, Proust or Joyce, and singer-songwriters for whom a characteristic voice quality acts as an additional identifying mark, such as Brassens or The Beatles, come to mind as obvious examples. At the other extreme, a message can be formulated in such a bland, neutral and ordinary way as to give away virtually no personal information about its author: the speaker/writer could be almost any member of the SL speech community.

Usually, however, a style will be recognized as characteristic of a certain *kind* of person, classified as belonging to some previously encountered social stereotype. This information is, obviously, distinct from information carried specifically by dialectal features. Perhaps less obviously, it is also distinct from information carried specifically by sociolect: a social register is different from a sociolect in that a sociolect corresponds to very broad conceptions of social grouping (limited to sociological notions of 'class structure'), whereas social register designates fairly narrow stereotypes of the sorts of people one expects to meet in a given society. (For example, the grammatical, orthographical and lexical features of the Pagnol text on p. 115 indicate a social register more immediately than they do a sociolect.) Since, in general, we organize our interactions with other people (especially those we do not know intimately) on the basis of social stereotypes to which we attach particular expectations, likes and dislikes, it is easy to give examples of social register.

For instance, encountering a man given to using four-letter expletives, one may perhaps infer that he is the vulgar, macho type. (Terms like 'vulgar' and 'macho' are typical stereotyping terms.) Difficulties of precisely pinpointing the appropriate stereotype are similar to those of precisely pinpointing an attitudinal meaning (see p. 103). Nevertheless, what is significant is that a whole section of the population is eliminated from conforming to this type – one's maiden aunt is never going to speak like this – while other types (such as young, unskilled urban manual worker) remain likely candidates. Similarly, a style full of 'thank you' and 'please' and other polite expressions is not indicative of just any speaker. A middle-class, well-bred, well-mannered person may be implied by such a style (note again the typical stereotyping terms).

As these examples suggest, whatever information is conveyed by linguistic style about the kind of person the speaker/writer is will often be tentative, and will require the support of circumstantial and contextual knowledge before it adds up to anything like the 'characterization' of an individual. For example, in the Pagnol text, while the regionalisms and certain points of lexis, grammar and spelling suggest that the speaker may be a Provençal *paysan*, it is circumstantial details like the references to cuttings and watering that allow one to be reasonably confident in this inference. (In any case, as we have suggested, that example also shows that sociolect is subordinate to social register as an indication of what 'kind of person' is speaking.)

Despite these reservations, the fact remains that the mere observing of linguistic style invites unconscious social stereotyping, both of people and of situations in which they find themselves. Linguistic style is an unconscious reflex of a speaker's perception of 'self', of situations and of other people present. All the time that one is unconsciously stereotyping oneself and others, and situations, into various social categories, one is also unconsciously correlating the various stereotypes with appropriate styles of language-use. Inferences from social stereotype to linguistic stereotype and vice-versa are virtually inevitable.

As soon as a particular stylistic indication places a speaker and/or a social situation into one of the relatively narrowly circumscribed social categories used in stereotyping personalities and social interactions in a given society, the amount of stylistic information is relatively rich. In such cases, the information is likely to include fairly clear pointers to a combination of specific characteristics of speaker and/or situation. Among these character-istics are likely to be the speaker's educational background and upbringing; the speaker's persona with regard to social experience (for example, social roles the speaker is used to fulfilling); the speaker's occupation and professional standing; the speaker's peer-group status, and so on – the list is in principle inexhaustible.

This, then, is the sort of information carried by what we are calling 'social register'. In other words, when speakers signal or betray details of their social personae and specific social milieux (as distinct from broad class affiliations), we say that they are using particular social registers, each one held in common with other speakers answering a similar social description. Equally, if the style reveals details of the way participants perceive the social implications of the situation they are speaking in, we refer to this style as the social register appropriate both to a type of person and to a type of situation.

When authors' social credentials are of some importance (perhaps because of the need to establish authority for speaking on a particular subject), they will select and maintain the appropriate social register for conveying a suitable social persona. This use of social register accounts for much of the use of jargon, not only the jargon in technical texts (which is at least partly used to maintain the author's self-stereotyping as a technical expert), but also jargon consisting of clichés, catch-phrases and in-words that build up other social stereotypes.

Using jargon very often has to do with expectations, and the fulfilling of expectations, with respect to social register. In moderation, this does work as a successful strategy in signalling social stereotype. However, when taken to excess, jargon easily becomes ridiculous, putting its users into stereotypes they do not intend. This is illustrated in R. Beauvais's intralingual rendering of a famous speech from Act I, Scene v of Corneille's *Le Cid*. It is worth analysing Beauvais's text in Practical 10, to identify the social registers he is caricaturing, to determine how the caricature is done and how successful it is, and to attempt a TT. We give Corneille's text first:

> O rage! ô désespoir! ô vieillesse ennemie!
> N'ai-je donc tant vécu que pour cette infamie?
> Et ne suis-je blanchi dans les travaux guerriers
> Que pour voir en un jour flétrir tant de lauriers?
> Mon bras qu'avec respect toute l'Espagne admire,   5
> Mon bras, qui tant de fois a sauvé cet empire,
> Tant de fois affermi le trône de son roi,

Trahit donc ma querelle, et ne fait rien pour moi?
O cruel souvenir de ma gloire passée!
Œuvre de tant de jours en un jour effacée!   10
Nouvelle dignité, fatale à mon bonheur!
Précipice élevé d'où tombe mon honneur!
Faut-il de votre éclat voir triompher le comte,
Et mourir sans vengeance ou vivre dans la honte?

O stress! ô break-down! ô sénescence aliénante! N'ai-je donc tant vécu
que pour cette perturbation culpabilisante! Et n'ai-je donc perduré dans
une escalade promotionnelle à vocation martiale, que pour déboucher sur
l'instantanéité de ce retour au degré zéro de l'investiture!

    Mon bras proposé comme archétype à l'hispanité, prise dans sa   5
globalité, mon bras qui tant de fois fut l'élément vecteur de l'autonomie
fondamentale de cette unité sociologique, tant de fois a conforté le trône
de son substitut du père, cesse donc de sous-tendre ma contestation, et
manifeste à mon égard une activité oppositionnelle de refus? O mémori-
sation éprouvante de ma saga! Réalisation pensée en termes de durée,   10
durant des décennies et soudainement néantisée! Promotion éclair
dommageable à mon confort moral! Champ gravitationnel où s'anéantit
ma bonne conscience! Faut-il voir le Comte en assumer le leadership
définitif? Et arriver au terme de mon processus biologique, sans assumer
ma catharsis? Ou perdurer dans l'être, déconnecté par un sentiment de   15
culpabilisation irréductible?

(Beauvais, 1970, pp. 136–7)

This example clearly shows the potential of exaggeration in social register as
a comic device, and also the attendant problem of finding an appropriate
social register, and getting the degree of exaggeration right, when translating a ST parodying a SL social register. The example also shows a
different, but related, problem in translating *serious* STs: while it is
important to choose an appropriate social register, it is just as important not
to over-mark it, otherwise the TT may become unintentionally comic.

In a narrative or play, an essential part of making sure the characters stay
plausibly true to type is to ensure that they express themselves consistently
in an appropriate social register. The extract from *L'Agression* on p. 121
shows this need for consistency even more clearly in respect of social register
than of sociolect. It would indeed be very odd for a street-corner 'hooligan'
suddenly to assume the social register of a contemplative intellectual or an
aristocrat, unless, of course, there were special textual/narrative reasons for
doing this deliberately. (Still more interesting in this extract is the social
register of the middle-class 'chorus': are there in fact distinguishable social
registers among these anonymous characters, or is their anonymity con-

firmed by their sharing a single social register – and, if so, which one?) Good
characterization demands two things: insight into the way in which people
belonging to identifiable social stereotypes express themselves, and the
ability to use consistently the stylistic quirks and constraints of these social
registers. (By *quirks* we mean the kind of thing representatives of a given
stereotype would say; by *constraints*, the kind of thing they would never
say.)

It is important to remember that, in literature and real life alike, social
register can be signalled on any or every level of textual variable, including
accent and delivery. Practical 10 may include discussion of two taped
extracts, the first spoken by an actress, the second from an interview. In
both, there is important speaker-related information to be gleaned from the
phonic features of social register, as well as from grammar and vocabulary.
The transcribed texts of the extracts are as follows:

Text 1

'Bonjour chou,' m'a-t-elle dit — elle était dans le noir, elle était en train
de penser — elle m'a dit: 'Vous savez qu'il est arrivé une chose ahurissante
à Gismonde.' (Taisez-vous Hannibal,[1] vous êtes odieux.) Elle dit — vous
connaissez Gismonde? Vous savez que c'est une fille absolument
sensationnelle? C'est une fille qui a dépassé Picasso depuis très long-   5
temps. C'est une fille qui peint à coups de marteau: elle envoie la couleur
dans la toile avec le marteau, et plus la toile est crevée plus elle se vend
cher. Une fille absolument sensationnelle. Restez tranquille Hannibal,
vous êtes odieux — ah! ce chien me tue . . .

(Adapted from Carton et al., 1983, p. 90)

[1] Hannibal is a dog.

Text 2

[*From an interview on the life-style of modern youth, in particular relations
between the sexes*]

Question. Et autrement, que ce soit dans ce milieu ou dans . . . dans celui
que vous fréquentez, vous, quelles sont les relations garçons-filles? C'est
toujours la même chose, ou ça a évolué depuis le féminisme et depuis un
certain nombre de . . .?
Réponse. Ça évolue un peu ouais, on s'y retrouve un peu moins, nous les   5
garçons, mais . . . Ouais ça évolue oui, euh . . . Disons que ça . . . ç . . .
on s'en rend pas complètement compte nous, parce que je crois qu'il faut
vivre avec une fille pour s'en rendre vraiment compte . . . euh, quoi . . .
Bon, on s'aperçoit que ça change dans . . . Ouais j'arrive pas . . . c'est . . .
c'est un problème qui me touche pas, alors j'essaye de vous en parler à   10
travers ce que j'ai entendu. Ouais, je dis dans le couple, on s'en aperçoit

parce qu'ils nous disent que . . . euh . . . bon, que . . . que les filles elles
veulent moins faire de choses, elles veulent plus partager . . . euh . . . plus
partager les tâches et cetera . . . euh . . .

(Adapted from Carton et al., 1983, p. 86)

It will be clear by now that in translating a ST that has speaking characters in
it, or whose author uses a social register for self-projection, the construction
of social register in the TT is a major concern. Equally clearly, in translating
P.G. Wodehouse into French, one would have to do something about the
fact that Jeeves speaks in the social register of the 'gentleman's gentleman',
and Bertie Wooster in that of the aristocratic nitwit. The fundamental
problem is this: how can British stereotypes like Jeeves and Bertie be
transplanted into a French-speaking context, produce plausible dialogue in
French, and still remain linguistically stereotyped so as to hint at the
caricatures of gentleman's gentleman and inane aristocrat? There are no
obvious global answers to such questions.

A choice of appropriate TL registers can, however, sometimes seem
relatively easy when the translator is operating between similar cultures,
where certain social stereotypes (such as the street-corner hooligan) and
stereotype situations (such as an Embassy ball) do show some degree of
cross-cultural similarity. It may well be that some social stereotypes can be
fairly successfully matched from one culture to another. The translator is
then left with two tasks. First, a ST stereotype must be converted into an
appropriate target-culture stereotype; and second, a plausible social register
must be selected and consistently applied for each of the target-culture
stereotypes chosen.

However, such 'parallels' in social stereotyping are in fact far from exact.
There are obvious discrepancies between, for example, the stereotypes of
British aristocrat and French aristocrat, or British hooligan and French
hooligan. In any case, is it desirable for Bertie Wooster to become every inch
the French aristocrat in a French TT? Does the translator not need to remind
the French reader of Wooster's essential Britishness (or even Englishness)?
These are important strategic decisions, and have to be taken at the outset.

There are still greater difficulties when it comes to matching social
stereotypes for which there are no likely parallels in the target culture. For
instance, what target-culture parallels are there for the British gentleman
farmer or the French *paysan*? Given either of these types in a ST, what social
register would be appropriate for the corresponding character in the TT? Or
should their speech be rendered in a fairly neutral style, with very few
marked features of social register? After all, for Marcel Pagnol's *paysans* to
lose all trace of their Frenchness in a translation of *Jean de Florette* might be
as disappointing – or as ludicrous – as for Bertie Wooster to come across as
completely French. Even once the strategic decision has been taken, there
remains the eternal double challenge to the translator's linguistic skill: to be

familiar with the quirks and constraints of TL language varieties, and to be able to produce a consistently plausible TL social register.

TONAL REGISTER

The fourth type of speaker-related information that can be inferred from the way the message is formulated is what we shall call **tonal register**. Tonal register is what is often called 'register' in dictionaries and textbooks on style. It often combines with any or all of dialect, sociolect and social register in an overall stylistic effect, but it is crucially different from them. Tonal register is *the tone that the speaker/writer takes* – perhaps vulgar, or familiar, or polite, or formal, or pompous. That is, the effect of tonal register on listeners is something for which speakers can be held responsible, in so far as they *are being* familiar, pompous, and so on. Dialect, sociolect and social register are different from tonal register in that they are not matters of an attitude that speakers intentionally adopt, but the symptomatic result of regional, class and social-stereotype characteristics that they cannot help. So a listener might reasonably respond to tonal register by saying 'don't take that tone with me', but this would not be a reasonable response to dialect, sociolect, or social register. If, in a given situation, Bertie Wooster *is being* polite, that is a matter of tonal register; but it would be odd to suggest that he *is being* an upper-class twit – he *is* an upper-class twit, as one infers from his sociolect and social register. (Of course, someone perceived as *putting on* an accent, sociolect or social register is in a sense 'being', say, Glaswegian or Sloane, but this mimicry or play-acting is in itself a matter of social register, not tonal register; in 'playing the Sloane', the speaker is not taking a tone with the listener, but is consciously or unconsciously projecting herself as belonging to the social stereotype of the code-switcher and mimic.)

Many of the labels dictionaries attach to certain expressions, such as 'familiar', 'colloquial', 'formal', and so on, are, in fact, reflections of the tone a speaker using these expressions can be said to be taking towards the listener or listeners. It is, therefore, helpful to assess levels of tonal register on a 'politeness scale', a scale of stylistic options for being more or less polite, more or less formal, more or less offensive, and so on.

Looked at in this way, tonal register is relatively easy to distinguish from social register. As we have suggested, being polite on a particular occasion is different from being stereotyped as a well-brought-up kind of person. Nevertheless, tonal register often overlaps with social register, in two ways.

First, there are ambiguous cases where it is not clear whether a style of expression is a reflection of social stereotyping or of the speaker's intentions towards the listener. For example, it may be impossible to tell whether a speaker is deliberately being pompous in order to convey a patronizing attitude (tonal register), or whether the pomposity is just a symptom of the fact that the speaker fits the stereotype of, for example, the self-important academic (social register). Thus, the difference in register between 'this essay isn't bad' and 'this essay is not without merit' might equally well be classified as social or as tonal.

Second, the characteristics of particular social registers are very often built up out of features of tonal register – and of dialect and sociolect, for that matter. This is especially true of social stereotypes characterized by 'downward social mobility'. For instance, a middle-class, educated person who is adept at the jargon of criminals and down-and-outs will have an active repertoire of vulgarisms and slang expressions. As we have seen, 'vulgarity' and 'slang' are points on the politeness scale of tonal register; but, at the same time, they go towards building up the complex of features that define a particular social register. Similarly, the girl pretending to be a Sloane is thereby also using the amalgam of tonal registers that helps to constitute the Sloane social register.

The notions of 'social register', 'tonal register', 'dialect' and 'sociolect' do therefore overlap to some extent, and all four are likely to occur inter-mingled in a text. Their separation is consequently something of a theoretical abstraction, but, practically speaking, it is still very useful to keep them as clearly distinct as possible in analysing style, because it helps the translator to discern what features are textually important, and therefore to take correspondingly important strategic decisions. Where it does remain unclear whether a particular case is an instance of tonal register or of social register, it is legitimate to use the cover-term 'register'. (Similarly, where dialect, sociolect and social register overlap indistinguishably, the cover-term 'language variety' can be used.)

The implications of tonal register for the translator are essentially no different from those of dialect, sociolect and social register. Since tonal register is linked to intended effects on the listener/reader, interpreting the impact of a ST depends very greatly on identifying its tonal register. Once this has been done, care has to be taken to match the tonal register of the TT to the effects intended to be produced on the audience. Inappropriateness or inconsistency in register can all too easily spoil a translation. For example, there would be unacceptable translation loss in mixing registers by rendering 'voilàtipas qu'alors jremarque un zozo l'air pied' by 'thereupon I spotted a doltish-looking jerk', or 'taisez-vous Hannibal, vous êtes odieux' by 'shut it, Hannibal, you're intolerable'. As with the other language varieties, looking for suitable renderings of tonal register puts translators on their mettle, giving ample scope for displaying knowledge of the SL and its culture, knowledge of the target culture, and, above all, flair and resourcefulness in the TL.

PRACTICAL 10

10.1 Language variety: social register and tonal register

Assignment

(i) Identify and discuss the salient features of language variety in the following text. Pay special attention to social register and tonal register, but do not ignore important instances of dialect and sociolect. In the case of features of social register, say what sort of social stereotype they signal.

(ii) Using appropriate English social and tonal registers, translate the ST expressions that you have identified as instances of register. Explain your decisions in each case.

Contextual information

The passage is from Armand Lanoux's *Le commandant Watrin* (1956). A group of officers is billeted in a country house in May 1940, among them Durroux, Vanhoenacker, Thomas Cavatini (nicknamed 'Toto' because he stammers), *capitaine* Bertuold and *sous-lieutenant* Soubeyrac. They know their battalion affectionately as 'le brave bataillon'. Watrin is the battalion's commanding officer. Bertuold commands a section of machine-gunners, Soubeyrac a section of *voltigeurs* (light infantry). Soubeyrac's section is a group of tearaways known by the nickname of 'les zèbres de Soubé'. There is intense, sometimes violent, but basically friendly, rivalry between the two groups. Bertuold has just been pulling Soubeyrac's leg, because the machine-gunners have appropriated some raspberry brandy which the 'zèbres' had looted but not hidden away: the 'zèbres' are still wet behind the ears, he teases.

Text

Soubeyrac — Je leur ferai la commission, mon capitaine.

Capt Bertuold — Ah! non. Pour qu'ils se foutent encore sur la figure avec mes mitrailleurs! Soubeyrac, l'esprit de corps, c'est bien, mais il n'en faut point trop. ⟧ Trans

– A propos de mes zèbres, dit Soubeyrac, vous vous souvenez de   5
Kirschweiler?

Le capitaine rit:

– Oui, dit-il, mais les autres ne la connaissent pas. Allez-y, Soubeyrac.

Narrator — Kirschweiler avait été le premier secteur dangereux du brave   10
bataillon, un gros bourg mort, vidé de ses habitants, avec sa chapelle ouverte comme une porte cochère, son cimetière occupé par les groupes de voltigeurs. Soubeyrac gardait Kirschweiler où logeait la

compagnie franche, Kirschweiler qui n'avait jamais vu un soldat
allemand depuis le 2 septembre et qui était pourtant pillé jusqu'aux   15
murs, avec des lits à colonne dans les prairies, des fauteuils de reps
pourpre sur les pavés, des prie-Dieu dans les barricades, son
presbytère éventré, Kirschweiler, cette première dent pourrie dans
la mâchoire de la guerre.

Soubeyrac — Eh bien, conta Soubeyrac, vous vous souvenez que nous avons   20
relevé des Catalans?

— Triste souvenir, dit Vanhoenacker, qui aimait peu les Méridionaux.
Il faut reconnaître que cette relève avait été surprenante d'humour
involontaire. Après quatre nuits de marche, le brave bataillon,
arrivé tout frais des cantonnements familiaux du Nord, avait trouvé   25
sur ses positions un régiment d'active du Midi, un caravansérail noir
et grouillant dans une odeur de chevaux et de campement gitan!
Naturellement les Chtimis avaient mis au compte de la crasse
méditerranéenne le désordre et la saleté qui n'étaient dûs qu'à la
guerre, ils le verraient bientôt.   30

François — Eh bien, continua François, sirotant la framboise des mitrailleurs,
mes zèbres relevaient la section qui occupait Kirschweiler. Un de
Catalan mes gars, aimable, Poivre, dit gentiment à un Catalan: 'D'où t'ch'est
qu' t'es, ti? – Hé, qu'est-ceu que tu me raconn'teu? chante l'autre.
– Mi, j' to dis, d'où d' ch'est qu' tê? – Oh! putaing, je neu comprin rien   35
de rieng!' Et ils se regardaient de travers, comme mes voltigeurs et vos
mitrailleurs, mon capitaine. Alors, j'interviens: 'Il te demande d'où tu es?
– Oh! moi, putaing, je suis de Cerbère! – Alors tu dois connaître
Vandarem, Carlos Vandarem? – Bien sûr, que je le connais, cet
essepéditionnaire, mon lieutenin!' Et mes Chtimis sont restés figés devant   40
ce miracle, leur lieutenant parlant avec des gitans olivâtres, les entendant
et se faisant entendre d'eux!

François — C'est drôle, dit Bertuold.

— Le plus drôle, mon capitaine, c'est bien Poivre. Il avait l'air à la
fois stupéfait, décontenancé et agressif. Il s'approche de moi et il me   45
confie: 'Mi, j'sauros jamais rien comprindre de leur parlet. I' pourro
p't'être pas apprendre el français, ches gars-là!'

Ils riaient de bon cœur.

François — Vous êtes en forme, Soubeyrac. Racontez-nous-en une autre. Et
après, si le commandant n'est pas rentré, nous irons nous coucher.   50

Soubeyrac— Bon, dit Soubeyrac, il s'agit justement du commandant. Les
Catalans relevés, je défends Kirschweiler, théoriquement, bien
entendu. J'avais un groupe dans une écurie et mon P.C. avec ce
groupe. Un jour, le Capim me tombe sur le poil avec Watrin. Il
faisait un froid à tout claquer, mais, dans l'écurie, mes zèbres étaient   55
en chandail et ça sentait la volaille bien rissolée! Watrin ressemblait
à un setter qui tombe en arrêt sur une compagnie de perdreaux. 'Ma

parole, dit Gondamini, vos hommes font du feu, lieutenant Soubeyrac.
— Ça m'en a bien l'air, dit Watrin, mi-figue, mi-raisin. — Mon com-
mandant, reprend le Capim, c'est insensé! Ils vont se signaler aux avions.' 60
Ça, c'était de la mauvaise foi. Mes zèbres savent camoufler un feu.

— On se demande ce que vos zèbres ne savent pas camoufler, dit
Bertuold, la framboise mise à part.

Le capitaine mitrailleur remplit encore une fois les verres, des verres
à vin. L'odeur de fruit embaumait la maison de l'avoué. 65
'Continuez votre édifiante histoire.'

— Eh bien, Watrin reste le nez au sol pour ne pas trop sentir l'odeur
du poulet, et le Capim devient blanc comme un linge, blanc de
fureur. 'Décidément, vous êtes fou à lier, Soubeyrac', crache-t-il.

Il était drôle, Soubeyrac, car il imitait très bien les autres. 70

'— Et les précautions en cas d'incendie? Hein? Où est votre piquet
d'incendie, je préfère ne pas vous le demander!' Naturellement, je
n'avais pas pensé au piquet d'incendie. 'Mais enfin, mon ami, où
avez-vous la tête? S'il y a le feu, qu'est-ce qu'on fera quand il faudra
rendre les locaux . . .' 75
— Re-rer-rrendre les locaux? dit Toto, incompréhensif.

— Parfaitement, dit Soubeyrac, rendre les locaux. Aux civils. Voilà
ce qu'il y avait dans la tête du Capim, le 20 décembre 1939. Il était
indigné! Les hommes aussi, mais plutôt pour d'autres raisons. Alors,
Gondamini a pris un seau d'eau et il est allé vers le poêle. J'avoue 80
qu'il ne donnait pas grande garantie de sécurité, le poele, vu que
c'étaient mes zèbres qui l'avaient monté. Mais le plus curieux, c'était
le commandant. Si je pouvais soupçonner le commandant Watrin
d'avoir eu un jour envie de rire, je crois bien que ce jour-là, il avait
envie de rire. 85
— Improbable, dit Durroux.

— Bref, Watrin arrêta d'un mot la charge de notre breveté. 'Enfin,
dit le Capim, se retournant vers lui, si la division nous tombe dessus,
ça va faire un drame, mon commandant. L'incendie, c'est grave! Et
les rapports! Et les enquêtes!' Moi, je suis allé à la fenêtre où j'avais 90
mis le thermomètre et je l'ai posé sur la table. Gondamini l'a pris.
Moins quinze. Le commandant le lui a arraché des mains, me l'a
rendu. Il a dit, un bon moment après: 'Lieutenant Soubeyrac, le
capitaine Gondamini a raison; je devrais vous mettre aux arrêts.'

10.2 Language variety

Assignment

(i) Listen to the recordings transcribed on pp. 127–8 above, and identify the salient features of language variety in each. Discuss the strategic problems confronting the translator in each, and outline your own translation strategy for each.

(ii) Working in groups, translate 'Bonjour chou . . .' into English, paying appropriate attention to language variety. The TT should be suitable for oral performance as part of a sketch.

(iii) Explain the decisions of detail you made in producing your TT.

10.3 Language variety

Assignment

(i) With particular reference to language variety, discuss the strategic problems confronting the translator of the Pagnol text given on p. 115. Outline your own strategy for translating it, bearing in mind that it is part of a novel.

(ii) Translate the text into English.

(iii) Explain the main decisions of detail you made in producing your TT.

11

Textual genre as a factor in translation: oral and written genres

At various times in this course, we have spoken of the ST both as a starting-point for translation and as a point of reference in evaluating TTs. However, before it is ever thought of as a ST, any text is already an object in its own right, and actually belongs to a particular genre of the source culture. Because any ST shares some of its properties with other texts of the same genre, and is perceived by a SL audience as being what it is on account of such genre-defining properties, the translator must be familiar with the broad characteristics of the source-culture genres. Furthermore, since any source culture presents a whole array of different textual genres, the translator must have some sort of overview of genre-types in that culture. This does not imply an exhaustive typology of genres – even if such a thing were possible, it would be too elaborate for a methodology of translation. All that is needed is an approximate framework of genre-types that might help a translator to concentrate on characteristics that make the ST a representative specimen of a particular source-culture genre.

The most elementary subdivision in textual genres is into *oral* text types and *written* ones. Both these major categories naturally break down into a number of more narrowly circumscribed minor categories, and ultimately into specific genres.

ORAL GENRES

In the case of oral genres, the ultimate breakdown into genres will include a long list of oral text-types. Some examples are:

oral narrative (that is, story-telling)
anecdotes
jokes
unrehearsed conversation
oral poetry (including recitation of written verse)
dramatized reading
reading aloud
speeches, lectures, talks, and so on
drama performances and film sound-tracks
song-lyrics and libretti

This list gives just a few suggestions. Other genres could be added, and many items could be further subdivided (for example, oral narrative into folk tales, ghost stories, autobiographical accounts, and so forth). However, even as it stands, the list enables us to pick out the basic features that concern translators of oral texts.

The defining property all these genres have in common is the fact that they are realized in a vocal medium. This truism has important implications. First, an oral text is in essence a fleeting and unrepeatable event that strikes the ear briefly and 'then is heard no more'. Second, vocal utterance may be accompanied by visual cues (such as gestures or facial expressions) that are secondary to it, and equally transitory, but which do form part of the overall text and play a role in colouring its meaning. This all means that, on every level of textual variable, oral texts must obey the 'rules' of a spoken language first and foremost. It also means that an effective oral text avoids the problems of comprehension arising from informational overloading, elaborate cross-reference, excessive speed and so forth. Of course, in all these respects, what is true for oral STs is true for oral TTs as well – an obvious fact, but one that is all too often overlooked.

Another important implication is the appearance of spontaneity that in general characterizes oral genres. This goes not only for impromptu conversation or unrehearsed narrative, but for prepared texts as well: stories told and retold in a carefully formulated version; memorized lines in a play or film; even such texts as speeches or lectures, where the speaker may stick closely to a script but the delivery is imitative of unscripted oral texts. Similarly, dramatized reading, recited verse, song lyrics and libretti, if well performed, all give the audience a chance to enter into the illusion of spontaneous vocal utterance.

As these remarks suggest, an oral text is always quite different in nature and impact from even the most closely corresponding written version. For instance, a recited poem is very different from its printed counterpart, and so is a performed song from the bare text set down on paper. Even a text that is obviously being read out from the printed page has nuances of oral delivery, such as intonation and stress, that make its reception quite different from the experience of silent reading.

An awareness of these properties of oral texts and genres is a necessary starting-point for discussing the particular types of problem that confront anyone wanting to translate an oral ST into an oral TT. The most specialized branch of oral-to-oral translating is on-the-spot interpreting. (In fact, terminologically, interpreting is usually distinguished from other kinds of translating.) There are three major types of interpreting.

The first is *two-way interpreting* of dialogue, where the interpreter acts as intermediary in unrehearsed conversation. Two-way interpreting can be the most relaxed of the three types; the interpreter can even clarify obscure points with the speakers. What this kind of interpreting involves mainly is a broad facility in understanding and speaking the languages involved, familiarity with the cultures involved, and sensitivity to the conversational nuances of both languages (including such things as tonal register and the visual cues of gesture or facial expression).

The second type is *consecutive interpreting*. This requires all the same skills as two-way interpreting, and more besides. The interpreter listens to an oral text, makes detailed shorthand notes and, from these, ad libs an oral TT that relays the content and nuances of the ST. The training for consecutive interpreting is intensive, and takes several months at least.

The third type is *simultaneous interpreting*. Here, the interpreter relays an oral TT at the same time as listening to the oral ST. This is the most specialized form of interpreting, and requires the longest training. Grasping the content and nuances of a continuous oral ST, and at the same time producing a fluent oral TT that does justice to the content and nuances of the ST, is very taxing indeed. Trainees do not usually start learning simultaneous interpreting until they have acquired considerable skill in consecutive interpreting.

Since it is a specialized skill, interpreting is not part of this course, and we shall not dwell on it. It is very useful, however, to try a session of two-way interpreting and one of consecutive interpreting, partly as an exercise in gist translation (as defined on p. 17), but mostly because it sharpens awareness of specifically oral textual variables, which may require special attention in translating any kind of text, spoken or written.

An exercise in interpreting will also confirm that spoken communication has stylistic quirks and characteristics that are very much language-specific. The eternal problem of translating jokes is a good example of this. We are not concerned here with jokes that are hard to translate because they depend on word-play, but with the fact that both humour itself and techniques of joke- and story-telling are to a great extent culture-specific. Translating spoken jokes is an especially clear illustration of the fact that oral translation is not simply a matter of verbal transposition from one spoken language to another: the genre-related techniques of the target culture must be respected as well, including gestures, facial expressions, mimicry and so on. A text in a particular oral genre is not only an utterance, but also a dramatic performance. This will have been vividly seen by anyone who tried putting 'Bonjour chou . . .' into English (p. 127). To do so, one is almost bound to produce a written TT, but this will only be an interim approximation to the combination of phonic and prosodic features essential to a successful, performed, oral TT.

Another oral genre, which we will meet in Practical 11, helps to highlight a second set of difficulties peculiar to oral translation. This is the genre of the song lyric. Assuming that the TT is to be sung to the same tune as the ST, the major translation problems will be on the prosodic and phonic levels of textual variables. It is therefore hardly surprising that translators of songs, and even libretti, sometimes take considerable liberties with the literal meanings of STs. Popular songs may have completely new TL lyrics written for them, of course; and if they are translated, it is very freely. Libretti cannot enjoy the same degree of freedom, since the TT still has to make sense within the framework of a plot that does not depart significantly from that of the original ST. Libretto-translators have an extremely demanding task, because they have to do three things: respect the dramatic needs of the ST (with its linguistic and stylistic implications); produce a dramatic TT matching the expectations that a TL audience has of the genre; and work under the very strict prosodic constraints imposed by the music. As we have seen (pp. 69–74), the prosodic properties of different languages are very different. Consequently, anyone translating a lyric needs to understand the prosodic features not only of the SL, but also of the TL, so that the TT can actually be sung without sounding ridiculous.

In addition, the song-translator must be alert on the phonic level, and pay attention to the quality of syllabic vowels as they correspond with notes on the score. For example, in a French song it is feasible to sing a long note on a syllabic [ə], as in Piaf's rendering of 'la vie'; but a [ə] on a long musical note in English is only possible in syllables that are stressed in ordinary speech – compare 'return', which is acceptable, and 'eternally', which is not. Consonant clusters must also be attended to, so that the performer is not given a tongue-twister to sing.

In Chapter 12, where we look at problems that arise in translating written STs for oral delivery and oral STs into written TTs, we shall need to keep in mind this brief survey of the main issues in oral-to-oral translation. First, however, we need to survey – equally briefly – the field of written genres.

WRITTEN GENRES

There are so many different varieties of written text that any typology of practical use for translation is bound to be even more approximate than the one suggested for oral genres. We shall approach the categorization of written genres by looking back to a time immediately predating the literary explosion that has continued to escalate since the sixteenth and seventeenth centuries. The approach implies that innovation in textual genres, for at least the past four centuries, has been limited to the invention of new subdivisions of five already existing genres, the seeds of which were probably sown in classical antiquity. On this assumption, the fundamental and most general categories of written genres are:

> literary/fictional
> theological/religious
> theoretical/philosophical
> empirical/descriptive
> persuasive/prescriptive.

This classification is primarily based on subject matter, or, more precisely, on *the author's attitude to the treatment of subject matter*.

Literary/fictional genres

The essence of texts in this category is that they are about a 'fictive', imaginary world of events and characters created autonomously in and through the texts themselves, and not controlled by the physical world outside. However close a text of this type may be to autobiography, it still approaches its subject matter by re-creating experience in terms of a subjective, internal world, which is fundamentally perceived as fictive, for all its similarities to real life. In texts in this category, the author is understood to be ultimately in control of events and characters.

Literary genres have, of course, subdivided and diversified very greatly. Even poetry, which is just one genre in this category, has split up over the last two centuries into innumerable sub-genres, each with different characteristic styles. (One need only compare the poems used in this course to get a good idea of this proliferation.) As for prose fiction, there are not just the genres of novel and short story, but a wide variety of minor genres such as detective stories, thrillers, historical romances and science fiction.

Theological/religious genres

The subject matter of theological and religious works implies the existence of a 'spiritual world'. Seen from outside (that is, by an atheist or agnostic), there may seem little difference between this and the fictive and imaginary subject matter of literary/fictional genres. However, that is not the point. The point is that, seen in terms of the author's attitude to the treatment of the subject matter, there is nothing fictive about the spiritual world treated in theological/religious texts: it has its own external realities and unshakeable truths. That is, this category has more in common with the 'empirical/descriptive' than with the 'literary/fictional' category. The author is understood not to be free to create the world that animates the subject matter, but to be merely instrumental in exploring it.

Of all five categories of genre, this one seems to have changed and diversified least of all. Even the Good News Bible represents only a minor diversion from the Authorized Version, and Thomas Aquinas or Julian of Norwich have only to be brought modestly up to date to feel remarkably modern.

Theoretical/philosophical genres

These genres have as their subject matter a 'world' of *ideas*, which are understood to exist independently of the individual minds that think them. So-called pure mathematics is the best example of the kind of subject matter and approach to subject matter that define theoretical/philosophical genres. The vehicle used by authors is not fictional imagination or spiritual faith, but reasoning. (In Western cultures, the primary form of abstract, rational thinking is deductive logic.) The author of a theoretical/philosophical text, however original it may be, is understood not to be free to develop theoretical structures at will, but to be constrained by standards of rationality.

The proliferation of genres in this category has been less spectacular than that of literary genres, but it is strikingly diverse nonetheless – compare, for instance, Leibnitz's *Theodicy*, Wittgenstein's *Tractatus* and Sartre's *Critique de la raison dialectique*.

Empirical/descriptive genres

Genres in this category purport to treat of the real objective world as it is experienced by observers. An empirical/descriptive text is one with necessarily 'factual' reference (though, again, sceptics may refuse to accept that factuality), and it is understood to take an objective slant on materially concrete phenomena.

This category has diversified in direct proportion to the creation and diversification of scientific disciplines. Each scientific topic and each school of thought tends to develop its own technical vocabulary and its own style. In this way, a virtually endless list of minor genres is being constantly generated.

Persuasive/prescriptive genres

The essence of these genres is that they aim at influencing readers to behave in textually prescribed ways. This aim can be pursued through various means: explicit and helpful instructions; statutory orders, rules and regulations; oblique suggestions. Thus, we are classifying in a single category the entire gamut of texts from instruction manuals, through documents stating laws, rules and regulations, to propaganda leaflets, advertisements, and so forth. Like the other four genre-categories, this one

can be broken down into an indefinite number of sub-categories. Nevertheless, it is held together by a common purpose, the purpose of somehow
getting readers to take a certain course of action, and perhaps explaining
how to take it.

The category of persuasive/prescriptive genres has also exhibited
immense proliferation, thanks not only to the growth of bureaucracy,
technology and education, but also to the modern escalation in advertising.

The reason why this classification is useful for translation methodology is
that *differences in approach to subject matter* entail fundamental *differences
in the way a text is formally constructed*. In other words, differences in genre
tend to correspond to characteristic differences in the use of textual
variables. So – to take a simple example – sound-symbolism and the
deliberate use of connotative meanings are inappropriate in English
empirical/descriptive texts. Apart from the interesting case of 'hybrid' texts
that cut across categories, linguistic and stylistic expectations are in general
different for different genre-categories.

The importance of genre-distinctions for the practice of translation is
actually very clearly illustrated by the phenomenon of 'hybrid genres'.
There are three main ways in which a particular text can cut across basic
genre-distinctions. Either it can belong by subject matter to one category,
but borrow stylistic features from another (as in Norman Mailer's *The
Armies of the Night*, or Goethe's scientific treatises in verse): hybrids of this
type have a double purpose, such as providing literary enjoyment along with
empirical description. Or a text can use genre-imitative subsections as a
conscious stylistic device. Thus a novel may contain passages that deliberately
imitate or evoke non-literary genres. A good example is this passage from
Pascal Lainé's *La Dentellière*, satirically couched in the persuasive style of a
travel brochure:

Le climat frais et vivifiant de Cabourg est particulièrement recommandé
aux enfants, aux vieillards, aux convalescents. Des leçons de gymnastique
sont organisées sur la plage, sous la direction d'un moniteur agréé. Les
adultes peuvent s'y inscrire. Outre le tennis et le golf, de nombreuses
activités sportives ou distractives s'offrent au choix des vacanciers: 5
équitation, école de voile, club de bridge, et, bien sûr, le Casino, avec son
orchestre typique, sa boule, sa roulette, et tous les samedis une soirée de
gala, animée par une vedette du music-hall.

   La plage de sable fin est large, surtout à marée basse; on peut louer une
cabine ou un parasol. Tout est prévu pour la distraction des enfants et la   10
tranquillité des parents: promenades à dos d'âne ou de poney, terrain de
jeux constamment surveillé, et chaque semaine un concours de châteaux
de sable doté de nombreux prix. Parmi les festivités régulièrement

organisées par le syndicat d'initiative, dirigé depuis vingt-trois ans par le
dynamique et toujours jeune P.L., on notera surtout le corso fleuri, à la   15
fin du mois de juillet. [. . .] Au cours de la même soirée les Messieurs de
l'assistance participent à l'élection de miss Cabourg, parmi les jeunes filles
présentées par le sympathique président du syndicat d'initiative.

(Lainé, 1974, pp. 101–3)

This passage repays discussion in class. It is also very instructive to compare
it with the following extracts, which are taken as 'genre-models' from a
genuine Cabourg tourist information leaflet:

CABOURG
UNE ANIMATION PERMANENTE

Vous connaissez CABOURG l'été, ses fleurs, ses fêtes, ses distractions.
Mais cette jolie station a l'ambition de vous accueillir toute l'année.

Déjà le mois de juin a ses lettres de noblesse avec le Festival de la   5
chanson pour enfants et le Festival international du cinéma romantique.
Le mois de septembre est animé par la braderie et la fête 'Guillaume le
Conquérant'.

Et tout au long de l'année, la station est équipée pour recevoir les
touristes qui souhaitent quitter les grandes villes pendant les week-ends et   10
les nombreuses vacances scolaires, novembre, décembre, février,
Pâques. Tous les équipements fonctionnent 7 jours sur 7 pendant toute
l'année avec un personnel d'accueil:

- accueil par un personnel spécialisé à CABOURG au Grand Hôtel, au
  casino et à l'Office du tourisme,   15
- professeurs au Garden Tennis-club,
- professeurs au golf avec leçons particulières et stages,
- maîtres-nageurs à la piscine,
- centre équestre avec initiation et promenades,
- professeur de bridge et tournois hebdomadaires,   20
- karting avec location de matériel, etc.

Cette organisation permet aux initiés de pratiquer leur sport ou leurs
distractions favorites et aux débutants d'apprendre et de découvrir les
joies d'une activité de détente nouvelle.

Profitez pleinement de la station que vous avez choisie.   25

LA VIE DIURNE

Cabourg offre en plus des plaisirs de la plage, des distractions variées:
promenades à bicyclette, en tandem ou en rosalie, flâneries dans les rues

commerçantes, au marché, aux terrasses des cafés, sur la digue longue de
2 kilomètres, dans les jardins publics, excursions dans les environs, 30
concours, rallyes, Festival du Film Romantique, défilé Guillaume le
Conquérant, feu d'artifice, concerts, bibliothèque, bridge, courses de
chevaux et de lévriers, etc . . .

LA VIE NOCTURNE

Cabourg vous propose tous les plaisirs nocturnes avec son Casino 35
nouvellement rénové:

- 'Le palace de la Côte Normande', le plus vaste night club de la côte,
  offre aux danseurs de disco et de reggae un véritable spectacle féerique
  où s'harmonisent les techniques les plus modernes de la lumière et du
  son. 40
- 'Le Privé', où vous trouverez une ambiance plus romantique.
- 'Du côté de chez Swann' bar musical sur la mer.
- Des galas avec les plus grandes vedettes de la chanson et du rire.
- La Boule ouverte à partir de 16 h.
- Le Cap's Club, un nouveau night club à l'ambiance sympathique sous 45
  les arcades de CAP CABOURG.
- Les cinémas, le Régent, le Casino.

There is a third way in which a text may be a hybrid of genres, and that is
when the overall text is explicitly made up of parts from different sources,
with different purposes and diverse in subject matter: components that, as a
result, are expected to represent different textual genres. Two major
examples of this type of 'hybrid' are, on the one hand, the Bible, and on the
other, newspapers and magazines. The separate books of the Bible vary not
only in origin and purpose, but also in genre. For instance, the book of Job
and the Song of Songs can be attributed to a literary/fictional genre, Paul's
Epistle to the Romans to a theological/religious genre, Acts of the Apostles
to a descriptive/historical genre, and Leviticus to a prescriptive one. The
various 'columns' in a newspaper or magazine – world news, business
section, literary reviews, fashion page, sports page, and so on – are produced
by diverse contributors on diverse subject matters, and are manifestly
diverse in genre and the stylistic characteristics attendant on different
genres. In fact, from the point of view of translation, it makes more sense to
consider individual newspaper and magazine articles as separate texts
representing particular genres than to think of a newspaper or magazine as a
single, integrated text. (In any case, while translators may be required to
produce TTs of particular articles, there can be no call for translating an
entire issue of a newspaper or magazine.)

'Hybrid' texts, especially literary ones, show why translators need to have a clear view of what genres are available and what their linguistic and stylistic characteristics are. For instance, the point of the Lainé text would be lost if the typical style of TL tourist information leaflets were not used (with appropriate exaggeration) in the TT. A sense of genre distinctions enables translators to set themselves clearly formulated targets before they start producing TTs. It also forewarns them about any special needs in translating a particular text, such as finding the necessary dictionaries and source materials, doing the necessary background reading, and so on. No translation can be undertaken without due preparation, and identifying the genre of the ST is the first step towards adequate preparation.

As the Lainé example also shows, awareness of genre is vital in that translators have to be familiar with the styles of presentation and language-use expected from particular genres in particular cultures. It is often genre that makes a communicative translation preferable to literal translation. For instance, if someone shouts 'Attention! il a un revolver' in a cops-and-robbers film, genre demands that this be rendered by 'Look out! he's got a gun', the familiar cry from countless English-language cops-and-robbers films. This generalizing translation could easily be avoided by translating literally – 'Look out! he's got a revolver' – but, as very often happens, the demands of the genre outweigh those of literal accuracy. These considerations are as true of written as of oral genres, and will be of central importance in Practicals 11–14.

Between textbook and poetry

There is another parameter on which genres can be compared in a way relevant to translation. This parameter can be visualized as a scale or continuum defined by the relative importance of explicit literal meaning at one extreme, and of implicitly conveyed connotative and/or stylistic meaning at the other. At one end of the scale are texts like scientific or legal documents, or textbooks, that require maximum attention to precision in literal meaning and minimum attention to 'aesthetic' effects. What stylistic nuances or overtones do exist in these texts can be virtually ignored by the translator – indeed, care must be taken not to let such effects creep into the TT inadvertently, as they could be a distraction from the literal meaning.

At the opposite end of the scale are texts that depend maximally on subtle nuances of non-literal meaning and aesthetic effect, and minimally on explicit, literal meaning. Poetry stands at this extreme. In poetry, understanding the literal content of sentences is often no more than perceiving the outer garb of a more subtle textual meaning, no more than a stepping-stone towards sensing a 'deeper' message-content of which the literal meaning is a symbol. Clearly, if the translator pays no attention to effects like these, there will (normally) be no point in trying to translate the poem at all. This is the prime reason why poetry is often said to be untranslatable. In our view, however, if one accepts that translation loss is *inevitable*, and that the translator's role is to reduce it as much as possible, then it is possible to contemplate at least highly honourable failure in translating poetry – witness Pierre Leyris's outstanding translations of Gerard Manley Hopkins (Hopkins, 1980).

Translators can usefully gauge the genre of a ST, and also of their own TT, by rating its position on this scale between textbook and poetry. Obviously, this cannot be done objectively or precisely, but it is possible roughly to assess the *proportions* in which literal meanings and emotive meanings are important in a given text. So, for example, poetry is to be taken as increasingly 'poetic' the less important literal meaning is in proportion to emotive meaning; and it will be taken as increasingly 'prosaic' the more important literal meaning is relative to emotive meaning. Certain examples of prose-poetry (such as Ponge's 'Les mûres', studied in Practical 3), as well as certain kinds of fictional prose (such as the Grainville extract studied in Practical 6), would seem to occupy the middle ground in the continuum; but, in principle, connotative meaning still has a slight edge over literal meaning in even the most prosaic forms of poetry. (It is, incidentally, important not to be misled by textual layout: verse is not necessarily poetry, and prose may well be.) Conversely, even the most poetic prose will be classified as prose if literal meaning has overall precedence over connotative meaning.

At the other end of the scale, while scientific texts represent the extreme point of meaning in directly expressed and logically structured form, one must be careful not to overrate their vaunted 'objectivity': it may on occasion be a consciously adopted social register, and therefore constitute a stylistic device requiring attention in translating.

In conclusion, then, we can say that even a rough-and-ready typology of oral and written textual genres concentrates the translator's mind on four vital strategic questions.

First, what genre is represented by the ST? What problems are expected in connection with this genre?

Second, given the genre of the ST, what ST features should be retained in translation? Does the ST have recognizable, perhaps clichéd, genre-specific characteristics that require special attention?

Third, what genre(s) in the TL provide a match for the ST genre? What can be learned from scrutinizing existing specimens of these TL genres regarding the manner in which the TT should be formulated?

Finally, what genre should the TT be ultimately couched in, and what genre-specific linguistic and stylistic features should it have?

PRACTICAL 11

11.1 Genre

Assignment
Working in five groups:

  (i)   Listen to the song, without following the printed text. *Treating it as an oral text*, discuss its genre, content and impact.

 (ii)   Examine the lyrics of the song (on p. 148) and discuss their salient features *as a written text*.

(iii)   Listen to the song again, following it on the text, and discuss the relations between the lyrics and the music.

(iv)   Listen to the English version of the song, without following the printed text, and discuss it as *an oral text*.

 (v)   Listen to the English version again, following it on the text (on p. 149), and discuss the relation between lyrics and music.

(vi)   Each group taking two verses, analyse the TT. Where you think the translation can be improved, give your own edited TT and explain your decision in detail. Remember that the TT must be singable to the original tune.

Contextual information
The ST is written and sung by Georges Brassens, a leading poet-singer, and is typical of his non conformism – witty, playful, sometimes poignant (and sometimes sarcastic). The TT is by Andrew Kelly, and is sung by Graeme Allwright.

After doing (i) turn to p. 148.

LA MARGUERITE

La petite
Marguerite
Est tombé',
Singulière,
Du bréviaire   5
De l'abbé.

Trois pétales
De scandale
Sur l'autel,
Indiscrète   (bis)   10
Pâquerette,
D'où vient-ell'?

Dans l'enceinte
Sacro-sainte,
Quel émoi!   15
Quelle affaire,
Oui, ma chère,
Croyez-moi!

La frivole
Fleur qui vole,   20
Arrive en
Contrebande   (bis)
Des plat's-bandes
Du couvent.

Notre Père,   25
Qui, j'espère,
Etes aux cieux,
N'ayez cure
Des murmures
Malicieux.   30

La légère
Fleur, peuchère!
Ne vient pas
De nonnettes,   (bis)
De cornettes   35
En sabbat.

Sachez, diantre!
Qu'un jour, entre
Deux ave,
Sur la pierre   40
D'un calvaire
Il l'a trouvé',

Et l'a mise,
Chose admise
Par le ciel,   45
Sans ambages,   (bis)
Dans les pages
Du missel.

Que ces messes
Basses cessent,   50
Je vous prie.
Non, le prêtre
N'est pas traître
A Marie.

Que personne   55
Ne soupçonne,
Plus jamais,
La petite   (bis)
Marguerite,
Ah! ça, mais . . .   60

Reprinted by kind permission of PolyGram Music,
Copyright © 1963 Editions Musicales 57.

Target text

THE DAISY

A daisy neatly
Pressed completely
Fell out – look!
From the pages
Of our good priest's　　　5
Holy book,

Some accusing
Petals losing
On the altar
'Tell me, sweet flower, } (twice)　10
Who put you there
In the psalter?'

Hide your faces,
Goodness gracious
What confusion.　　　15
'No, my dear, it's
True I fear, it's
No illusion:

Stolen – shame – this
Pressed flower came, I　　　20
Say, what fun
From the garden, } (twice)
Beg your pardon,
Of the nuns.'

Lord our Father　　　25
Who, I gather,
Art in Heaven;
In your Glory
Spurn this story
Quite unproven.　　　30

It's just hearsay
That the daisy
Graced, serene, a
Novice nun } (twice)
In witches' coven　　　35
At hallowe'en.

Surely, God's truth,
You don't need proof,
You were there.
Bishop found it　　　40
In the church grounds
After prayers:

(a) He confessed it,
Plucked it, pressed it
In his missal　　　45
In Your eyes
Beneath Your skies the
Deed's permissible

(b) He confessed it,
Plucked it, pressed it　　　50
In his hymnal
In Your eyes be-
neath Your skies the
Deed's not criminal.

Stop these rumours,　　　55
End those murmurs,
They're absurd;
Bishop's chaste, there's
No disgrace to
Our Good Lord.　　　60

No-one should sus-
pect the goodness
Of this daisy } (twice)
Neatly pressed com-
pletely blessed – No　　　65
That's just crazy.

11.2   Genre: crossover between oral and written genres

This assignment is designed as a bridge between Chapters 11 and 12. While
it may be completed in Practical 11 or Practical 12, it is best started in
Practical 11 and then finished either in time for, or during, Practical 12.

Assignment I
Working in five groups:

(i)   Discuss the strategic problems confronting someone asked to trans-
      late the following text for a literary magazine, and outline your own
      strategy for doing so.
(ii) Each group taking four lines, produce an English translation for a
      literary magazine.
(iii) Explain the main decisions of detail you made in producing your TT.

Contextual information
The poem is by René Guy Cadou (1920–51), a village schoolmaster in the
Loire-Atlantique. His poetry is, for the most part, nature poetry and love
poetry, often with a mystical or pantheistic Christian tinge. It is simple,
domestic, sometimes verging on the sentimental. He once wrote: 'Je
cherche surtout à mettre de la vie dans mes poèmes, à leur donner une odeur
de pain blanc, un parfum de lilas, la fraîcheur d'une tige de sauge ou d'une
oreille de lièvre. Est-ce ma faute à moi si mon amour est sans histoire? [. . .]
La poésie a besoin de chlorophylle et j'en ai assez de trouver dans chaque
livre les vomissures et les poumons de ces jeunes aliénés de la littérature. Je
parle de la fraîcheur comme d'un paradis perdu et je pense aux arbres, aux
femmes, aux chevaux qui piaffent de volupté sans se soucier du style et de
l'homme.' Jealous of his independence, he refused to join any clique or to
compromise his talent and taste by writing Resistance or political poetry.
This poem was written at the end of the Second World War.

Text

                Liberté couleur des feuilles
                Liberté la belle joue
                Jeune fille qui dénoues
                Tes cheveux blonds sur le seuil
                Flamme neige épaule nue   5
                Arc-en-ciel de la rosée
                Haut visage pavoisé
                De cent regards inconnus
                Oiseau la plume légère
                Seins jaillis odeur de pain   10
                Blanche vague de la main

A tâtons dans la lumière
La plus pauvre du village
La plus belle sous les coups
Toi qui fais chanter les fous   15
Et qui fais pleurer les sages
Liberté je t'ai nommée
Pour que nous vivions ensemble
Tu me vêts et tu ressembles
Au portrait de mon aimée   20

Reprinted by kind permission from Cadou, R. G., *Pleine poitrine et quelques poèmes*
(Périgueux: Fanlac, 1972), copyright © Seghers 1972.

Assignment II
You will be played a recording of 'Liberté couleur des feuilles' sung by Gilles
Servat to his own musical setting. The song is taken from the finale to a
television documentary (see contextual information below).
  Working in five groups:

  (i)   Discuss the effect of the musical setting on the listener, the relation
        between the text and the music, and the function of the song in the
        film.
  (ii) Discuss the strategic decisions confronting the translator asked to
        translate the song for subtitles for the film, and define your own
        strategy for doing so.
  (iii) Each group taking four lines, discuss the subtitles from the film, which
        will be given to you by your tutor. Where you think they are defective,
        give your own edited TT and explain your decisions of detail.

Contextual information
The film is one of a militant television series entitled *How to be Celtic*. It
examines the fortunes of the Breton language and Breton culture, notably
music and song, during the twentieth century. In the film, the struggle to
renew the culture and to protect the language from official extirpation by
central government is related to the rise in Breton self-awareness and to the
growing support for the Front de la libération bretonne. Among other
things, the film shows violent scenes from demonstrations against the
proposed siting of a nuclear power station near Plogoff, on the Finisterre
peninsula. Farmers and fishermen objected passionately to the proposal,
and were joined by activists of both the Breton national movement and the
international anti-nuclear campaign. After three years of protests,
demonstrations and jailings, the plans were cancelled when the Socialist
government came to power in May 1981. After this scene, the film traces the
fight in schools and universities to save the Breton language, and ends with
the song sung by Gilles Servat. Servat is from Nantes, capital of the Loire-

Atlantique, which is now officially in Brittany for cultural, but not political, fiscal or educational, purposes. He was active in the Plogoff protests, and because of his sometimes militant songs and his part in the campaign to have the Loire-Atlantique reintegrated into Brittany, he was banned from television and radio during the 1970s. Servat often sings 'Liberté couleur des feuilles' at gigs, getting the audience to join in.

12

Genre marking and the crossover between oral and written genres

In Chapter 11 we concentrated on the ST as an object belonging to a given genre. We outlined certain major categories of oral and of written genres, and suggested that translators should be familiar with the characteristics of SL and TL genres and have the ability to couch a TT in a form appropriate to the chosen TL genre. We also suggested that demands of genre often outweigh those of literal accuracy in a TT. In this chapter, we shall explore two related themes, one of which follows on from the other. The first of these themes concerns the use of features that mark a TT as being a plausible text in a particular TL genre. The second concerns the problems attendant on the fact that, in the course of translation, there is very frequently a 'crossover' between oral and written texts and their corresponding genres. As we shall see below, a careful view of such a crossover is of vital importance for minimizing translation loss. At the same time, such a view invites direct comparison between oral and written texts, providing the clearest and most economical way of bringing out features specific to each. The theme of 'crossover' also builds on lessons drawn from Practical 11, linking these to Practical 12.

GENRE MARKING

A TT must stand, independently of any knowledge of the ST, as a plausible text in terms of the expectations of a TL audience. While this is true of any genre, it is probably most immediately obvious in the case of certain oral genres, since the audience can publicly applaud, or boo, or walk out.

Making a TT 'fit' a particular genre means not only tailoring it to the standard 'grammar' of the TL genre, but also giving it features that conform to typical stylistic properties of that genre. Some of these features may be simply formulaic; certainly formulaic features give the most tangible examples of what we mean. For instance, in translating a traditional fairy story told by a French story-teller, it would be reasonable to open the TT with the phrase 'Once upon a time . . .'. This is a genuine choice, since one *could* translate the formulaic French beginning 'Il était une fois . . .' literally as 'There was once . . .'. Choosing 'Once upon a time' is an autonomous, TL-biased decision based on the fact that English fairy tales commonly begin with this standard formula. This formulaic expression is a simple genre-marking characteristic of fairy tales, and is a good example of genre-marking as a significant option for the translator. Similarly, TL linguistic etiquette suggests that the French expression 'Mesdames, Mesdemoiselles, Messieurs' should, in an appropriate TL genre, be rendered by the English formula 'Ladies and Gentlemen'. Even ordinary conversation has its share of genre-marking formulae, such as 'ritualized' greetings, to which interpreters need to be sensitive and where the choice of a given formula is a matter of TL etiquette. So, for example, whether to render ST 'Bonjour' by 'How do you do', 'Good morning' or 'Hello' has to be an autonomous decision made in the light of target-culture etiquette, with ST tonal register acting as a guideline.

As these simple examples show, genre-marking a TT influences the process of translation in the direction of TL-orientation. This may affect small details or general translation strategy; both types of effect are illustrated in the following extract from Georges Michel's play *La Promenade du dimanche*. (*Contextual information*. The grandmother, mother, father and son are at a café. The father has asked the mother what she wants, and has ordered a beer, a coffee and two grenadines.)

LA MERE	Tu pourrais demander à mémé ce qu'elle veut . . .
LE PERE	Mais elle prend toujours une grenadine . . .
LA MERE	Cela ne fait rien, tu peux toujours lui demander . . .
LE PERE	Qu'est-ce que vous voulez, mémé?
LA GRAND-MERE	Une grenadine . . . tu sais bien que je ne peux pas 5
	supporter tout ce qui est gazeux . . . l'alcool c'est encore
	pire, ça me donne des douleurs à l'estomac pendant des
	semaines . . . le café, n'en parlons pas, un fond de tasse
	et je ne ferme pas l'œil de la nuit . . . les tisanes, j'aime
	pas ça . . . et je ne vais pas me mettre à boire du vin à mon 10
	âge . . . mais je prendrais bien une petite grenadine . . .
LE PERE	Oui, mémé, je sais bien.

(Michel, 1967, p. 79)

This text, especially the Grandmother's slightly querulous old persons' litany of woes, is clearly intended for oral delivery in a petty-bourgeois social register and a colloquial tonal register. Michel's text is not, of course, a **transcript** – that is, it does not represent and record a pre-existing oral text. It may (perhaps deliberately) be inconsistent in register in some details – compare 'je *ne* ferme *pas* l'œil' with 'j'aime *pas* ça', and the Mother's '*Cela* ne fait rien' with the much more plausible '*Ça* ne fait rien'. Nevertheless, Michel has included enough features drawn from everyday, informal conversation to act as genre-marking cues. Whatever other components there are in the genre to which this play belongs (theatre; realism of setting/ symbolism of plot; social and political satire; black comedy), an essential one is use of colloquial conversational prose. In the following literal TT, there is no allowance made at all for these genre-marking features of the ST; this translation strategy yields a poor text for stage performance:

MOTHER	You could ask Granny what she wants . . .
FATHER	But she always has a grenadine . . .
MOTHER	That does not matter, you can still ask her . . .
FATHER	What do you want, Granny?
GRANDMOTHER	A grenadine . . . you know very well that I cannot 5 tolerate anything that is gassy . . . spirits, they are even worse, they give me stomach pains for weeks . . . coffee, let us not say anything about that, a drop in the bottom of a cup and I cannot close my eyes all night . . . herbal teas, I do not like those . . . and I am not going to start 10 drinking wine at my age . . . but I would gladly have a small grenadine . . .
FATHER	Yes, Granny, I know very well.

Compare this TT with one that, in strategic approach, resembles the ST in being a **script** – that is, a written text designed for oral performance. In detail, this TT makes plausible use of communicative translation, italics (to indicate emphasis in speech) and contracted forms, all as genre-marking features:

MOTHER	You might ask Granny what she wants . . .
FATHER	But she always has a grenadine . . .
MOTHER	Never mind, you could still ask her . . .
FATHER	What do you want, Granny?
GRANDMOTHER	A grenadine . . . You *know* anything fizzy disagrees 5 with me . . . spirits are even worse, I get stomach cramps for weeks . . . and you can forget about coffee . . . one drop and I can't get a wink . . . I don't like herbal teas . . . and I'm not going to start drinking wine at my time of life . . . But I do quite fancy a drop of grenadine . . . 10
FATHER	Yes, Granny, *I* know . . .

As we saw in Chapter 3, communicative translation is a form of cultural transposition. It is usually a crucial factor in genre-marking a TT. In the case of the Michel extract, the translator might decide to go still further by introducing an element of cultural transplant, in order to prevent the TL genre being deformed by unwanted exoticism: 'grenadine' might then give way, say, to 'tomato juice', and 'herbal teas' to 'tea'. (Whether to go this far would, of course, depend on an initial strategic decision about whether to keep the French setting, with its inevitable exoticism, or transpose the whole play into a target-culture setting.)

TL genre-marking characteristics can be over-used, of course. Compare, for example, these four lines from Prévert's 'Complainte de Vincent' (about van Gogh) with the TT that follows:

> [. . .]
> Et montre à la pauvre enfant
> Son oreille couchée dans le linge
> Et elle pleure sans rien comprendre
> Songeant à de tristes présages
>
> (Prévert, 1949, pp. 230–1)

> [. . .]
> And presents to the poor child
> His ear on the linen reposed
> And she weeps without understanding
> Musing on omens so cruel

Unlike the ST, the TT is heavily marked for some kind of archaic or folksy 'poetic' genre. This is done through lexical items ('reposed', 'weeps', 'musing', 'cruel'); inversion ('on the linen reposed', 'omens so cruel'); and the dominant anapestic/dactylic metre bought at the cost of the inversion in line 2 and the padding ('so') in line 4.

The lesson to be learnt from all these examples is simple but important: there is a middle course to be steered between under-marking genre-features, as in the literal translation of the Michel extract, and over-marking them, as in the Prévert TT.

A particular genre-marking translation problem occurs in the case of STs heavily marked by slang. Sociolect and register are crucial here, but so is the fact that languages differ from one another in respect of the referential domains covered by slang, and even in the kinds of slang available. The example given below comes from *Le corbillard de Jules*, a novel by A. Boudard; we suggest devoting time in Practical 12 to the translation problems it raises, and to attempting a TT. (*Contextual information*. Jules has fallen in battle. His father is bringing the body home in his old van, to give it a decent burial. However, the young soldiers accompanying the coffin in the back of the van are managing to keep cheerful. The extract is the opening passage of the novel.)

. . . beau faire, s'escrimer, il glisse Jules, on n'arrive pas à le caler correct. De guerre lasse, on le retient avec nos grolles[1] comme on peut. On finit par se le repasser, on se le pousse en se marrant, on n'a plus le respect de rien, on fait une sorte de partie de baby-foot. [. . .] C'est pas possible de rester des heures entières en gravité, surtout à nos âges. On n'est déjà pas 5 si confortable, s'il fallait être triste de surcroît ça serait à se couper la bébête.[2] Les rafales nous parviennent à travers les interstices de la bâche. [. . .] Et les panards,[3] s'ils sont au frais! . . . de se repousser Jules, ça leur donne de l'exercice, ils s'engourdiraient sans ça. On les sent déjà plus lerche.[4]   10

Bing! Badaboum! Cahote, brinquebale . . . tressaute . . . le tape-cul,[5] le tape-Jules!

(Boudard, 1981, p. 15)

[1] grolles: boots; [2] bébête: willy; [3] panards: feet; [4] plus lerche: not a lot any more;
[5] tape-cul: rattle-trap

CROSSOVER BETWEEN ORAL AND WRITTEN GENRES

Except in most forms of interpreting (barring *consecutive* interpreting), translators actually do a great deal of their work in a written medium. This means that when their ST is in an oral medium, or is in a written medium but has its basis in an oral genre, or when the eventual TT is meant for oral performance, the translation process crosses over the important boundary between oral and written genres. This is easily overlooked, but merits serious attention by translators. Given that both ST and TT are, ideally, carefully genre-marked, one should not lose sight of the inevitable metamorphoses resulting from the conversion of an oral text into a written one, and conversely, of a written text into an oral one. These meta- morphoses are due partly to the lack of precise correspondence between speech and writing (see Chapter 5, p. 51–3), which makes writing a pale copy of speech in terms of expressive force, and partly to the different genre- marking expectations associated with oral and written genres. The point is that in crossing over from oral to written versions of a ST the translator may lose sight of the presence of important genre-marking features of an oral nature (for example, the oral register features of the Michel extract on p. 154); and, in producing a written TT that is ultimately to be con- verted into an orally performed one, the translator may fail to indicate, or even allow for, the inclusion of suitable oral genre-marking features in the TT (as in the first version of the Michel TT on p. 155). There is also the analogous problem of transposing or implanting into written texts genre-marking features with oral properties, like the slang in the extract from Boudard.

Crossover in the process of translation may take a number of forms. Four in particular deserve mention here. In the first, the translator starts with a live or recorded ST in an oral medium, transfers to the use of a written transcript, and then composes a TT which is on paper but suitable for transfer to oral performance: *song lyrics* are typically translated in this way. In the second form of crossover, the translator starts with a written script, transfers to considerations of oral performance of the ST and then composes a TT which is on paper but suitable for a final transfer to oral performance: this is the usual process by which *plays* are translated. Or, third, the translator starts with an oral ST and its transcript, but produces a TT suitable for silent reading (though perhaps with some suggestion of the oral origins of the ST): *film subtitles* are typically produced in this way. In the fourth type, the translator starts with a written script, has recourse to oral performance of the ST, but produces a TT suitable for silent reading (though, again, perhaps with a hint of the oral properties of the ST): *poetry* will usually be translated in this way.

In discussing crossover between oral and written genres, drama texts deserve special mention. Dramatic traditions in different cultures are usually markedly different, despite various degrees of cross-fertilization. This implies that the translation of stage-plays will often involve an element of genre-transposition, in deference to the different expectations and tastes of TL audiences. (In any case, as the Michel example shows, the appearance of spontaneity essential to a stage performance often implies that a faithful ST-oriented translation is inappropriate, since it would not sound plausible.) On the other hand, complete transposition of the TT into some traditional TL genre may mean that the point is lost, and with it the merits of the ST. Thus, a translation of Racine as an imitation of the genre of Shakespearean tragedy would fail on two counts: the TT would convey none of the merits of the genre of Racinian tragedy, and retain little or nothing of the merits of the genre of Shakespearean tragedy. The translations of stage drama that are most successful from the performing point of view are usually based on compromises between reflecting some of the features that confer merit on the ST and adopting or adapting features of an existing TL dramatic genre.

(There are, of course, plays that deliberately trade on incongruity for the creation of absurd effects, effects resulting from the clash between the improbability of the plot or dialogue and the apparent spontaneity of performance. Ionesco's *Rhinocéros*, featured in Practical 8, is a good example. In such cases, one of the translator's main tasks is to preserve the absurdity of this clash, otherwise the TT could become pointless.)

Related to theatre is film, but film dialogue presents special problems for translators. Putting aside the alternatives of subtitling and voice-over (which is normally only used in certain kinds of documentary), actual oral translation of film dialogue requires dubbing – that is, creating the impression that the TT heard by the audience is actually the text spoken by the characters on the screen. This impression depends entirely on the skill of the dubbing specialist in synchronizing the oral TT with the movements, facial expressions and lip movements of the screen actors.

Dubbing is very difficult to do successfully, and a more feasible alternative is subtitling. A subtitle is not an oral TT, but an excellent example of crossover between an oral ST and a written TT. It has special requirements, however. First, it is essentially a form of gist translation. Second, while working in a written medium, under very tight constraints of time and space, the translator will usually want to produce a TT that, within reason, hints at some of the characteristics of the oral style of the ST. These may include features of social register, tonal register, dialect, sociolect, and so on. While it would be difficult (and potentially ludicrous) to pay attention to every little quirk of the oral delivery of the ST, it could also be unfortunate to produce an over-polished TT suggesting that the ST speaker 'talks like a book'. Here, as ever, compromise seems to be indicated, between making the subtitles easily readable as a written text and injecting into them features reminiscent of an appropriate oral style.

The special requirements of subtitling make it into a very useful exercise for students, because it forces them to focus especially clearly on many of the issues raised in this chapter and the previous one. Even without the equipment for subtitling film or videotape, a useful practical can still be done simply using an audiocassette. An exercise of this type figures in Practical 12. To assist in preparation for it, we end this chapter with some general notes on subtitling as practised by professionals (for which we are indebted to John Minchinton), followed by a sample of the amateur version using an audiocassette.

NOTES ON SUBTITLING

The subtitler-translator usually has a dialogue list, consisting of all the speech and song in the film. The dialogue list does not include details of cuts. The subtitler runs the film on a viewing/editing table, measuring the time of each phrase, sentence and shot to determine when titles should start and stop. This process is called 'spotting'. The technicalities of spotting vary, depending on whether one is working with 35mm film or videotape, but the essential rules are the same:

- One line of subtitle requires at least two seconds' viewing time.
- Two lines of subtitle require at least four seconds.
- Never show a title for less than one second or more than six seconds.

- Never carry a title over a cut (except, for example, in newsreel with many cuts).
- Voices off, such as telephone voices or narrations, are in italics (unless the speaker is present but simply not in camera view).
- Observe the basic rules of punctuation. However, if the end of the subtitle coincides with the end of a sentence, there is no need for a full stop.
- If the title has two lines, try to make the second line shorter than the first, but do not be inflexible: it is most important that the first line should read well and not end clumsily.
- Make every title a clear statement. Avoid ambiguity (unless the ST is deliberately or significantly ambiguous): viewers have only a limited time in which to take in the message, and cannot turn back as they can with a book or a newspaper.
- When a sentence is broken into more than one title, end the first one with three suspension points, and begin the next one with three suspension points.
- Do not use telegraphese, because viewers do not have enough time to work it out.

When timings are short, it is sometimes possible to have two speakers' dialogue as a double subtitle (ideally for question and answer). In such cases, use a dash to introduce each line, and justify left, so that the titles are not centred on the screen. For example:

— Where have they gone today?
— To the country

Here is an example of how to spread a text over two or more titles. The text itself conveys the point we are making: 'In such cases, it is especially important to make each title sensible in itself, unless the speaker is rambling, delirious, or similar, so that viewers maintain a steady understanding of the dialogue.' This sentence might be effectively subtitled as follows:

Title 1 In such cases . . .
Title 2 . . . it is especially important to make
           each title sensible in itself . . .
Title 3 . . . unless the speaker is rambling,
           delirious, or similar . . .
Title 4 . . . so that viewers maintain a steady
           understanding of the dialogue

Here is an example of how *not* to do it:

Title 1   In such cases, it is especially . . .
Title 2   . . . important to make each title sensible . . .
Title 3   . . . in itself, unless the speaker is rambling,
            delirious, or similar . . .
Title 4   . . . so that viewers maintain a steady
            understanding of the dialogue.

The weakness in this version is that the breaks between the first three titles correspond to neither the logic nor the oral phrasing of the sentence. Despite the suspension points, Title 2 looks like the end of a sentence or clause, and Title 3 like the start of one. The result is that Title 4 looks like a consecutive clause inserted in mid-sentence: the text looks as if it may be saying 'In itself, unless the speaker is rambling so that viewers maintain a steady understanding [. . .]'. But the awaited resolution of this apparent sentence does not materialize, so that the viewer is (at best) momentarily puzzled.

N.B.   The maximum number of spaces allowed for a line of title varies, depending on the equipment used. We shall take as an example a maximum of 36, which is not untypical. This includes letters, spaces between words and punctuation marks. So, for instance, the following line of title is exactly 36 spaces long:

. . . so that viewers maintain a steady

Sample subtitling exercise using audiocassette

Dialogue list (from the television interview in Practical 9)
Voilà. Par exemple je . . . je me fais d'abord une petite cabane, hein. Tout en . . . broussailles, quoi, voyez. Et je plante des petits arbustres tout le tour. Alors à l'intérieur je me fais des petites . . . fenestrons. Sous ce . . . toujours à l'intérieur, je regarde que j'y ai mis sous ces petits arbustres des . . . des verguettes.

Spotting
Following the taped text on the dialogue list, mark off convenient sections coinciding, if possible, with pauses and intonational cues in the spoken delivery. Each of these sections will subsequently coincide with a sub-title. At the end of spotting the dialogue list should look something like this:

Voilà. Par exemple je . . . je me fais d'abord une petite cabane, hein./ Tout en . . . broussailles, quoi, voyez./ Et je plante des petits arbustres tout le tour./ Alors à l'intérieur je me fais des petites . . . fenestrons./ Sous

ce . . . toujours à l'intérieur,/ je regarde que j'y ai mis sous ces petits
arbustres des . . . des verguettes./

Timing
The sections marked off in spotting are numbered, and the time between the
start of one section and the start of the next is measured (with a stopwatch if
possible, but the second-hand of a watch will do very well for our purposes).
The timing of the subtitles is based on these measurements. *Remember that
pauses in and between sentences are part of the overall time the text lasts*. They
are invaluable allies for the subtitler, because they give extra time for
viewers to read and register the titles. The timed list should look like this:

Title 1	6.0 sec	Voilà . . . hein.
Title 2	3.5	Tout en . . . voyez.
Title 3	3.0	Et je . . . le tour.
Title 4	5.0	Alors . . . fenestrons.
Title 5	3.5	Sous ce . . . intérieur,
Title 6	5.0	je regarde . . . verguettes.

Creating subtitles
Each of the sections into which the dialogue list has been divided is
translated into English, observing the following three constraints:

(i)   *Not more than two lines* can be shown on the screen at once.
(ii)   *Lines should not be longer than 36 spaces*, as explained on p. 161.
(iii) The time available for reading each subtitle is given by the timing
       measurements above; allow at least *two seconds for a single-line title*,
       and at least *four seconds for a double-line title* (but not more than six
       seconds for any title).

Here is a possible TT:

Title 1	6.0 sec	Well, first I get some brushwood . . .
Title 2	3.5	. . . and I build myself a little hut
Title 3	3.0	I put small shrubs all around it
Title 4	5.0	Then I put perches under the shrubs
		and go into the hut
Title 5	3.5	I make little windows in the hut . . .
Title 6	5.0	. . . and look out to check I can see
		the perches under the shrubs

Note that the order of the speaker's sentences has been changed, for the
express purpose of subtitling. The TT follows the order in which he
originally performed the actions, not the order in which he mentions them in
his narrative. To see why this is so, compare our TT with the following one,
which keeps the ST order:

Title 1	6.0 sec	Well, first I get some brushwood . . .
Title 2	3.5	. . . and build myself a little hut
Title 3	3.0	I put small shrubs all round it
Title 4	5.0	Then I go inside, and make little windows in it
Title 5	3.5	I look out through the windows . . .
Title 6	5.0	. . . to check that I can see all the perches I've put under the shrubs

As with any subtitled text, the message is given in a series of short bursts, each of which disappears for good after a few seconds. Therefore, as we have seen, viewers need to concentrate harder than readers (who can see the whole sentence on the page and go at their own pace) or even listeners (who have phonic and prosodic cues to help them assimilate new information). These factors create a particular problem in the last sentence of this ST and our second TT, where important new information is fed in 'retrospectively', in a subordinate clause. That is, although the speaker actually put the perches under the shrubs before going into the hut and looking out, he only tells us this as an afterthought, at the end of the last sentence. Assimilating this requires a certain mental agility of anyone, but most of all of film viewers. Keeping the ST order in the subtitles may well lead viewers to panic momentarily and to ask 'Which perches? Have I missed something?' While they are sorting that out, they will not register the next subtitle properly, and could end up losing the thread altogether. (A similar problem arises in lines 5–6 of the same interview (see p. 121). Both examples should be discussed in class before the set exercise is started.)

This, then, is why we changed the ST order in our first TT. Normally, 'improving' a ST in this or any other way is not necessary or desirable, but it is sometimes a serious option in oral-to-oral translating (especially interpreting), in cases of crossover between oral and written texts (in either direction, but especially in subtitling), and, as we shall see in Chapter 13 and its practical, in empirical/descriptive or persuasive/prescriptive texts where the paramount concern is absolute clarity.

PRACTICAL 12

12.1   Subtitling

Assignment
Working in groups:

(i)   Listen to the recording of the following ST, and discuss the strategic decisions that have to be made before translating it into film subtitles; outline your own strategy for doing so.

(ii)   Taking the text as a dialogue list, use a stopwatch or wristwatch to convert it into a list with spottings.

(iii) Translate the text into English subtitles; lay your TT out as shown on p. 162.

(iv)   Explain the main decisions of detail you made in producing your TT.

Contextual information

The extract is taken from the television interview on bird-catching on which you worked in Practical 9. N.B. A true dialogue list does not contain details of cuts, but, since this is an audiocassette, you are here given details of the cuts; these are marked by asterisks, as indicated below.

Text

Q.   *Mais alors, dites-moi maintenant: comment se passe une chasse aux grives avec les appelants que vous avez capturés et élevés?

R.   **Bien ça se passe que vous prenez encore les cages, vous les mettez par terre, vous vous mettez dans une autre cabane, constituée pour, et vous avez plusieurs pins à droite ou à gauche, ***ou en face,   5
simplement, selon l'endroit où il[1] est, et vous en avez même derrière, et vous entendez vos bêtes qui chantent. ****Tic tic tic, qui appellent, vous écoutez le s . . . vous savez où vous avez mis vos cages, 'ah! tiens, elles chantent de . . . de là-bas.' Alors vous regardez, vous la voyez sur l'arbre, la bête se pose, vous prenez le   10
fusil, c'est simple, vous leur tirez dedans. *Tan!* vous l'aurez attrapée, *tan!* vous l'avez manquée, hein.

*	cut to interviewer
**	cut to interviewee
***	cut to clearing in pine wood, with hut
****	cut to interviewee

[1]il: a slip in gender, perhaps because the speaker has in mind the word *cabanon*, commonly used in Provence for a small hut in the country.

Adapted by kind permission from Carton, F. et al., *Les accents des Français* (Paris: Hachette, 1983), copyright © HACHETTE.

12.2   Speed translation

Assignment

You will be asked to translate a text given you in class by your tutor, who will tell you how long you have for the exercise.

13

Technical translation

In so far as all texts can be categorized in terms of genre, there is no reason to give special attention to any one genre rather than any other. However, since most language students are not trained in science or technology, they are often in awe of 'technical' texts, and this chapter is devoted to problems confronting the translator of texts in this genre-category. By 'technical' translation, we mean translation of empirical/descriptive texts written in the context of scientific or technological disciplines. In fact, of course, any specialist field, from anthropology to zymurgy via banking, history, numismatics and yachting, has its own register, its own 'technical' jargon, its own genre-marking characteristics, with which translators have to be familiar if they are to produce a convincing TT in the appropriate field. In any case, the problems met in translating technical texts are to a great extent no different from those met in translating in any genre, specialized or not. A textual variable is a textual variable, a hyponym is a hyponym, whatever the genre and whatever the subject matter; and the relative merits of literal and communicative translation need to be considered in translating any text. Nevertheless, the very fact that technical texts are at the far extreme of unfamiliarity for most language students makes them especially clear illustrations of all these points. There are two reasons, then, for giving a chapter to technical translation: first, because it is often so unnerving for language students; and second, because it is so exemplary of issues crucial to translation methodology.

A notable generic property of technical texts is that they are seldom aimed at complete non-specialists. Thus, in terms of subject matter and interpretation, the typical technical ST is not easily accessible to most native SL speakers, let alone to those who have learnt the SL as a foreign language. There are three main reasons for this relative inaccessibility. One is lexical and the other two are conceptual. All three can be illustrated from the following text, to which we shall refer in our discussion:

CONSTRUCTION ET CARACTERISATION D'UN ELECTROLYSEUR
POUR LA REDUCTION ELECTROCHIMIQUE DE LA VAPEUR D'EAU
A 850°C. RAPPORT FINAL

Une nouvelle cellule plane d'électrolyse de la vapeur d'eau utilisant un
disque d'électrolyte solide de zircone yttriée de 50cm² de surface utile a   5
été mise à l'épreuve à 850°C. Les problèmes d'étanchéité ont été résolus,
mais l'épaisseur du disque reste le paramètre critique de la technologie de
cet assemblage. Vers 300 microns une fissuration apparaît, soit au
moment de l'usinage soit, dans la cellule, au cours de la montée en
température.   10
    L'effet de dopage de l'interface cathodique par oxyde de cérium a été
étudié sur des cellules de petite dimension. Sous l'effet du changement de
l'état, d'oxydation du cérium, la réactivité de la cathode se trouve
augmentée quand la concentration en eau du mélange gazeux décroît. On
a calculé que cet effet peut élever le rendement des cellules tubulaires   15
connectées en série de 50%. Cette amélioration électrochimique, donne
un regain d'intérêt au dispositif tubulaire, dont la technologie d'assemblage
est par ailleurs bien maîtrisée.

LEXICAL PROBLEMS IN TECHNICAL TRANSLATION

There are three sorts of problem arising from the specialized use of technical
terms. First, there is the obvious problem of terms not used in everyday,
ordinary language, and which are, therefore, totally unfamiliar to the lay
translator. The text given above contains an example of this problem. A
term such as 'zircone yttriée' is instantly recognizable as belonging only to
specialized scientific contexts. Without specialist knowledge, therefore,
translators can neither guess the exact meaning of the term nor make an
informed guess at its correct TL rendering.

The second problem is that of terms whose ordinary, everyday uses are
familiar to the translator, but which are manifestly used in some other,
technically specialized, way in the ST. That is, the familiar senses of the
terms do not help the translator to understand their technical senses. The
noun 'enceinte' is an example. This word has a familiar everyday use,
normally rendered as 'enclosure', 'precinct', 'area' or some such. However,
when 'enceinte' is encountered in a specialized hi-fi context, its familiar
everyday use is clearly inappropriate. That much will be obvious, but
knowing the commonsense meaning of the term is no help at all in guessing
what the technical meaning might be. (It is in fact 'speaker'.)

Third, a term may have an ordinary, everyday sense that is not obviously wrong in the context. This is the most dangerous sort of case, because the translator can easily fail to recognize the term as a technical term, and mistakenly render it in its ordinary sense. There are good examples in the text given above. The first is the term 'étanchéité', which appears to be used in its ordinary sense of 'watertightness'. This sense seems to fit the context perfectly adequately, and a translator might be tempted to render the term as 'watertightness' without even recognizing that there is a translation problem here. The problem, as closer scrutiny of the text shows, is that the apparatus requires to be impermeable not to liquids, but to gases. The appropriate contextual rendering of 'étanchéité' is therefore not 'watertightness', but 'gas tightness'.

Similarly, in the same text, 'cellule plane' is apparently a perfectly ordinary collocation of everyday words, 'cellule' ('cell') and 'plan' ('flat'). The non-specialist might well translate this expression simply as 'flat cell', without recognizing it as a technical term with an English synonym, 'planar cell'.

As these examples show, access to technical dictionaries and up-to-date databanks is indispensable for translators of technical texts. However, not even these source materials can be guaranteed to keep the translator out of difficulties. For one thing, technical texts are liable to be innovative – why publish them unless they make some new contribution? This means that dictionaries and databanks must always lag slightly behind the most up-to-date use of technical terms. Second, even the best source materials do not necessarily give a single, unambiguous synonym for a particular technical term, so that the translator may still have to make an informed choice between alternatives. Finally, even established technical terms are sometimes used loosely or informally in technical texts, in which case it may be misleading to render them by their technical TL synonyms. All of this suggests that the normal limitations on the use of dictionaries apply also to technical translation, but in a particularly acute form. That is, translators can only select the appropriate TL terminology from a range of alternatives offered by the dictionary if they have a firm grasp both of the textual context and of the wider technical context. The problem is not lessened, of course, by the awkward fact that some of the context may remain obscure until the correct sense of the ST terms has been identified. This brings us to the two conceptual reasons why technical texts may be difficult to translate.

CONCEPTUAL PROBLEMS IN TECHNICAL TRANSLATION

The first type of conceptual problem is caused by failure to understand underlying suppositions and knowledge taken for granted by experts in a science, but not understood by non-specialists and not explicit in the ST.

This is another point that can be illustrated from the text on p. 166. Take the sentence: 'On a calculé que cet effet peut élever le rendement des cellules tubulaires connectées en série de 50%.' Constructionally, the sentence is ambiguous or even misleading, because of the position of 'de 50%'. Purely syntactically, 'de 50%' may modify either 'série' ('a 50% series') or 'élever' ('increase by 50%'). If 'de 50%' had been placed immediately after 'élever', there would, of course, have been no ambiguity. Yet the possibility that the sentence is ambiguous would presumably never even occur to an expert who knows that there is no such thing as 'connecting cells in a 50% series'. However, this 'obvious' piece of background knowledge is not explained in the immediate textual context, and may not be obvious at all to the non-specialist. Without the conceptual equipment of such background knowledge, the translator may suspect that 'tubular cells connected in a 50% series' is a mistranslation, but cannot be certain that 'increase the yield of tubular cells by 50%' is the right translation. Translation problems like this are generally easily resolved by TL speakers with a basic grasp of the technical discipline in question. Non-specialist translators, however, may reach a conceptual impasse from which no amount of attention to syntax or vocabulary can rescue them. In that case they have only two options: learn the concepts of the technical field in which they are translating, or work in close consultation with experts.

The most intractable problems in technical translation arise in translating the development of new ideas. In such an instance, even basic grasp of background knowledge may be insufficient to save the translator from a conceptual impasse. This is the second conceptual reason for inaccessibility in technical texts. What one might call the 'logic' of a discipline – methods of argumentation, the development of relations between concepts – is normally specific to that discipline. There may therefore be translation problems that hinge crucially on that logic. It may transpire that the translator is quite unable to solve a conceptual problem of this nature, and that the only alternative is to consult either an expert or, if necessary (and if possible), the author of the ST.

In a minor way, the text on p. 166 illustrates the kind of conceptual difficulties raised by grasping the 'logic' of a discipline, in particular the relationship between concepts. Without a grasp of the principles of electrolysis, and the ideas behind the development of the new type of cell, one cannot be absolutely sure whether 'dispositif tubulaire' refers to the same thing as 'cellule tubulaire' or to something different. Unless the relationship between the two notions is understood, one cannot be sure how to translate the last sentence of the text.

To summarize thus far: the non-specialist is not well equipped for producing a reliable technical TT guaranteed to be useful for technical experts in the target culture. Would-be technical translators must acquire as soon as possible some degree of technical expertise in the field in which they intend to work. Training in technical translation usually has this as its main target. Such training cannot be general, however: technical translators can only train by specializing in particular fields. Naturally, a combination of an academic degree in a science and a qualification in a foreign language is an ideal background for a technical translator. However, not even people with that kind of qualification can expect to keep abreast of research while at the same time earning a living as translators, and they will sooner or later come up against problems that can only be solved by consulting technical experts.

These remarks about the need for consultation are not to be taken lightly. They raise the important question of the responsibility – and perhaps the legal liability – of the translator. There is a difference here between literary translation and technical translation. It is not that literary translators are not held responsible for their published TTs, but the implications of mis-translation are generally less serious for them than for technical translators, whose one mistake could cause financial damage or loss of life and limb. This is another respect in which technical translation is exemplary, bringing out extremely clearly a golden rule which is in fact essential to all translation: *never be too proud or embarrassed to ask for help or advice*.

The spectre of legal liability is a reminder that even the minutest error of detail on any level of textual variables is typically magnified in a technical text. This is not surprising, given that matters of factual correctness rank maximally high in empirical/descriptive genres. Some such errors are in the category of *faux amis* – banal, but no less potentially embarrassing. For example, in a text on automobile engineering, translating 'le starter' as 'the starter' instead of 'the choke' could at least lead to an infuriating waste of time.

Much more dangerous (and more likely, if the translator is not a specialist) is confusion between closely similar technical names. Consider, for example, how similar are some of the prefixes and suffixes that can be attached to the root 'sulph', and how many possible permutations of them there are:

$$
\left.\begin{array}{l}
\text{per-} \\
\text{bi-} \\
\text{de-} \\
\text{hypo-} \\
\text{hydro-}
\end{array}\right\} \quad \text{sulph} \quad \left\{\begin{array}{l}
\text{-ate} \\
\text{-ite} \\
\text{-ide} \\
\text{-onate}
\end{array}\right.
$$

Obviously, the slightest error in affixation here will be a major factual error, whereas, in non-technical language, affixation may sometimes be a matter of style. For example, in French, there is a distinction in meaning between 'continu' and 'continuel', if they are precisely used. Something that is 'continu' lasts without interruption, in space or time; something that is 'continuel' may last without interruption, but may also occur as a succession of repetitions, with possible intervals, in time. In English, 'continuous' and 'continual' correspond very closely to 'continu' and 'continuel' respectively. Yet, in non-technical texts, the translator into English often does not need to make a careful choice, in terms of literal meaning, between 'continuous' and 'continual'. Similarly, there is little difference in general between English 'disbelieving' and 'unbelieving', or between 'unexcusable' and 'inexcusable'. In literary texts, then, one can, to some extent, base such choices on questions of euphony or style. But that temptation must be resisted absolutely in translating technical texts.

Again, in a literary text, choosing the wrong synonym is, at worst, a stylistic error; but in a technical text it might create a serious misnomer showing ignorance, thus undermining the reader's confidence in the text. For example, it may not be immaterial, in a given context, whether vanilla is referred to by its trivial name 'vanilla', its technical name 'vanillin', its old systematic name '4–hydroxy–3–methoxybenzaldehyde', or its empirical formula $C_8H_8O_3$.

The unfamiliarity of technical texts is such that it is easy to misconstrue the syntax. A single such mistake can make the TT factually nonsensical. A simple example is found in the text on p. 166: 'un disque d'électrolyte solide de zircone yttriée de 50cm² de surface utile.' This phrase translates correctly as: 'a solid electrolyte disc of yttriated zirconia with a working surface of 50cm².' But the uninformed or hurried translator could all too easily misconstrue the syntax in a number of ways, for example like this: 'a solid electrolyte disc of zirconia yttriated with 50cm² of working surface.' – And how is the non-specialist to be sure that this is nonsense?

Some parts of technical texts may be expressed with mathematical precision. Indeed, they may actually be formulated in mathematical symbols, in which case they only need a minimum of effort in translation. (They cannot always be literally transcribed, however; for example '0,35 . 10^{-4} bar^{-1}' in a Continental ST must be given in English as '0.35 × 10^{-4} bar^{-1}'.) In these cases, the most important thing is for the TT to achieve the same standard of mathematical precision.

However, even the driest technical text is bound to have more informal passages – perhaps introductory, parenthetical or concluding remarks in ordinary, or even colloquial, prose. Such passages pose another kind of problem for the technical translator, for it is there that the technical author may let personality intrude, or even deliberately cultivate a persona. Thus, although technical translators are chiefly accountable for the literal and factual content of the ST, they cannot always remain insensitive to such stylistic ploys as register, connotation, humour, polemic, and so on. The TT should at least not spoil, cancel or contradict what is to be read between the lines in the ST. The overall register of the text – if only the question of pompous versus casual style – is also a matter of concern. To this extent at least, no text can avoid being the result of stylistic choices. In short, as we suggested at the beginning of this chapter, technical translators should not see themselves as having nothing in common with, for example, literary translators. On the contrary, because problems of style affect all texts, all translators have problems and methods in common. To this it should be added that, while 'factuality' may on the face of it appear antithetical to 'style', textual factuality can itself be a kind of style, or even a pose.

To return finally to the question of error and accuracy, there is – as with any text – the problem of what to do if the ST is badly written or even ungrammatical. Should the infelicities of the ST be reflected in the TT, or should they be ironed out? This is in fact a general and controversial issue. In our view, translators are not in principle responsible for 'improving' defective STs. However, we saw in the last chapter that this may sometimes be necessary in dealing with oral texts. It is more often necessary in the case of technical texts – or indeed any empirical/descriptive or prescriptive text – because the paramount concern is factual accuracy. If there is any accidental ambiguity or obscurity in the ST, and it is potentially misleading or dangerous, there is every reason to keep it out of the TT – if necessary (as ever) after consultation with the author or an expert.

We have quoted several times from the text on p. 166 in this chapter. In preparation for Practical 13, the problems this text poses should be analysed, and a translation attempted. Quite apart from the technicalities of electrolysis, it is worth considering the author's style and what, if anything, to do about it. What the exercises in Practical 13 will show is that, apart from the lexical and conceptual problems outlined above, technical translation is not essentially different from most other sorts of prose translation: as long as specialist help can be called on, there is no reason why anyone should not confidently tackle technical translation in most fields.

PRACTICAL 13

13.1 Technical translation

Assignment

  (i) Discuss the strategic problems confronting the translator of the text given on p. 166, and outline your own strategy for translating it.
 (ii) Translate the text into English.
(iii) Explain the main decisions of detail you made in producing your TT.
(iv) Discuss the published TT, which will be given to you by your tutor.

N.B. We give no contextual information for this text (apart from the points made in Chapter 13). This is so that you can distinguish clearly between the problems requiring specialist knowledge and those raised by the usual characteristic differences between French and English.

13.2   Technical translation

Assignment

Working in groups:

(i)   Discuss the strategic problems confronting the translator of the following text, and outline your own strategy for translating it.

(ii)   Translate the text into English.

(iii) Explain the main decisions of detail you made in producing your TT.

(iv)   Discuss the published TT, which will be given to you by your tutor.

Contextual information

The text is part of an abstract of a study on safety in mines.

Text

PRESENTATION DU PROBLEME A ETUDIER

Les moyens de lutte contre les feux ont considérablement évolué au cours de ces dernières années, en particulier grâce à l'utilisation de l'azote.

Cela a permis une intervention plus rapide, mais aussi plus progressive, la fermeture de l'enceinte dans laquelle se développe un feu pouvant être   5
limitée à des barrages légers qui seront ensuite déposés en cas de retour dans le chantier traité ou renforcés dans le cas contraire.

La réussite de la méthode est d'autant plus probable que sa mise en œuvre est plus rapide.

D'autre part, l'édification de tout barrage à proximité d'une zone en   10
échauffement ou en feu présente certains risques qu'il est nécessaire de réduire au minimum.

PLAN DE TRAVAIL

Une voie de recherche consiste en l'utilisation de matériaux plus légers ou plus facilement transportables afin d'en accélérer l'acheminement au lieu   15
du barrage. A cet égard, l'utilisation de mousses incombustibles est susceptible d'apporter une amélioration considérable.

Une autre voie vise à réaliser le barrage, ou au moins la plus grosse partie du barrage, à distance. Il pourra s'agir d'essais de nouvelles structures gonflables, mais surtout d'un mode approprié de mise en œuvre   20
de mousses à prise rapide.

Un troisième domaine sera exploré: la réalisation de barrages rapides et adaptés pour la fermeture des tubbings[1] de dressants.

[1] tubbings: segmental linings. The reference is to the technique of lining a tunnel with metal or concrete as it is dug. The lining is prefabricated, and is installed in segments ('tubbings').

Reprinted by kind permission from *Euroabstracts Section II*, Vol. XII, No. 1
(Luxembourg: Commission of the European Communities, 1987),
copyright © Commission of the European Communities.

14

Translation of consumer-oriented texts

A real translation, as distinct from translation as an academic exercise, is always produced in response to the specific demands of an audience, a publisher or whoever is paying for the translation. This puts a particular kind of pressure on the translator. We have tried to simulate such demands and pressures in some of the practicals in this course, for example by asking for a TT that can be sung to a particular tune, or a TT suitable for subtitles. These exercises are necessarily artificial, but they do make it clear that TTs are purpose-made texts, their manner of formulation heavily influenced, both strategically and in detail, by who and what they are intended for. It is to emphasize this vital point that we are giving an entire chapter to consumer-oriented texts, for the determining influence of 'translation-for-a-purpose' is nowhere more strongly felt than in translating such texts.

Of course, all texts are in a certain sense consumer-oriented. One may assume that every genre, and in every genre every type of text, appeals to the tastes of a particular audience. In that sense, short stories are consumer-oriented to satisfy those who enjoy short stories, television soap operas are consumer-oriented to satisfy those who like watching soap, and so forth. The first thing a publisher asks when offered a manuscript is what potential readership there is for the text. The whole question of saleability turns primarily on this kind of consumer orientation.

However, consumer orientation comes up in a much more acute form in texts that do not merely 'sell' themselves, but have other things to 'sell'. These are texts that fall into the persuasive/prescriptive genre, texts whose main purpose is to recommend commodities, attitudes or courses of action.

The most transparently consumer-oriented sub-category of this genre is advertising. Indeed, one may initially think of this genre as epitomized by advertising copy. The self-evident consumer-oriented purpose of advertising is to boost the sales of particular commodities. On the other hand, many advertising campaigns show that sales promotion techniques shade into the promotion of opinions, beliefs, attitudes and courses of action. Examples are government health warnings about smoking, drug-abuse and AIDS. All these examples point to a flourishing genre of texts directly aimed at instructing and persuading audiences to do or not to do (as well as to think or not to think) a wide gamut of things. That is, whether the consumer is meant to buy a product, or subscribe to a particular opinion, or actively behave in a certain way, consumer-oriented texts share common properties: they must capture attention and hold it, they must in some sense speak directly to their public and they must convey their message with neatly calculated effect.

That much is clear. What is perhaps less immediately clear is that the range of texts suitably grouped under 'publicity' is wider than one would think at first sight. It includes, for instance, things like tourist brochures and information leaflets, public notices, posters, and even some construction manuals, instructions for the use of appliances, recipe books, and so on.

It is therefore necessary to bear in mind that the title or explicit description of a text (for example, 'Instructions for Use') does not always clearly indicate that the text belongs to the same persuasive genre of consumer-oriented texts as those that are explicitly labelled as advertisements. It could be argued, in fact, that some of the most successful advertisements are those that are not recognized as advertisements at all, but appear to belong to some other genre, masking their consumer-oriented purposes under the guise of being 'informative' or 'educational', or even 'literary'. The upshot of this is that translators may sometimes have to look carefully at STs in order to recognize and identify their covert consumer-oriented persuasive/prescriptive features.

Take the average recipe book, for instance. On the face of things, it may seem to belong to the category of empirical/descriptive genres, for it appears to classify different cooking techniques in a descriptively systematic manner, to offer factual and objective accounts of the contents and appearance of dishes, as well as of their preparation. In itself, this almost makes recipe books sound like scientific texts. But it does not account for a number of manifest textual features of recipe books: the fact that even the most 'objective' recipe books are rarely written in a technical and scientifically neutral style; the fact that their use of tonal register is often calculated to draw the reader into a comfortable, possibly flattering, relationship; the fact that they have a transparently helpful organization, beyond what could be expected of the most indulgent scientific textbook; and the fact that recipe books are often lavishly furnished with glossy pictures. (Some of these features are illustrated in the three extracts from recipe books on pp. 181–2.) Such features indicate a consumer-oriented purpose in recipe books that contain them, and are well worth looking out for when translating certain kinds of 'commercial' ST. Even if not directly consumer-oriented to the sale of particular foodstuffs or the promotion of fashionable cuisine, most recipe books are, at the very least, specimens of a hybrid genre characterized by the dual purpose of description and persuasion.

One must, then, be on the lookout for covertly persuasive STs, in order to be able to translate them into suitably persuasive TTs; but this is only the tip of the iceberg. The more methodologically interesting aspects of consumer orientation in STs and TTs are revealed when it is realized that literal translation of persuasive STs is likely to produce TTs that are far from persuasive for TL audiences.

This point, too, shows up most transparently of all in the case of advertising copy. To find examples hinging on cultural differences, it is not even necessary to look at interlingual examples; one need only observe differences of style and impact in different English-speaking cultures. For instance, hectoring and hard-sell styles appear in general to be more acceptable in American advertising than in British advertising, where overpraising a product is seen as unpleasantly boastful, and any kind of overkill can only be used for humorous purposes. A lot of successful British television advertising is based on comic effects of some kind or another, whereas American-style advertisements may strike the British customer as bombastic and unsubtle. For the rest, the tendency in British advertising is to stereotype the customer as a discerning equal, not someone to be browbeaten or condescended to; consequently, the tonal register of some American advertisements might be considered 'insulting' to British customers.

In cultures where they are in favour, hard-sell techniques may spread over the entire range of persuasive genres – not just commercial, but also ethical and political publicity, as well as many of the less obviously consumer-oriented textual types. To the extent that this is so, analogous differences in stylistic tendencies are likely to hold for all consumer-oriented genres. Naturally, one can only speak of tendencies here, not of general norms. Nevertheless, importing, for example, an American-style consumer-oriented text without modification from an American to a British context runs the risk of producing adverse effects on British consumers.

There is a lesson for translators in this intercultural comparison. The fact that different cultures (even those that nominally speak the same language) build up different norms, tendencies and expectations with regard to style in consumer-oriented genres explains why a literal translation of a persuasive ST is likely to turn out less than persuasive in the TL. In other words, persuasiveness in consumer-oriented texts is culture-specific.

The advice to the translator of persuasive/prescriptive texts is therefore the same as for translating any other kind of text. Look not only at the style of the ST, but also at the style(s) of other SL texts in the same or similar genres. Look not only at the surface literal meaning of the ST, but also at the details of the stylistic choices made in the ST. From detailed observation of stylistic choices in a number of texts in a given genre it is possible to build up a general picture of the stylistic tendencies or expectations associated with particular types of text in a given culture. Naturally, only the specialist will have the requisite time and experience to develop a clear and detailed sense of stylistic appropriateness in a given genre. (Practical 14 may be seen as a first step towards becoming a specialist translator of instruction manuals, by considering some general tendencies in the style of French manuals as compared with English ones.)

Further recommendations to the translator of consumer-oriented texts concern the nature of TTs. Here again, the same principles apply as to any other text: do not be afraid to break away from literal translation where the needs of persuasive effect indicate such a break; do not produce TTs without having first-hand knowledge of the style of specimen TL texts in genres similar to the genre of the TT. First-hand analysis of such TL specimens means building up, through careful observation, certain generalizations concerning the stylistic tendencies and expectations typical of the genre of the eventual TT. This does not mean that the TL specimens are necessarily models to be slavishly copied; but comparing the stylistic tendencies of the ST genre with those of the TT genre is the best starting-point for tackling the issue of how far to depart from literal translation.

Conducting the kind of observation we are talking about may typically involve comparing texts relating to the same product in SL and TL. An example is given here from the English and French versions of the Renault 5 owner's handbook. This should be prepared for discussion in Practical 14. Corresponding passages are given in the order in which they come in the original texts, and are, as far as possible, arranged opposite one another. Our omissions are shown by three points within square brackets. The numbers and letters in bold type refer to the accompanying illustrations.

Comment changer une roue		**Changing a wheel**	
Roue de secours		The spare wheel, wheelbrace	
Située dans le compartiment		and jack are fixed in the engine	
moteur, elle est fixée par		compartment.	
un tendeur élastique.	5	Depending on the version or	5
		equipment, the spare wheel may	
		be held in place by a strap or by	
		a cross-bar. [. . . (how to use	
		cross-bar)]	
Cric		The wheelbrace is held to the	10
Situé sous la roue de secours,		bonnet lining by wing nut **B**. The	
il se sort en dévissant l'écrou		jack lies under the spare wheel	
2, et en basculant la tige de		(it is secured to the L.H. front	
fixation. Tirez: il sort de	10	inner wing panel on Right Hand	
son support **3**. Pour le		Drive vehicles).	15
remettre en place, repliez-le		Unscrew wing nut **C**, tilt the	

complètement.
Le cric s'encastre en l'un des
points **4** prévus à la partie   15
inférieure de la carrosserie,
près des roues.

Manivelle
Elle est fixée sur le doublage
du capot du compartiment   20
moteur **5**.
La manivelle sert au démontage
des écrous de roue et à
l'utilisation du cric.
[. . .]   25

[. . .]
● Débloquez légèrement les
écrous de la roue en plaçant la
manivelle **5** de façon à appuyer
dessus, et non à tirer vers le   30
haut (fig. 1).
● Pour lever la voiture: il
faut présenter le cric
horizontalement, le crochet **6**
de la tête du cric doit être   35
tourné vers vous (le faire
pivoter si nécessaire), la
tête du cric étant sous la
voiture, le crochet doit être
encastré dans le logement du   40
support prévu à la partie
inférieure de la carrosserie
et le plus proche de la roue
concernée.
● Commencez à visser le cric   45
à la main pour placer
convenablement sa semelle
(légèrment rentrée sous la

fixing rod and lift the jack up.
The jack must be lowered
completely before stowing
away.   20

[. . .]
Raising the car
Two jacking points are provided
on the sidemember on each side
of the car to accept the jack head.   25
Use the jacking point nearest
the wheel to be raised.
Proceed as follows to change a
wheel:
[. . .]   30
Loosen the nuts on the wheel to
be changed with the wheelbrace
(leave nuts on).
Fit the wheelbrace on each nut
in turn so that you press down-   35
ward and not upward to unscrew.
Fit the jack head to the jacking
point nearest the wheel to be
raised.
Offer up the jack horizontally so   40
that it slips into jacking slot **A**.
(The jack head must be
positioned so that the hook
portion is on your side.)
Screw the jack up by hand at   45
first so as to be able to align the
baseplate slightly inwards under
the body. Use a small plank of
wood under the baseplate if the
ground is soft.   50
Insert the wheelbrace into jack
head **B**, by placing the pin in the

voiture). Sur un sol mou,
interposez une planchette   50
sous la semelle.

● Introduisez la manivelle
dans la chape **7** en engageant
l'un des ergots dans la
boutonnière, et donnez   55
quelques tours pour décoller
la roue du sol:

● démontez les écrous;

● retirez la roue;

● mettez la roue de secours   60
en place sur la tige de
fixation supérieure, et
centrez-la sur les autres
fixations;

● serrez les écrous et descendez 65
le cric;

● roues au sol, serrez les
écrous à fond.
[. . .]

closed slot end of the jack head
first. Turn the wheelbrace and
raise the vehicle until the tyre   55
is just clear of the ground.
Unscrew all the wheel nuts with
the wheelbrace.
Remove the punctured wheel.
Fit the spare wheel.   60
Place it on the top stud first,
then line it up on the others.
Tighten the fixing nuts and
lower the jack.
When all the wheels are on the   65
ground, use the wheelbrace to
tighten the wheel nuts finally.
[. . .]

These parallel texts are not simply a ST and a TT; to some extent, they are
two different presentations of the same subject matter. The contrasts
between them may, therefore, suggest possible culture-specific differences
between French and British maintenance manuals.

We have recommended departures from literal translation in translating
consumer-oriented STs, and have just illustrated wide divergences in literal
meaning between two parallel texts in French and English. However, this
does not mean licence for distortion. The example of translating maintenance manuals (or instruction manuals in general) aptly illustrates what we
mean. The translator's prime responsibility to the manufacturer is absolutely
clear: the TT must give a correct, unambiguous and comprehensible account
of maintenance procedures. This places tangible limits on possible
departures from the substance of the ST. It does not, however, imply that
the TT should be a carbon copy of the ST. There are two reasons for this.

First, as the Renault 5 example illustrates, textual cogency and the
conventions by which information is presented are to some extent culture-
specific. Consequently, readers from one culture might find the logic of
presentation of a given text patronizingly over-explicit, whereas readers
from another culture might find it over-economical and, therefore, unclear.
The literal exactitude of such corresponding texts is more a matter of both
texts being congruent with the technical details described than of a TT
necessarily matching the form of the ST.

Second, it may be that, in certain fields, different pieces of background knowledge will be expected from SL consumers and TL consumers respectively. For example, the English instructions with an imported *pétanque* set might well include details of where and how to play that a French person takes for granted. In such cases, there will be points on which the TT needs to be more specific, and spell out procedures in more detail than the ST: expecting TT readers to guess information that cannot be taken for granted is risky. There will also be points on which the TT needs to be less specific and explicit than the ST, for fear of insulting readers by expecting them not to know information that is taken for granted in their culture.

All this implies that when, for cultural reasons, a higher degree of sophistication is to be expected from either SL or TL consumers, the difference in sophistication needs to be reflected for formulating TTs in either more technical or less technical ways than the corresponding STs.

Closely related to these considerations is the question of register. The social and tonal registers of ST and TT may need to differ in ways reflecting different consumer expectations. Features of register in consumer-oriented texts tend to stereotype three things: first, the 'author' (more precisely, the purveyor of the commodity); second, the consumer (more precisely, the group of consumers aimed at); and third, the relationship between purveyor and consumer.

For example, it may be that the relationship between purveyor and consumer in the ST is stereotyped as being, for example, one of the expert to poorly informed non-experts, while, for cultural reasons, the relationship in the TT is more accurately stereotyped as being one of expert to other experts, or of non-expert to non-experts. Again, recipe books are a case in point: it is probably a fair assumption that a British reader of a recipe book is less likely to feel insulted by being addressed as a non-expert than would most French readers. (There will be a chance to put this assumption to the test in Practical 14.)

Where the need arises for differences in stereotyping, it follows that the register of the TT will differ from that of the ST in terms of a number of things: vocabulary; grammatical/syntactic structure (for example, active and personal constructions may be preferable to passive and impersonal ones); sentential structure (for example, the presence or absence of parenthetical clauses; colloquial or formal use of sentential markers, illocutionary particles and connectives); discourse structure (for example, obvious or less obvious use of devices signalling textual cohesion); and so on. In principle, every level of textual variable may be drawn on to signal register.

In particular, features of tonal register may need to be altered between ST and TT in order to establish and maintain a certain desired relationship between TT and consumer which is different from that between ST and consumer. The genre-specific tendencies of the ST may, for instance, lead one to expect a text that addresses the SL consumer in a formal tonal register, whereas the chosen genre of the TT may lead one to expect a text that addresses the TL consumer in an informal tonal register. In a situation like this, the knock-on effects of a change of register may imply quite drastic departures from the framework of the ST, on a number of levels of textual variables.

These sorts of consideration will arise in Practical 14. It is important to remember, however, that changes in structure, vocabulary and register are as much a matter of standard differences between languages as of genre-specific cross-cultural differences. For instance, compare these corresponding sentences from the section on changing headlight bulbs in the French and English Renault 5 handbooks:

Après remplacement d'une lampe de phare, faites vérifier le réglage du phare.	It is advisable to have the head-light beams adjusted after changing a bulb.

Whatever the genre, if the French text were translated literally into English, the nominalization and the greater degree of abstraction would sound pompous and unidiomatic, and the imperative might sound brusque or rude. (For a discussion of nominalization, see Chapter 16.) Here is a second example, from one of a series of D.I.Y. books published in the Collection Marabout (the blurb on the cover says that the book will show you how to turn your home into 'un véritable palais, grâce à Marabout–Flash, l'encyclopédie permanente de la vie quotidienne'):

Une façon simple de vérifier l'intégrité des charnières consiste, la porte étant ouverte, à la saisir par les poignées de la serrure, et à tenter de la faire 5 branler verticalement (dessin D, fig. 17). Si la porte obéit à la sollicitation, c'est-à-dire si vous sentez un jeu, c'est le dévissage de la charnière qui est en cause. 10 Un examen de la charnière supérieure vous révélera que les vis (généralement trois) sont sorties de leur logement.	A simple way of checking the state of the hinges is to open the door, take hold of the handles and try moving it up and down (see Fig. 17 D). If the door 5 responds, i.e. you feel it give, then you know the screws holding the hinge are loose. Look at the top hinge, and you will see that the screws are 10 coming out (there are usually three).

Finally, there is an extract from an article on the microwave oven in a magazine on kitchens and bathrooms. The article does not discuss specific makes, but explains what microwave ovens are, and how and whereabouts they can be used:

Il est raisonnable, pour ne pas
avoir de problèmes par la suite,
de prévoir dès la conception de
la cuisine, l'emplacement de
tous les appareils dont on ne　　5
pourra plus se passer dans
quelques années, comme cela
sera le cas du micro-ondes.

To avoid problems later on, it's
a good idea when you're
actually planning the kitchen to
look ahead and decide where
you're going to put all those　　5
appliances – like a microwave –
which you won't be able to do
without in a few years' time.

All these considerations apart, choosing a register for a consumer-oriented TT can be quite problematic in itself. For instance, there may be little in common between the groups of consumers aimed at by the ST and the TT respectively. In any case, any TL genre selected as a prototype for the TT is likely to provide specimens in widely divergent styles and registers, leaving the translator with a number of possible models. We finish this chapter with extracts from three different recipe books in English that amply illustrate these potential problems of choice. Thanks to their manifest consumer orientation, the extracts are also clear concluding reminders that every text – and therefore also every translation – is made for a specific *purpose* and a specific *audience*:

BOUILLABAISSE

NOTE: This, the most famous of all fish soups, is made chiefly in the South of France, different districts having particular recipes. It is a kind of thick stew of fish, which should include a very wide mixture of different kinds of fish. The original French recipes use many fish not available in　　5
Great Britain. The following recipe is adapted to use the available fish. In order to get a wide enough variety a large quantity must be made.
　　[Ingredients listed]
Clean the fish, cut them into thick slices and sort them into 2 groups, the firm-fleshed kind and the soft kind. Chop the onion, slice the leek, crush　　10
the garlic, scald, skin and slice the tomatoes. In a deep pan make a bed of the sliced vegetables and the herbs, season this layer. Arrange on top the pieces of firm-fleshed fish; season them and pour over them the oil. [. . .]

(Beeton, 1962, p. 119)

ZUPPA DA PESCE

It doesn't matter whether you call it bouillabaisse, cippolini, zuppa da pesce, or just fish stew; whether it has lots of liquid, or, like this, is simmered in its own richly aromatic juices. It's not just good, it's wonderful. To put it in the oven is somewhat illegitimate, but you are less　　5
apt to overcook it. Serve with Spanish rice (for the hearty ones), tossed green salad, French bread to sop up the juices.

[Ingredients listed]

Put the olive oil and garlic in a warm, deep casserole and heat. Place the large fish on the bottom, then the mussels and shrimp. Season, and **10** sprinkle the parsley over all. [. . .] Baste from time to time with the juices, using an oversized eyedropper called a baster. Serve in deep hot plates. Serves 6 generously. Time: 45 minutes.

(Tracy, 1965, n.p.)

FISH CAKES

[Ingredients listed]
1. Chop the parsley with both hands, one on the knife handle and one on the top of the knife blade. This chops the parsley smaller and keeps your fingers safely out of the way of the knife.   **5**
2. Put the potatoes on one plate and mash them up with the fork. Add the fish and mash it up too. Add the butter, parsley, salt and pepper. Mix them all together.
3. Turn the mixture out on to the board and make it into a roll with your hands like a big sausage. Cut off rounds with the knife.   **10**
    [. . .]

(Anderson, 1972, p. 26)

PRACTICAL 14

14.1   Consumer-oriented texts

Assignment

(i)   Compare and contrast the texts from the French and English versions of the Renault 5 owner's handbook, given on pp. 176–8.
(ii) Determine what general conclusions can be drawn from the comparison.

14.2   Consumer-oriented texts

Assignment
Working in four groups, each taking about a quarter of each text:

(i)   Compare and contrast the following French and English texts (on pp. 184–5), discussing in particular the salient details of stylistic difference between them.
(ii) Determine what general conclusions can be drawn from the comparison.

Contextual information

The texts are taken from the English and French introductions to the user's manual for the Braun Multipractic Plus and Multipractic Plus Electronic food-processors. The English title of the manual is *The Cookbook for the Braun Multipractic Plus and the Multipractic Plus Electronic*; the French title is *Cuisiner avec Multipractic Plus et Multipractic Plus Electronic de Braun*. (Of the two versions of the machine, the 'Electronic' is the more sophisticated.)

Turn to p. 184.

INTRODUCTION

Ce livre de cuisine ne prétend pas vous apprendre à cuisiner. Au contraire, nous supposons que vous le savez déjà. Non, ce livre de cuisine voudrait vous ouvrir d'autres horizons en vous présentant des exemples de recettes de tout genre réalisables plus facilement, plus rapidement et   5 mieux encore à l'aide du Multipractic Plus.

Le principe du Multipractic Plus est très simple: il fait tout ce qu'il fait en une fois tout en ne nécessitant, dans la majorité des cas, qu'un seul accessoire, le bloc-couteau. Il en résulte trois avantages.

D'abord, il ne vous sera plus nécessaire, avant de commencer votre   10 cuisine, de monter et démonter les pièces de l'appareil avec plus ou moins de difficulté. Ainsi vous aurez moins de vaisselle à laver et à ranger. Deux grands avantages que n'ont pas la majorité des appareils de cuisine ménagers: ils ne sont que peu ou pas utilisés, non pas en raison d'un fonctionnement déficient, mais parce que leur assemblage, démontage et   15 entretien prennent trop de temps.

Ce n'est certainement pas le cas avec le Multipractic Plus qui présente encore un troisième avantage et non des moindres. La majorité des recettes se prépare dans le bol unique, à l'aide du seul couteau du Multipractic Plus. Par conséquent, il est possible d'effectuer plusieurs   20 opérations successives sans avoir à vider ou nettoyer le bol à chaque reprise.

Pour profiter de cet avantage, il est indispensable de réfléchir d'abord à l'ordre de succession des opérations. Il convient ensuite de bien connaître comment le Multipractic Plus transforme les ingrédients selon qu'ils sont   25 séparés ou mélangés.

Douze chapitres de ce livre y sont consacrés pour vous en parler et vous le démontrer. Chaque chapitre traite une fonction essentielle du Multipractic Plus, depuis le hachage des fines herbes jusqu'à la préparation d'une pâte à brioche. Toutes les opérations nécessaires sont expliquées et   30 illustrées, les résultats obtenus décrits et les tours de main révélés.

Chacun de ces chapitres est suivi de recettes illustrant une fonction de base de l'appareil. Ainsi on trouvera de nombreuses recettes utilisant des fines herbes hachées, ou une pâte à brioche, etc.

Afin de vous permettre de vous y retrouver plus facilement, nous avons   35 classé les recettes de façon habituelle en 'entrées', 'potages', 'viandes', etc.

English text

COOKING THE MODERN WAY

The object of this book isn't to teach you how to cook – we assume you're past the beginner stage! But now you have your Multipractic Plus to help you, there are so many recipes (not just complicated ones) that you can make faster, easier – and better.   5

Basically, the Multipractic Plus is a very simple unit that does everything in just one working bowl. And for most purposes, you'll only need to use one attachment (the blade). This has three important advantages.

First, you don't have to go through all the fuss and bother of sorting out   10 which attachments you're going to need for a given recipe, and getting them all assembled and ready to use. Second, there's hardly anything to wash up and put away afterwards – the major timesaver. Too many kitchen appliances sit around in the cupboard and are hardly ever used, simply because they're more trouble to set up and clean than they're   15 worth. But your Braun Multipractic Plus has been specially designed to be quick to use and quick to clean.

The third major advantage of the Multipractic Plus is that everything is done in the same working bowl. Which means that you can often go through several stages in the preparation of a dish without having to   20 empty the bowl – or at least without having to wash it out after every step.

This sometimes means getting used to a new method of making a favourite recipe, so that you make the best use of your Multipractic Plus, but you will soon know which ingredients can be processed together and which processes can be speeded up or combined.   25

Each of the twelve chapters of this book has been planned to show you a basic function of your Braun Multipractic Plus, from chopping and grating through to kneading yeast doughs. All the important stages of each function are fully described with illustrations, including suggestions on how to get the best results.   30

Each explanatory section is followed by a series of recipes which give practical applications of the basic function – dishes using large quantities of chopped herbs, or yeast dough recipes.

There is a full index of recipes under the familiar headings ('Soups', 'Meat dishes' etc.), so that you don't have to try and remember whether   35 that delicious chicken soup was in the chapter on purées or the one on blending.

Reprinted by kind permission from *The Cookbook for the Braun Multipractic Plus and the Multipractic Plus Electronic; Cuisiner avec Multipractic Plus et Multipractic Plus Electronic de Braun* (Kronberg: Braun A.G., 1981), © Braun A.G.

14.3   Consumer-oriented texts

Assignment

(i)   Discuss the strategic decisions confronting the translator of the following text, and define your own strategy for translating it.
(ii) Translate the text into English.
(iii) Explain the main decisions of detail you made in producing your TT.

Contextual information
The text is from *Cuisiner avec Multipractic Plus et Multipractic Plus Electronic de Braun*. The Multipractic Plus Electronic is a more advanced model.

Text
Parmi toutes les fonctions du Multipractic Plus de Braun, celle de hachoir devrait être la plus fréquemment utilisée. Avec son bloc-couteau[1] et ses différentes vitesses, le Multipractic Plus joue le rôle d'un couteau de cuisine universel.

Travaillez à plusieurs reprises sur la position 'instantané'[2] en observant   5
à travers le couvercle la façon dont les ingrédients sont hachés. Dans la majorité des cas, 5 à 10 reprises suffiront: nombre réduit pour les ingrédients mous comme tomates ou œufs durs et nombre plus élevé pour les ingrédients plus fermes comme, par exemple, les carottes.

Le Multipractic Plus Electronic permet en plus le dosage de l'effet   10
obtenu en position 'instantané' en faisant varier la vitesse. Normalement la plus grande vitesse est celle qui donne les meilleurs résultats. Cependant, certains produits comme les tomates ou les œufs sont hachés avec plus de ménagement si on choisit une vitesse réduite (1 . . . 2). Il est recommandé d'employer cette vitesse pour les produits contenant   15
beaucoup d'eau comme les pommes de terre, les pommes – mais aussi les oignons – afin qu'ils restent secs.

Avant de mettre les ingrédients dans le bol, il est nécessaire de les couper en morceaux plus ou moins gros. (Voir les illustrations des deux pages suivantes.) Vous constaterez qu'il sera alors plus facile d'obtenir un   20
hachis régulier.

Les ingrédients tels que le persil ou d'autres fines herbes seront traités de préférence à l'état sec dans un bol sec. De ce fait, il semble indiqué de hacher le persil avant de passer à la préparation du plat pour lequel on en aura besoin. Cela évitera d'avoir à nettoyer et essuyer le bol du   25
Multipractic Plus.

Si vous avez à préparer des quantités plus importantes de hachis, passez vos ingrédients portion par portion dans l'appareil, car il est souvent difficile d'obtenir des résultats réguliers si le bol est trop rempli. Les quantités maximales à mettre dans le bol sont d'environ 400 g pour, par   30 exemple, les carottes ou les oignons. Une fois de plus, le persil ou les autres herbes, ingrédients moins compacts et plus légers, font exception. Vous constaterez qu'il sera beaucoup plus facile de les hacher, le bol bien rempli.

[1] le bloc-couteau: the blade; [2] la position 'instantané': the pulsator setting. (Both English terms are as used by Braun in the English version of the handbook.)

Reprinted by kind permission from *The Cookbook for the Braun Multipractic Plus and the Multipractic Plus Electronic; Cuisiner avec Multipractic Plus et Multipractic Plus Electronic de Braun* (Kronberg: Braun A.G., 1981), copyright © Braun A.G.

14.4 Consumer-oriented texts

Assignment

(i) Discuss the strategic decisions confronting the translator of the following text (on p. 188), and outline your own strategy for translating it.
(ii) Translate the text into English.
(iii) Explain the main decisions of detail you made in producing your TT.

Contextual information

The text is that of an advertisement for a very expensive car. The advertisement is spread over two pages of a motoring magazine, and appeared in 1986. The text, in large print, occupies the bottom third of the advertisement; the rest consists of a photograph of the car.

N.B. In reality, firms like Volvo are unlikely to want this type of advertisement translating. They are more likely to ask an agency to produce a tailor-made advertisement for the British public. Nevertheless, it is by no means rare for translators to be asked to translate advertisements; and intra-trade publicity is very commonly translated. Translating this Volvo text is a good exercise not only in discerning a genre and producing an appropriate style, but also in coping with some of the trickier problems likely to be encountered in translating any text in any genre.

Text

CERTAINS HOMMES EVOLUENT PLUS SUREMENT QUE D'AUTRES

Vérité première, l'évolution concerne la vie, conjugaison plusieurs fois millénaire du hasard et de la nécessité. Pourtant, pas de hasards chez Volvo, seulement l'impérieuse nécessité d'être toujours en accord avec notre idéal: évoluer plus loin, donc évoluer plus sûr.   5

Nos constantes découvertes, fondamentales, sur le bien-être auto-mobile nous ont permis d'être ici aujourd'hui, plus forts et plus sereins que jamais.

Assurés d'une base plus sûre et plus solide, Volvo est à même de vous présenter le futur de la voiture: la toute nouvelle Volvo 480 ES.   10

Celles ou ceux qui approcheront ce coupé à la ligne résolument futuriste, auront immédiatement l'impression que seul Volvo pouvait réaliser la délicate alchimie entre la sécurité maximale et le plaisir de conduire le plus égoïste.

Cette impression devient une certitude lorsqu'on s'installe au volant. 15 Coupé pour conducteurs hors du commun, la 480 ES doit beaucoup à l'ordinateur qui a guidé sa conception. Ainsi, sa gestion est assurée des roues au toit par une électronique de pointe. La Volvo 480 ES est également garantie 8 ans contre la corrosion, comme toutes les Volvo.

Pour évoluer plus fort, plus sûrement, plus longtemps. Comme ceux, 20 rares et privilégiés, à qui cette voiture s'adresse.

15

Stylistic editing

Throughout the course, we have considered translation sometimes as a process, and sometimes as a product (a TT). The assessment of existing TTs has been an important feature in practicals, even before we started discussing the question of genre. In this chapter, we turn our attention to the final stage of translation as a process, where the proposed TT is actually examined as a product. This stage is known as **editing**. A TT is only really complete after careful stylistic editing.

Any form of textual editing, stylistic or otherwise, is intrinsically an operation carried out in writing on a pre-existent written text. (Even editing spoken dialogue is normally performed on a written transcript.) That is, the editor already has at least an approximate draft form of a text. Basic editing, of course, is concerned with eliminating gross errors – anything from incorrect spelling or punctuation, through ungrammatical constructions to obscure, ambiguous or misleading sentential configurations; all the linguistic levels of textual variables require checking for mistakes. When the object of editing is a TT, this process has to include checking back to the ST to make sure that its basic literal meaning has not been misrepresented in the TT. Nevertheless, a lot of this stage of textual editing is done on the TT as a TL object in its own right, without reference to the ST. In a sense, therefore, the transitional process of stylistic editing is a post-translational operation used for tidying up an almost complete TT, and is done with as little reference as possible to the ST.

In principle, no TT is ever 'finished' and 'polished' to the point where it could not be edited further. The practical question is whether further editing will actually improve it. In practice there must, sooner or later (and for busy professional translators it is likely to be sooner), come a point where one has to stop tinkering with a TT. However, there is plenty of work to be done before that point is reached.

Just as basic editing presupposes at least a draft written text, so stylistic editing presupposes that the text to be edited is reasonably exact in such things as literal meaning, grammar and spelling. This may turn out in practice to have been an unwarranted assumption, but it has to be the methodological starting-point. (A text might be rejected as unsuitable for stylistic editing if it were clearly not substantially correct.)

In the stylistic editing of a TT the translator considers only alternative ways of expressing the literal meanings of parts of the text, rather than the possibility of altering the substance of what is expressed. This is admittedly a thin dividing line, because the way something is expressed is, to a great extent, part of what is expressed. Nevertheless, methodologically speaking, stylistic editing is purely a process of tinkering with stylistic effects in a TT. That is, it is not, in essence, a bilingual operation. It is perfectly possible for someone with no knowledge of, for example, Arabic to be called in to help with the stylistic editing of a TT translated from Arabic. As this observation suggests, the primary concern in editing is to enhance the quality of the TT, less as a translation than as a text produced in the TL for the use of a monolingual audience. Indeed, it is not uncommon for translations to be done by collaboration between one translator whose contribution is knowledge of the SL and another translator whose contribution is knowledge of the TL. With any luck, such collaboration would help in avoiding blunders like these classic newspaper headlines:

MAGISTRATES TO ACT ON STRIP SHOWS

FRENCH PUSH BOTTLES
UP GERMAN REAR

Stylistic editing is most effective if the editor lays the ST aside and concentrates on assessing the likely effects of the TT on a putative TL audience. One of the biggest problems in translating is that it is hard to put oneself in the shoes of a TL reader looking at the TT with a fresh eye. This is why translations from French often contain gallicisms which immediately signal that the text is a translation. Even the translator who manages to avoid gallicisms is not best placed to judge whether the TT on its own would convey particular meanings or create particular effects for the reader who did not know the ST. There is therefore a lot to be said for asking an independent TL-speaking observer, who does not know the ST, to help with the editing.

Perhaps the most important objects of stylistic editing are connotative meanings, because they require to be triggered by the context of the TT alone. The translator, who cannot escape the influence of the ST context, is unlikely to be able to assess objectively whether a connotation that is crystal-clear in the context of the ST and the SL is equally clear to someone who only looks at the TT from the viewpoint of the TL culture. It is vital that this be checked. It is just as vital to check the converse – that there are no obtrusive unwanted connotations evoked by the TT. At best, such unwanted connotations show that the translator has failed to anticipate the stylistic effects the TT is liable to produce on its TL audience, and is not fully in control of its style. At worst, they may distort and subvert the overall content and impact of the TT, or they may create textual anomalies, contradictory connotations clashing either with one another or with the literal meaning.

Of course, it is easier for the independent editor to help with the second of these constraints than with the first. For instance, whatever the ST expression may be, the phrase 'a well-hung door' in a D.I.Y. manual just will not do, and the editor will suggest that the translator think again. (Going back to the ST, the translator may then decide that the TT is too much of a calque, and render 'une porte bien montée' as 'a properly fitted door' instead.) But, without knowing the ST, how can editors tell when connotations are *missing* from a TT? The best thing is to give them the ST and hope that they do not get so deeply immersed in it that they, too, cannot see the TT objectively. Otherwise, if there is time, the translator can put the TT away for a month and then look at it again with fresh eyes; even so, there is no guarantee that missing connotations will become apparent.

The twin constraint of spotting both missing connotations and unwanted ones is best illustrated in cases of connotative clash. The elimination of connotative clashes is one of the principal objects of stylistic editing. Thus, for instance, only an objective reading of the TT may reveal that two or more juxtaposed literally exact expressions in the TT have conflicting attitudinal meanings which make the text anomalous by virtue of the clash between contradictory attitudes attributed to the author or speaker. Such textual anomalies leave the TT audience in doubt as to how to take the attitudes connoted in the text. Attitudinal anomalies are what spoil the TTs in these two examples from the Ionesco text in Practical 8:

Dire que le mal vient de chez   And to think it all started here!
nous!

The connotations of this TT sentence are likely to convey a favourable attitudinal meaning, the sentence reading as an expression of pride, not horrified regret. This clashes with the attitudes of the speaker conveyed elsewhere in the TT. Stylistic editing might produce a better suggestion: 'And to think the rot started here!'

Ils sont très efficaces, très efficaces.   They are very potent, very.

'Potent' has inappropriate collocative associations, because it is more likely to qualify inanimate than animate things (here, it is qualifying humans-turned-rhinoceroses). In addition, the attitudinal connotations of 'potent' are significantly favourable, whereas the context demands an expression of, at best, grudging admiration: 'efficient' is exactly the right word, given the contextual connotations of 'ruthless Nazi efficiency'.

Clashes like these tend to reduce the connotative content of the TT to absurdity or paradox. Where the ST is not itself deliberately enigmatic and paradoxical, this constitutes a distortion of its overall meaning. However, even where no actual clashes occur, translators should be careful not to let gratuitous attitudinal meanings insinuate themselves into the TT. These should be picked up and eliminated, as far as possible, at the stylistic editing stage.

The same problems apply for all other types of connotation. Thus, for instance, the loss of a reflected meaning having a subtle but thematically important role in the ST is a significant translation loss. Here is an example from the article on the bread war of 1980 which we have looked at earlier. The author foresees the imminent disappearance of real hand-made bread, and its replacement by tasteless, factory-produced bread, and he relates this to the spiritual and cultural lifelessness of the modern world. The article finishes like this: 'mais qui, au fond, s'en soucie dans un monde qui a perdu le goût du pain?' Relevant here are the reflected meanings of the idioms 'perdre le goût du pain' ('to kick the bucket') and 'faire passer le goût du pain à quelqu'un' ('to do somebody in'). A literal translation ('a world that has lost its taste for bread') would, therefore, be inadequate (although, as we have suggested, it is hard to see how an external editor would pick this up). A possible rendering is: 'but does anyone really care, in a world where life itself comes tasteless, sliced and wrapped?'

Likewise, unforeseen and potentially embarrassing reflected meanings can create translation loss by jeopardizing the serious content of a TT through unwanted comic effects or innuendo, as in the example of the well-hung door given above.

As regards collocative meanings, the most obvious flaws to look out for are mis-collocations. These are a likely result of the translator's immersion in the ST and SL at the earlier stages of translating. (Even where, strictly speaking, they do not motivate problems of collocative meaning as such, they are a common source of translation loss on the grammatical level. Our discussion here embraces mis-collocations in general, as well as collocative meaning.) Some mis-collocations may actually amount to outright grammatical errors, not merely stylistic ones. For example, the collocation of definite article and proper name is not ungrammatical in French, but generally is in English; compare 'la Jeanne' with 'the Joan'. This kind of grammatical mistake will presumably be eliminated at an early editing stage. However, there may be collocations that are not categorically ungrammatical in the TL, yet introduce a jarring note. It is sometimes hard to say just why a certain collocation does not ring true, or seems ungainly. At best, one can suggest that speakers of a language have a sense of 'euphonic order' by which they judge certain collocations as being more acceptable than others. For example, French 'droite et gauche' is more felicitous than 'gauche et droite' (as in 'elles regardent à droite, elles regardent à gauche'; 'je m'agite, je voyage, je déjeune à droite et à gauche', and so on), whereas English 'left and right' is more felicitous than 'right and left'. Similarly, French 'va-et-vient' needs to be rendered as 'comings and goings', just as 'aller et venir' is 'to come and go'.

When differences between felicitous collocations in one language and those in another are overlooked, a TT will often signal, by its ungainliness, the fact that it is a translation and not an indigenous text. Here are some examples:

de fond en comble	from bottom to top (*edit to*: from top to bottom)
Elle vint me rejoindre derrière le bureau.	She came to join me behind the desk (*edit to*: she (came and) joined me behind the desk).
promesses non tenues	unkept promises (*edit to*: broken promises)
Si je plagie Géraldy, c'est parce qu'on ne peut pas mieux parler d'amour.	If I plagiarize Géraldy, it's because there's no better way of talking about love (*edit to*: the reason I plagiarize Géraldy is that there's no better way of talking about love).
N'en parlons plus.	Let's not talk about it any more (*edit to*: let's forget it).

Other things that often create collocational problems of a stylistic rather than grammatical nature are deictic and anaphoric elements. Deictic elements like 'this', 'that', 'the' and 'a' are often involved in subtle and complex collocational euphonies. So, for example, 'this England' seems to be felicitous, 'that England' is less so, while 'the England' is downright ungrammatical. 'That which the butler saw' is ungainly, while 'what the butler saw' is felicitous. Anaphorics, too, show clearly that there are collocational choices to be made on the basis of felicity or infelicity in a given language. For example, 'Pierre, il ne vient pas' is usually better rendered as 'Peter isn't coming' than as 'Peter, he isn't coming'. The translation of deictics and anaphora is far from being a straightforward matter of literal translation. Here are some examples:

Et l'on peut songer à *ces* scènes de trompe-l'œil qu'admire Tournier chez Escher.	And it is reminiscent of *the* trompe-l'œil scenes Tournier admires in Escher.
[*Response to a question at a press conference*] *La* question est immense.	*This/that* is a vast question.
Les parties différentes du couchant exposées dans les glaces des bibliothèques [. . .] semblaient comme *ces* scènes différentes que *quelque* maître ancien exécuta jadis pour une confrérie.	The different parts of the sunset displayed in the glass fronts of the bookcases looked like *the* different scenes once painted by *an* old master for a religious fraternity.
[*To a woman vamping a man*] Florence, *c'*est indécent.	*This* is indecent, Florence.
[*Reference to 'rhinoceritis'; see Practical 8*] Vous allez voir que *ça* va s'étendre à d'autres pays.	*It'*s going to spread to other countries, you just wait.
Il est fou, *ce* type!	*The* guy's mad!
Enfin, du poisson digne de *ce* nom.	At last, fish worthy of *the* name.
si tu le taquines de *la* sorte	if you tease him like *that*

Infelicity in anaphora and deictics may in some cases originate from a factor of tedious repetition. That is, collocational possibilities may be stylistically affected by some kind of textual 'boredom factor'. If this is the case, however, it must be said that different textual genres in different languages have very different tolerances to repetition. In an English novel, for example, there may be countless repetitions of 'he said', without this repetition being thought obtrusive or tedious. If the dialogue is translated into Hungarian, however, the translator soon feels the need to vary the formula through translating 'he said' by various verbs descriptive of the manner of utterance (the Hungarian counterparts of 'he replied', 'he queried', 'he whispered', 'he affirmed', and so on). Thus it would seem that, in certain genres at least, the English-speaking reader's tolerance to the 'boredom factor' caused by continual use of 'he said' is higher than the Hungarian reader's tolerance of repetitions of the corresponding formula in Hungarian.

Along similar lines, it is clear that French has in general a lower tolerance for lists of words and phrases joined by 'et' than English has for lists joined by 'and'. Here is a typical example, a passage from Tom Sharpe's *Wilt* and the published French TT:

She had made breakfast for Henry and Hoovered the front room and polished the hall and cleaned the windows and Harpicked the loo and been   5 round to the Harmony Com- munity Centre and helped with Xeroxing an appeal for a new play group and done the shopping and paid the milkman 10 and been to the doctor to ask if there was any point in taking a course of fertility drugs and there was.
 	
            (Sharpe, 1978, p. 221)
	Elle avait préparé le petit déjeuner de Henry, passé l'aspirateur dans la pièce de devant, nettoyé le hall, fait briller les fenêtres, mis du 5 Harpic dans les toilettes, était allée au Centre communautaire 'Harmonie' faire des photo- copies pour la nouvelle troupe de théâtre, avait fait des courses 10 et payé le laitier, et était allée chez le docteur pour savoir si elle devait commencer un traitement contre la stérilité.
	
	      (Sharpe, 1982, pp. 288–9)

The repetition of 'and' in the breathless ST sentence has a specific function: to convey, with a measure of satire, Eva Wilt's febrile, childish excitement and energy. The French translator has nevertheless felt unable to do this by repeating 'et', even to the extent of leaving out the last, paroxysmic, comic 'and there was'. (We have already seen many examples of the converse, conjunctionless lists being more acceptable in French than in English; see Practicals 2, 6 and 7, for instance.)

It is clear from these examples that stylistic editing is in part an exercise in taste. Even if it means taking liberties with the literal faithfulness of TT to ST, rooting out unidiomatic collocations is a recommended editing process, except of course where the ST deliberately exploits them. This last proviso, however, makes clear a vital point in respect of all stylistic editing: while it is highly desirable to enlist the aid of people who do not know the ST, and to listen carefully to all their suggestions, *the ultimate editing decision must always be taken by the translator, with reference to the ST*.

Rooting out unidiomatic collocations is one thing, but there is, of course, also the converse case to consider, where a TT collocation is idiomatic to the point of being clichéd. Clichés can be obtrusive in their own way, and are therefore capable of creating their own unwanted stylistic effects. In particular, if the ST typically avoids hackneyed expressions, their use in the corresponding TT amounts to a significant translation loss, trivializing the text or even falsifying it. Both effects are seen in an example from Practical 8:

Tout le monde est solidaire.	Everybody is in the same boat (*edit to*: It's a matter of solidarity).

As we have suggested, it should not be forgotten that collocative clashes may be used deliberately. In such cases it will usually be appropriate for the TT to coin equally deliberate mis-collocations. The main thing then is to make sure that the contrived mis-collocations in the TT are still stylistically plausible, and that they are clearly recognizable as deliberate ploys and not stylistic hitches. Here is a good example from the Desnos text in Practical 8:

Une neige de seins qu'entourait la maison	A snow of breasts that the house surrounded (*edit to*: A breasty snow surrounded by house)

For affective meanings and allusive meanings, as well as stylistic uses of language varieties of all sorts, the same considerations hold as for the types of connotative meaning we have been discussing. These considerations can be summed up as calling attention to four problems: the problem of losing from the TT important connotations contextually triggered in the ST; the problem of creating unwanted connotative effects in the TT; the problem of bringing about connotative clashes in the TT; and the problem of intro-ducing gratuitous connotations into the TT. These are the main points to look for in stylistic editing.

One other thing that should be reviewed at the stylistic editing stage is the textual effects of language variety – alternatives associated with different social registers, dialects, sociolects and tonal registers. Even though conscious choices have been made about these things at the drafting stage, stylistic editing offers one more chance to weigh up how success-ful the outcome of these choices is over the TT as a whole. The four problems outlined above are all likely to arise here as well, *mutatis mutandis*.

It is particularly important, in using marked language variety in a TT, to avoid the two extremes of 'not enough' and 'too much'. Editing offers the chance to make sure that the TT contains enough features of language variety to prevent its coming across as a neutral, standard sample of the TL, but not so many that it seems caricatural. The 'boredom factor' we referred to earlier can also be invoked here, and so can an 'irritation factor': over-using stylistic features all signalling the same language variety very easily leads to tedium, embarrassment or exasperation (as witness some of the dialectal features in D. H. Lawrence's writing).

There is always a threat of connotative clash in the stylistic use of language variety. There is only one genuine excuse for mixing features from different registers, dialects and sociolects in a TT, and this is when the ST itself deliberately and consciously uses this ploy for specific thematic effects. (If the mixture is accidental, then the ST will probably not be worth translating anyway, unless it is a potboiler that has sold a million copies and been turned into a television series with an all-star cast – in which case, the last thing the likely readership is going to be interested in is accuracy of language variety.)

Finally, here are three passages manifestly in need of stylistic editing, and which amply repay discussion in class:

(i)   'Sartre, be clear, be brief: we have to discuss the adoption of a number of regulations.' These words were scribbled on a sheet of paper, abandoned on the lectern of the Mutualité just before Sartre's speech on 10 February 1969. [. . .] 'I immediately realised that I had nothing to do there,' Sartre wrote a few days after. He knew exactly how to explain this first gesture of scorn on the part of his favourite public.

(ii) This superb novel, carved in passion and burning with a secret irony, is a must for readers. It is both weighty and a bit strident in tone. [. . .] The secret of their life is contained in the some 500 pages of this novel, a tonic for blasé readers.

(iii) June 10th was a day of agony. The Government was to leave Paris that evening. The withdrawal of the front was accelerating. Italy was declaring war. The obvious fact of collapse was now borne in on all minds. But at the top of the State the tragedy was being played through as though in a dream. At certain moments, one might even have thought that a sort of terrible humour was seasoning the fall of France, as she rolled from the crest of History down to the deepest hollow of the abyss.

PRACTICAL 15

15.1   Stylistic editing

Assignment
Discuss the three passages given immediately above and edit them to read better where you think they are stylistically or idiomatically defective. Earmark points where you think editing may be necessary but can only be done with reference to the ST.

15.2   Stylistic editing

Assignment

(i)   Working in four groups, each taking about a quarter of the text, edit
        the first 23 lines of the following English TT to read better where you
        think it is stylistically or idiomatically defective.

(ii)   Earmark points where you think editing may be necessary but can be
        done only with reference to the ST.

(iii) After discussion of your provisional edited version, you will be given
        the ST and asked (a) to assess the accuracy of the TT and (b) to
        complete the editing of the TT.

(iv)   Working individually, assess the accuracy of the last paragraph of the
        TT, edit it to read better where necessary and explain your decisions.

Contextual information

The novelist Marie Cardinal is one of France's best-known feminists. The
extract is from the translation of *Les Mots pour le dire* (1975). This is an
autobiographical novel, the story of her gradual recovery from a condition
of acute anxiety, bordering on catatonia and suicide, and involving
chronic menstrual bleeding. It is dedicated to the 'docteur qui m'a aidée
à naître'. The doctor who helped her put herself together was a psycho-
analyst, whose consulting room was in a cul-de-sac in Paris. The analysis,
which lasted for seven years, was often stormy at first, with the patient
driven to anger or sulky silence by the analyst's calm detachment. The
passage comes at a point where Marie Cardinal has finally come to
terms with the strict, unloving Christian upbringing inflicted on her by
her mother, and the analysis is nearing completion. The translation is by
Pat Goodheart.

Target text

The first encounter with my real shortcomings gave me an assurance
I had never had, enhancing my virtues, which I was also discovering and
which interested me less. My virtues did not allow me to progress until
stimulated by my shortcomings. They took precedence over sin, that
infamous mark designating the wicked, the evil and the damned. My   5
shortcomings were dynamic. I felt deeply that as I learned about them
they became useful tools for the construction of my life. It had ceased
to be a matter of pushing them aside or passing over them in silence,
still less of being ashamed of them, but rather of mastering them and
in case of need, making use of them. My shortcomings were in some   10
way virtues.

Now I came to the cul-de-sac as in the past I had gone to the university
to learn. I wanted to know everything.

I had conquered such strong resistances that I was no longer afraid to find that I was face to face with myself. The anxiety attacks had completely disappeared. I could (and I still can) feel the physical symptoms of anxiety (perspiration, accelerated heartbeat, cold extremities), but there was no longer any fear. These symptoms now served to unearth new keys: my heart is beating! Why? When did it start? What was the provocation? What word struck me, what colour, what smell, what atmosphere, what idea, what noise? I would regain my composure and I would save the episode to be analysed by the doctor when I was incapable of doing it all by myself.

It often happened that I would be floundering, unable to get back to the origin of my malaise, only to find comfort in the knowledge that it did have an origin. On the couch with my eyes closed, I would try to disentangle the knotted threads. I no longer got excited as I used to, I no longer sought refuge in silence or insults, whose meaning I now understood, and about which, consequently, I knew that they were as eloquent as calm words, though more tiring.

Reprinted by kind permission from Cardinal, M., *The Words to Say It*, translated by Pat Goodheart (London: Picador, Pan Books, 1984), UK & Commonwealth rights © 1984 Pan Books Ltd; American rights © Van Vactor & Goodheart.

Contrastive topics
and practicals: introduction

The next four chapters will be devoted to a selection of topics from the 'contrastive linguistics' of French and English. Each of these topics is self-contained, and can be used at whatever stage of the course it seems most useful. The aim of including these topics is to sharpen students' awareness of certain characteristic difficulties in translating grammatical structures of French into English, and their awareness of the full range of options open to them in translating these structures.

The fundamental structural differences between different languages, which we have discussed at various points in the course (in particular in the sections on 'equivalence' and translation loss, Chapter 2, p. 22–5), assure the importance of contrastive studies concentrating on specific points of differentiation that can be isolated in comparing the structure (in particular the grammatical structure) of one language with another. Since such characteristic differences are a stumbling-block to literal translation and may present difficulties for the novice translator, contrastive studies are an extremely useful component of a course on translation. They enable students to recognize instantly those SL structures in a ST that are likely to present difficulties in translation and to require structural alteration in the TT.

In principle, a contrastive study of French and English offers a vast number of structural differences between French and English usage; complete chapters could have been devoted to many of these. 'Compensation in kind', which we discussed in Chapter 3, is generally made necessary by one or more of these numerous differences between the two languages. Anaphora and deictics, which we looked at briefly in Chapter 15, offer good examples of such points of interlingual contrast. The common feature these contrasts present from the translator's point of view is the need for **grammatical transposition**. By grammatical transposition we mean the replacement or reinforcement of given parts of speech in the ST by other parts of speech in the TT, wherever this is made necessary by significant differences of syntactic configuration between the SL and the TL. Many other writers designate this phenomenon simply as 'transposition', as we shall also do in what follows; we have used the full term 'grammatical transposition' here in order to prevent confusion with 'cultural transposition' (see above, pp. 28–34). Transposition is illustrated in the following examples:

Ils ont *massivement* répondu à son appel.	*The vast majority* responded to her call.

(What is conveyed in the ST by a pronoun and an adverb is conveyed in the TT by an adjective and a noun.)

Je *persiste à* croire qu'ils ont raison.	I *still* think they're right.

(What is conveyed in the ST by a verbal phrase is conveyed in the TT by an adverb.)

Je viens *chercher* un couteau.	I've come *for* a knife.

(What is conveyed in the ST by a verb is conveyed in the TT by a preposition.)

Observez *la façon dont* les ingrédients sont hachés.	Watch *how* the ingredients are chopped.

(What is conveyed in the ST by a nominal phrase is conveyed in the TT by an adverb.)

L'après-midi du vendredi est *consacré à* votre éducation.	Friday afternoons are *for* your education.

(What is conveyed in the ST by a preposition reinforced with an adjectival past participle is conveyed in the TT by a preposition alone.)

Translation problems like the ones in these examples have already been encountered in all the texts used in this course. Furthermore, they are abundantly dealt with in a number of useful works – for example, Astington (1983), Ballard (1987), Chuquet and Paillard (1987), Grellet (1985), Guillemin-Flescher (1981), Vinay and Darbelnet (1958). Since the present book cannot devote more space to contrastive studies, which are just one aspect of what the translator has to think about, we analyse only a small selection of contrastive problems. For the rest, we refer readers to the specialist works cited above. This enables us to stress the importance of contrastive studies for the translator, to encourage students of translation to consult contrastive textbooks, and to suggest that practising translators need to form their own repertoire of contrastive strategies.

As the handful of examples given above show, contrastive analysis is doubly useful, because it not only identifies SL expressions that need grammatical transposition, but also suggests 'standard' solutions for translating such expressions. It does only *suggest* them, of course – it can never *impose* them. Nevertheless, the contrastively aware translator is 'automatically' prompted to consider a range of well-tried transpositional alternatives available in dealing with a particular type of SL construction. A subsequent choice between these alternatives can then be made in the light of such considerations as genre, register and TT purpose. The contrastive chapters that follow will, we hope, suffice to establish this strategic practice as part of the routine of students of translation.

The choice of just four contrastive topics out of the many that could have been chosen was a difficult one. We have picked out four of the most common and multiform contrastive sources of translation difficulties between French and English, and illustrated each through a variety of classroom exercises. (It is important that these exercises be done as they arise, and not out of sequence with the expository material they relate to.)

There are two ways in which the contrastive exercises differ from other practicals in the course. First, students will be translating sentences taken out of context, so that attention can be focused specifically on the contrastive problems themselves – problems that, in textual context, tend to be masked or blurred by considerations of style or genre. Naturally, we do not mean to imply that context is, after all, less important than we have insisted hitherto. However, the strategic routine we are suggesting depends on fostering a contrastive awareness of available options in transposition, to which strategic considerations of context can be subsequently applied. The availability of options can only be properly assessed by taking sentences out of textual context.

Second, in the contrastive chapters we frequently reverse the direction of translation to translating from English to French. This is in order to bring into the open certain possibilities *in English* which it is easy to overlook when translating *from French*. For many French sentences, the option of translation into English without significant grammatical transposition is actually available, although this option frequently entails significant translation loss in terms of TT idiomaticity and appropriateness of register. Most of the English STs in the exercises contain perfectly acceptable constructions which, however, cannot pass into French without (sometimes drastic) transposition. These are instances of precisely those idiomatic English constructions which it is easiest to overlook as possible options when one is translating a French ST whose structure can be replicated in English. Our hope is that, having stumbled over these constructions as obstacles in translation *into* French, students will remain aware of their existence as options in translating *from* French.

16

Contrastive topic and practical: nominalization

This chapter constitutes the material for all or part of a practical. If possible, the following exercise should be handed in before the practical. It should in any case be completed before going on to the material in the rest of the chapter.

PRELIMINARY EXERCISE

Translate the following sentences into French, using only a monolingual French dictionary.

1 Army life seemed appallingly insipid to me.
2 These analogies occur too insistently and coherently.
3 Scandalously, they refused us any help.

4 It was a hopeless undertaking.
5 This attempted insurrection failed.
6 But Father, I was expecting you to be more understanding.

7 [*In a D.I.Y. manual*] Anyone can replace a broken window.
8 When I was in London I went round all the museums.
9 [*Imploringly*] You might stop parroting Baudelaire.

10 [*On a label on a coffee jar, announcing a competition*] Soak off and see back.
11 She motioned him in.
12 Sometimes I think back to when we met.

The preliminary exercise focuses on nominal expressions, that is, expressions consisting of a noun or having a noun as their nucleus. Here are four English examples of nominal expressions, each followed by a version using a different part of speech from a noun:

A coat of green.	A green coat.
With incredible speed.	Incredibly quickly.
Difficult of access.	Difficult to get to.
He shed his sandals with a kick.	He kicked his sandals off.

We shall use the term *nominalization* to denote the use of a nominal expression where, either in the same language or in a different one, an expression using a part of speech other than a noun would be possible.

Nominalization can be considered on two levels, the quantitative and the qualitative. The first is the simpler level. As will have become clear in previous practicals, French tends very readily to use a nominal expression where English would not. Commenting on this question, Vinay and Darbelnet (1958, p. 102) quote two authorities: A. Chevrillon (a literary critic), who writes: 'Le français traduit surtout des formes, états arrêtés, les coupures imposées au réel par l'analyse. L'anglais peut rendre bien plus facilement ce que M. Bergson appelle du *se faisant*'; and Ch. Bally (a linguist), who makes a similar point in comparing French and German: 'Bien loin de rechercher le devenir dans les choses, [le français] présente les événements comme des substances.' These venerable observations are as relevant today as when they were first made (Chevrillon's in 1921, Bally's in 1931). They suggest that, to some extent and in some way or ways, English texts are typically more 'dynamic' and 'concrete' than French ones. This raises important questions about whether French-speakers and English-speakers perceive the world, and think, differently from one another. To answer these questions is beyond the scope of a course on translation methodology, but the very fact that they can be asked is one of the reasons why, in Chapter 2, we warn against unconditional acceptance of the concept of 'equivalent effect' in translation. They are not, in any case, questions which translators can ignore altogether, because some writers and speakers overcome the relatively 'static', 'generic' and 'abstract' quality of French by recourse to specific stylistic devices. The Grainville text in Practical 6 is an example; and much surrealist writing may be seen as an attempt to win for French certain 'dynamic' and 'concrete' qualities inherent in English.

On the qualitative level, we are not going to attempt a taxonomy of nominalization in French. For our purposes, a broad division into four categories is enough. These are cases in which, translating from French into English, a noun or nominal expression translates most readily into an adverb, an adjective, a verb, or a preposition or phrasal verb. In each section, comments on the sentences done in the exercise are accompanied by further examples for discussion and translation in class.

16.1 Transposition from noun to adverb

The first sentence in the preliminary exercise will not translate literally into French. Although grammatically possible, 'La vie militaire me semblait désespéramment fade' is grotesque: whereas English very readily turns adjectives into adverbs by adding 'ly', French is more reluctant to do so by adding 'ment'. A much more likely translation is:

ST 1   La vie militaire me semblait d'une fadeur désespérante.

This is a good example of a very common French construction, *'de' + noun + adjective*, which is usually best rendered in English by *adverb + adjective*. Following the French structure is possible in English:

TT 1(a)   Army life seemed to me (to be) one of appalling insipidness.

But this sounds frankly pompous, where the ST does not. This question of register is important, as we shall see. Once register is taken into account, there seems little alternative to a TT along these lines:

TT 1(b)   Army life seemed appallingly insipid to me.

What are the differences between the French ST and TT 1(b)? The French is certainly not pompous (whereas TT 1(a) is), but it *is* more static, in that the insipidness is *discerned* (isolated) and then *described*. In the English, on the other hand, the insipidness *actively appals* the speaker. Similar remarks can be made about this English-French example:

ST 2   This detail is crucially important.

This will not translate with 'décisivement important', but has to be rendered with *'de' + noun + adjective*:

TT 2   Ce détail est d'une importance décisive.

Again, if this French phrase were translated into English as 'of crucial importance', the register would be quite different. As with 'd'une fadeur désespérante', there are, in respect of register, more possibilities open to the English-speaker than to the French-speaker. Examples of this structure are common, and translators must remember the range of possibilities at their disposal if they are to avoid inappropriate register (at best) or translationese (at worst). The deciding factor in choice of register will usually be provided by the context.

Another common French structure usually calling for an adverb in English is *'avec/sans' + noun*. Here is an example (from which sentence 2 in the preliminary exercise was derived):

ST 3   Ces analogies se répètent avec trop d'insistance, trop de cohérence.
TT 3   These analogies recur too insistently and coherently.

'With too much insistence and coherence' is implausible and pedantic –

though less implausible than French 'trop insistamment, trop cohéremment'! Here too, in so far as the adverbs induce the reader to visualize the analogies actively recurring thick and fast, the TT may be said to be more 'dynamic' and 'concrete' than the ST. The translation loss consists in the TT being less of a detached *perception and definition* of what is *involved*, and more an *account* of what is *happening*. The distinction is a relatively fine one here, and sensitivity to it will vary from language-user to language-user; but such sensitivity notwithstanding, a whole article or book can be made or marred by how the translator renders the numerous such expressions as:

Avec agitation: With excitement/in agitation? Excitedly/agitatedly?

Sans effort: Without effort? Effortlessly?

Avec nostalgie: With nostalgia/longing? Nostalgically/longingly?

Very often, then, a French adverbial phrase containing one or more nouns is most idiomatically rendered with an adverb in English. Indeed, such is the English-speaker's readiness to use adverbs that one adverb is frequently qualified with another in juxtaposition, something which is rare in French (at least with adverbs in '-ment'). For example,

ST 4   Elle a été élue à la quasi-unanimité

readily translates as

TT 4   She was elected virtually unanimously.

Now, with this example and the question of register in mind, the possibilities for translating the following sentences should be considered:

ST 5   Le travail avance avec une rapidité rassurante.
ST 6   Le travail avance avec une lenteur décourageante.

In cases like these, the translator may have little or no choice. The following example, however, is different: 'Elle joue avec une délicatesse étonnante.' Here, a translation juxtaposing two adverbs – 'amazingly delicately' – is idiomatic and acceptable, but 'with amazing delicacy' is equally acceptable. There is a genuine choice between adverb and noun, a choice which, as with STs 1 and 2, seems to depend mostly on what register is required. Similar remarks, in respect of 'stasis' and 'abstraction', apply to the nominal construction in English as in French. The only difference is that, since French-speakers do not have this choice, they will not find 'avec une délicatesse étonnante' unduly marked in terms of register, whereas 'with amazing delicacy' is less conversational than 'amazingly delicately', belonging more to the critics' page or the lecture platform.

An interesting conclusion emerges from the discussion so far. If one changes ST *preposition + noun* into a TT adverb, or vice-versa, a perhaps inevitable consequence is overlapping translation (as defined in Chapter 7, pp. 96–7). Take, for example, 'amazingly delicately' translated into French as 'avec une délicatesse étonnante'. While the core meaning is retained, the French TT both *loses* something and *adds* something. It loses something in that it makes two things more *implicit* than the ST does: the pianist actively amazing the listener, and her delicate finger-movements, which the adverb encourages the reader to visualize. It adds something in that it makes *explicit* the delicacy, which is an abstract quality or category implied in the pianist's playing. (In the French, two things have been *inferred* from the experience of listening to the playing. From her finger-movements, the quality of delicacy has been inferred; and from people's reactions when listening to her, the fact that her delicacy is amazing has been inferred. In other words, it is as if one has stood back from one's reactions and assessed them, allotting them to a category; this is no doubt why this noun-construction so often sounds academic, or even pedantic, to English-speakers.)

Overlapping translation is also clearly seen in another typical construction (see sentence 3 in the preliminary exercise):

ST 7   Chose monstrueuse, ils nous ont refusé tout soutien.
TT 7   Scandalously, they refused us any help.

Using an adverb in this position is possible in French, but much rarer than in English. It would in any case shift the meaning. 'Monstrueusement' would describe the manner in which the refusing was actually done, and would therefore also convey a stronger impression than 'chose monstrueuse' does of the speaker's *first reaction* on hearing that help had been refused; 'chose monstrueuse' is more a mature assessment than a first reaction. The English 'scandalously' has a similar effect, and is therefore an overlapping translation: while retaining the core element of scandalousness, it adds the implication of initial emotional reaction and loses the implication of later balanced judgement. As ever, this translation loss has to be balanced against different ones involved in different alternative TTs. Compare, for instance, the following possibilities with TT 7(a):

TT 7(b)   It is/was a scandalous thing, they refused us any help.
TT 7(c)   It is/was a scandal, they refused us any help.

A symptom of the French predilection for the noun is seen in the comparative readiness with which it turns adverbial phrases into nouns, as in 'l'au-delà', 'the beyond'. Here, to complete this section, are two examples for discussion and translation:

L'au-jour-le-jour de l'existence.

Mourir par absence et par à-peu-près.

16.2   Transposition from *preposition + noun* to adjective

Translating our earlier example, 'Elle joue avec une délicatesse étonnante',
the adjective 'amazing' may be said to be more 'static', less immediately
related to her 'action', than the adverb 'amazingly'. There is a clearer
implication in the adjective that both the pianist's playing and the listener's
reaction have been scrutinized and allotted to appropriate categories before
the sentence is uttered. It may indeed be the case that there is less difference,
in respect of dynamism, between a noun and an adjective than between a
noun and an adverb. At all events, it certainly is the case that translators very
often find themselves needing to render French *preposition + noun* with an
English adjective. Almost any page of French chosen at random will throw
up a crop of cases in which adjectival or adverbial noun becomes English
adjective; here are some examples for discussion and translation:

C'était une entreprise sans espoir (see p. 203).

Elle est dans l'incertitude quant à l'avenir.

J'ai l'air d'avoir de l'ordre, mais . . .

C'est pas possible de rester des heures entières en gravité (see p. 157).

Planté, roulé dans la prédominance de la fange (see p. 81).

As with adverbs, the tendency to nominalization in French is such that
adjectives are readily used as nouns, as in the following examples:

Ses pittoresques frappaient (see p. 81).

Il reste dans le vague.

Le tragique de l'histoire, c'est qu'elle a perdu son bébé l'année suivante.

Dans la mesure du possible.

Je suis sensible à l'absurde de cette hypothèse.

A symptom of this contrast between the two languages is found in such
fossilized everyday expressions as 'J'ai faim/froid/de la chance', where there
is little or no choice but to translate with an English adjective. Fixed
expressions like these may be closer to true synonymy than in the case of
transposition from noun to adverb, but the element of analysis and
categorization is often more evident in the use of a noun as opposed to an

adjective. A symptomatic example comes from the language of road signs: does 'Chute de pierres' mean 'fallen rocks' or 'falling rocks'? 'Chute', an abstract noun, is 'generic' in the sense that it includes all the possibilities – that there *has been*, or *may be*, or *will be* or *is being* a fall of rocks; and any idiomatic English translation of this phrase is bound to be 'particularizing' (as defined in Chapter 7, pp. 95), and more concrete.

The element of analysis and abstraction in the use of a noun as opposed to an adjective is especially clear where there is a choice between the two, as for example in 'she wore a coat of green' versus 'she wore a green coat'. In translating from French into English, there is frequently no choice; but when there is one, it will be determined to a great extent by what register is required, just as with the choice between *preposition + noun* and adverb. This is illustrated in sentence 5 of the preliminary exercise, which is, in fact, a translation of a French ST, 'Cette tentative d'insurrection a échoué'. 'This attempt at insurrection' would be rather wordy and pompous, and would in any case carry an implication that the French ST does not – that a fairly pathetic attempt to mount an insurrection had been made, but that no insurrection worthy of the name actually materialized. 'Insurrection attempt' is an unlikely collocation (although English *attributive noun + noun* is a common counterpart to French *noun + 'de' + noun*). If there is a choice in translating this French sentence, it must surely, as so often with this type of construction, be in favour of an adjective: 'This attempted insurrection failed.'

Sentence 6 in the exercise is also a translation from French:

ST 8   Mais mon père, je m'attendais à plus de compréhension de votre part.

In principle, there are three possibilities for translating this sentence into English:

TT 8(a)   But Father, I was expecting more understanding on your part.
TT 8(b)   But Father, I was expecting more understanding from you.
TT 8(c)   But Father, I was expecting you to be more understanding.

The choice between these versions depends, as ever, on the context in general, and on the son's use of 'votre' rather than 'ta' in particular. This last consideration probably rules the first two versions out of court, because neither has a register that one would expect from junior speaking to senior.

Our next example, from a D.I.Y. text on replacing window panes, contains another adjectival construction that is common in French, *'de' + noun*:

ST 9   Même si le mastic est de première fraîcheur, pétrissez-le jusqu'à le rendre très malléable.

In this sentence, 'fresh/brand new' is virtually the only possible translation of 'de première fraîcheur'. Here are some more examples of the *'de' + noun* construction, each requiring to be rendered with an adjective in English:

Les précautions d'usage.

Un cas d'espèce.

Le détail est d'importance.

(In the third of these examples, a noun could be used: 'this detail is of importance'; what is the effect?) The French *preposition + noun* structure often translates most idiomatically into English with a noun used attributively, without analytic prepositions like 'of', 'for' or 'on'; for example:

Mesures de sécurité.

Feux de circulation.

Tentative d'évasion.

Locomotive à vapeur.

Gravure sur bois.

Défense contre avions.

Here are two final examples for discussion and translation in class. In the first, from a book on the medieval writer Chrétien de Troyes, the choice between adjective and noun in translating 'sans témérité' is governed above all by concerns of register:

ST 10   Je crois pouvoir conclure sans témérité qu'avant Chrétien la Sainte Lance
         n'était pas une lance qui saigne.

The second is from an account of the fall of France in 1940. (For the published TT and context, see extract (iii) on p. 197.) Register is again an important consideration:

ST 11   L'évidence de l'effondrement s'imposait à tous les esprits.

16.3   Transposition from noun to verb

Here, the likely difference between 'static' noun and 'dynamic' verb is obvious. Once again, French is seen to deal in abstract categories. There is something of a generic flavour about the noun, as seen for example in this sentence from the D.I.Y. book:

ST 12   Le remplacement d'un carreau cassé est à la portée de n'importe qui.

The French *definite article + noun* is a generic concept – 'the replacement/

replacing of' – whereas in the natural English expression ('replacing a broken window') the gerund is strongly verbal, focusing on the *action*, more than the *concept*, of replacing the window. Keeping the ST structure in English is possible, but it elevates the register, perhaps inappropriately. Here are four alternative translations, for discussion:

TT 12(a) The replacement of a broken window is within anyone's capability.
TT 12(b) Replacing a broken window is within anyone's capability.
TT 12(c) Replacing a broken window isn't too difficult for anybody.
TT 12(d) Anyone can replace a broken window [sentence 7 in the preliminary exercise].

Translating either way, rendering a noun with a verb inevitably gives a particularizing translation when the verb is in a finite tense, as for example in:

ST 13   Quelques rides à la surface marquèrent sa disparition.

There are two possibilities here, between which one can only decide by reference to the context:

TT 13(a) A few ripples showed where she had gone down.
TT 13(b) A few ripples showed that she had gone down.

A TT that avoided particularization by using a noun ('showed/marked her disappearance/descent') would be distinctly donnish. The same is true of this example: 'Ils poussaient d'étranges cris, comme à l'apparition d'un fantôme': 'as at the appearance/apparition of a ghost' is preposterous; 'as if they had seen a ghost' or 'as if a ghost had appeared' is particularizing. In cases like these, then, the movement from generic concept to specific event is invariably particularizing. This translation loss has to be measured against that entailed in using an inappropriate register.

Using a noun instead of a subordinate clause is a typical and useful way of avoiding the subjunctive constructions necessitated by such conjunctions as 'avant que' and 'bien que':

Six mois avant ma naissance.   Six months before I was born.

Malgré mon absence de Paris.   Although I am away from Paris.

Yet again, in examples like these, keeping the French structure usually gives a more elevated register, while using a finite verb is particularizing. Translating 'malgré mon absence de Paris', for instance, once the decision has been taken to use a verb, one has to select a particular tense, aspect or mood: 'although I am/was/will be/would be', and so on.

The following sentence shows clearly the static and generic nature of noun as compared with verb:

ST 14   Dès son entrée en fonctions, en 1969, elle avait déclaré devant la Knesset qu'Israël n'en démordrait pas.

TT 14   On taking office   } in 1969, she told the Knesset that
         When/As soon as she took office } Israel would not back down.

The context will show which of these options is best. As this example suggests, phrases like *'lors de'* + *noun* or *'dès'* + *noun* resemble *'avant'* + *noun* or *'malgré'* + *noun* in that they are virtually always rendered in English with a particularizing translation. For example, 'lors de' can be followed by the whole gamut of indicatives and conditionals, as can be seen from these variations on the French translation of sentence 8 in the exercise:

ST 15   Lors de mon passage à Londres j'ai visité/j'aurai visité/j'aurais visité/je visite/je visitai/je visiterai/je visiterais tous les musées.

'Lors de mon passage' contains no precise temporal, aspectual or modal indication at all, and could be rendered by:

TT 15
$$\left\{ \begin{array}{l} \left\{ \begin{array}{l} \text{If I had been} \\ \text{If I were} \end{array} \right\} \\ \left\{ \begin{array}{l} \text{When} \\ \text{While} \\ \text{Whenever} \end{array} \right\} \left\{ \begin{array}{l} \text{I am} \\ \text{I was} \end{array} \right\} \end{array} \right\} \text{in London} \ldots$$

Only the context (usually the tense of the main verb) will show which of these particularizing options is the right one; and only the most pompous of contextual registers would prompt an English TT with a noun-construction like that of the ST ('On the occasion of my passing through London').

The relative predilection for the noun in French is neatly illustrated by two opposite tendencies in English and in French. Where English can, and does, easily use nouns as verbs, French usually cannot, as in this example from the exercise (sentence 9):

ST 16   Tu pourrais cesser de sortir du Baudelaire comme un perroquet.
TT 16   You might stop parroting Baudelaire.

Other examples are easy to find:

Jeter un pont sur une rivière.   To bridge a river.

Atteindre son niveau plancher.   To bottom out.

Mettre en bouteille(s).   To bottle.

Conversely, just as French readily turns adverbs and adjectives into nouns, so also it typically uses verbs either in the infinitive, *as* nouns, as in

Le laisser-aller.

Le savoir-vivre.

L'être et le paraître.

J'sauros jamais rien comprindre de leur parler (see p. 132):

or, in the third person singular present indicative, *in* nouns, as in:

Le porte-bagages.

Le passe-partout.

Le tire-bouchon.

English does of course sometimes use infinitives as nouns, as in 'the hijack'. However, the English verbal noun is usually a gerund ('replacing', 'belonging', and so on), which has a stronger verbal force than the corresponding French noun. This is doubtless because, unlike French, English does not need a definite article in such cases: contrast '*le* remplacement *d*'un carreau' (and English '*the* replacing *of* a window') with 'replacing a window'.

Here, to finish consideration of the noun/verb contrast, is, first, an example for translation, which exhibits other modes of nominalization as well:

J'avais plus que jamais conscience de son appartenance à la religion musulmane.

and, second, a sentence from Cardinal de Retz (1613–79), with an intralingual translation into modern French (Godin, 1964, p. 127); it is particularly revealing to compare the two versions in respect of particularization and generalization:

La Reine avait, plus que personne que j'aie jamais vu, de cette sorte d'esprit qui lui était nécessaire pour ne pas paraître sotte à ceux qui ne la connaissaient pas.

La Reine possédait plus qu'aucune autre personne de ma connaissance, cette sorte d'esprit nécessaire pour ne pas paraître sotte en présence d'étrangers.

16.4 Transposition from preposition reinforced by a noun phrase to a preposition or phrasal verb

We draw attention to two problems in this section. The first is that French prepositions cannot in general bear as much weight as English ones – consider the many possible meanings of 'de' and 'à'. Consequently, they are often reinforced with a noun, which does not as a rule need translating into English; for example:

Dans un délai de trois semaines.	In three weeks.
C'est de la part de qui?	Who's it from?
Je ne suis pas spécialiste en matière de sculpture.	I'm not an expert on sculpture.

The second, and bigger, problem is that of phrasal verbs. Most of the following sentences bring out clearly constructions which are common in English but do not exist in French, and which translators from French into English often overlook. It is, of course, often possible to keep the French structure and use a noun in English, but it is very often much more idiomatic to substitute a phrasal verb for the noun. The first three examples are the French originals for sentences 10–12 in the exercise:

ST 17   Décoller à l'eau et voir au dos.
TT 17(a) Unstick with/in water and see on back.
TT 17(b) Soak off and see back.

ST 18   Elle le fit entrer d'un geste.
TT 18(a) With a gesture, she made/had him come in.
TT 18(b) She motioned him in.

ST 19   Parfois je reviens en pensée au moment où nous nous sommes connus.
TT 19(a) Sometimes I return in my thoughts to when we met.
TT 19(b) Sometimes I think back to when we met.

In each of these cases, if one were asked to put TT(b) into French, it could only be translated with the help of nouns.

Proper attention to prepositions and phrasal verbs is one of the surest ways of avoiding translationese. It will be useful to conclude with discussion and translation of some further examples, which also bring in other categories of nominalization:

Il marchait à longues foulées, remontant l'avenue Montaigne, et Tony devait trotter pour se maintenir à son niveau.

[*Of a diver underwater*] D'un coup de jarret il revint à la surface.

[On retrouve la] même philosophie en matière de rémunérations: là encore, il s'agit de donner la priorité aux moins favorisés, tout en évitant les rigidités.

[*Tokor is taking his guest for a drive through the city*] On dévala en trombe une rue large où Tokor klaxonnait comme un fou, se frayant de la force du poignet un fulgurant passage dans les attroupements de la cohue bariolée, braillarde du matin.

16.5 A final word of common sense

We have been talking here about a notable contrast between French and English. This does not, however, mean that one has to get rid of all ST nouns when translating from French into English, or that one has to replace all ST adverbs or adjectives or verbs with nouns when translating into French. The initial assumption will always be that a noun will be rendered with a noun, an adjective with an adjective, and so on. The purpose of this chapter has simply been to sharpen awareness of the fact that, in the many cases where transposition from one part of speech to another is necessary, one is statistically more likely to transpose *to* a noun in English-French translation and *from* a noun in French-English.

The transposition between noun and other parts of speech is, therefore, not one-way. Exceptions to the statistical norm are easy to find; for example:

Il était borgne.	He only had one eye.
Je gémis de douleur et tordis brutalement le levier.	I yelped in pain and gave the lever a savage twist.
Le monde entier a tressailli quand il a su que Paris émergeait de l'abîme.	A tremor shook the whole world when they [sic] heard that Paris was rising from ruin (see p. 57 for this TT).
Elle aime bien rire.	She likes a good laugh.
C'est pas dramatique.	It's not the end of the world.
L'appareil possède des effecteurs simples lui permettant de saisir les objets pour les identifier et les expliquer le cas échéant.	The machine has simple effectors that enable it to take hold of objects for identification and, if necessary, explanation.
Il risquait de se faire arrêter.	He was in danger of arrest.
[*On the telephone*] Ça ne répond pas.	[There's] no reply.
Il écoutait, stupéfait.	He was listening in amazement.

17

Contrastive topic and practical: adverbs

This chapter constitutes the material for all or part of a practical. If possible, the following exercise should be handed in before the practical. It should in any case be completed before going on to the material in the rest of the chapter.

PRELIMINARY EXERCISE

Translate the following sentences, using only a monolingual French dictionary.

1 – Rentrer en France? dit Jeanne, pensive.
2 'Someone should tell him about the pill,' said another youth raising his head somnolently.
3 – Ça c'est une bonne idée, s'exclama Léa joyeuse.

4 Pour lui aussi, la durée s'écoule à un rythme implacablement ralenti.
5 'I've given up trying with Patrick,' said Mavis Mottram studying Eva's vase critically.
6 Ils accomplissaient leur besogne sans hâte, méthodiquement.

7 L'autre reluquait les garçons sans se gêner.
8 'Two bananas?' yelped Sherwood uncomprehendingly.
9 Tous étaient prêts à mourir, sans poser de questions, pour le IIIᵉ reich.

10 Elle gagne difficilement sa vie.
11 You don't laugh at Margaret Thatcher and get away with it.
12 Les jeunes gens s'éloignèrent sous l'œil faussement désespéré de Raoul.

The preliminary exercise was designed to draw attention to a specific set of problems in translation between French and English, namely problems arising from contrasts between the two languages in respect of adverbs and adverbial phrases. The English sentence in each section contained the section's 'hidden agenda' – that is, it is a clue to an option in English which is not available in French, but which is often hidden from the translator by the fact that the grammatical structure of a given ST expression can be reproduced in the TL. To borrow an example from Vinay and Darbelnet (1958, p. 127), the following sentence can be translated literally into English:

ST 1   Il fait constamment allusion à ses propres sources, dont l'anonymat est
           compréhensible mais tout de même agaçant.

TT 1(a) He constantly refers to his own sources, whose anonymity/the anonymity
           of which is understandable but nevertheless annoying.

Because the ST's grammar does have a structural counterpart in the TL, the translator's initial reaction is most likely to be to reproduce the French structure, as in TT 1(a). The tonal register of the TT is formal, and the social register is that of a slightly old-fashioned scholar; but since the ST is clearly taken from a scholarly work, the translator might decide that the element of pompousness entailed by keeping the French structure is not inappropriate. These are two good reasons why the following English structure – more idiomatic and no less appropriate – might not occur to the translator:

TT 1(b) He constantly refers to his own sources, which are understandably, but
           nevertheless annoyingly, anonymous.

This recourse to two adverbs qualifying the adjective is on the translator's 'hidden agenda' precisely because it is a pattern that is acceptable in English but is unlikely ever to appear in a French ST: 'qui sont compréhensiblement mais tout de même agaçamment anonymes' is unacceptable in any but a comic or satirical text.

As this example suggests, there are two main reasons why adverbs can pose translation problems. First, English *forms* adverbs, by adding 'ly' to an adjective or a past participle, much more readily than French does by adding 'ment'. Second, English *uses* adverbs much more frequently than French – even to the extent of sometimes qualifying one adverb in 'ly' with another. There is also a third source of translation difficulties: despite the more frequent use of adverbs in English, French not uncommonly uses adverbs in a way that would be unidiomatic or ungrammatical in English.

The four sections of this chapter reflect the four parts of the exercise. Each section is devoted to a major contrastive category. The first three categories consist of cases where French adjective, noun and verb respectively are best rendered by an English adverb; the fourth consists of cases where a French adverb is best rendered by a different part of speech in English. In each section, comments on the sentences used in the exercise are accompanied by further examples for discussion and translation in class.

17.1   Transposition from French adjective to English adverb

Sentence 1 in the exercise is an example of a very common structure in French, an adjective used in apposition to the subject:

ST 2   – Rentrer en France? dit Jeanne, pensive.

In English, the most plausible way of translating such adjectives is usually to use an adverb, as here:

TT 2   'Go back to France?' said Jeanne thoughtfully.

Another possibility is 'said the thoughtful Jeanne', which, like the ST, does refer more to Jeanne's state of mind than to the way she says the words. However, this is a less favoured construction in English than the adverbial one, perhaps because – to take this example – the definite article implies either that Jeanne was already thoughtful before going back to France was suggested, or that she is thoughtful by nature. In any case, this type of construction is more common with an adjectival past participle, as in 'said the excited Jeanne'. A further possibility is 'said a thoughtful Jeanne', but this construction, too, tends to occur more with an adjectival past participle, and it is in any case more likely in journalism, as in ' "I knew it would work out this way," said an elated/emotional/obviously dejected Bloggs'. The most unlikely solution of all, however, is to keep the ST structure: 'said Jeanne, thoughtful' is a calque that borders on translationese.

Sentence 3 in the preliminary exercise is a variant on the same construction as that found in ST 2:

ST 3:   – Ça c'est une bonne idée, s'exclama Léa joyeuse.
TT 3   'That's a great idea,' cried Léa joyfully.

Here, as is commonly the case with such a construction, there is no comma between the subject ('Léa') and the adjective ('joyeuse'). This often conveys a nuance of suddenness, the construction being an elliptical form of 's'exclama Léa devenue tout à coup joyeuse'. In such cases – that is, *verb + subject + adjective* with no comma – the impact of the adjective is often slightly closer to that of the English adverb. This is because, in so far as the absence of comma conveys a sudden change in state of mind, the reader is invited to picture a change taking place in the protagonist's behaviour, notably in facial expression and tone of voice. Since facial expression and tone of voice are part of the way in which something is said, the absence of comma gives the adjective, to some extent, the function of an adverbial complement of manner.

French is thus capable of nuances that English, because it is compelled to use an adverb, tends to blur. The following three sentences illustrate this clearly:

– T'es salaud, siffla Philippe, malveillant.

– T'es salaud, siffla Philippe malveillant.

'You bastard,' snarled Philippe malevolently.

Note that if the subject were not a proper noun, the construction without a comma would be capable of two readings. For example, '– T'es salaud, fit le gosse malveillant' could be taken to mean that the boy is habitually, or by nature, malevolent. Only the context will show whether 'the kid said malevolently' or 'said the malevolent kid' is the appropriate translation.

Apart from the question of the comma, ST 3 raises similar translation problems to ST 2: compare 'cried Léa joyfully', 'cried the joyful Léa', 'cried a joyful Léa' and 'cried Léa (,) joyful'. (For similar cases see the three examples on p. 235.)

As we have seen, French both forms and uses adverbs more sparingly than English. Nevertheless, the option of using an adverb does of course exist in many cases. Here is a simple example:

ST 4   Le chien aboya joyeusement.
TT 4   The dog barked joyfully.

Comparing ST 4 with ST 3 brings out very clearly the difference between adverb and adjective. 'Joyeusement' directly qualifies the barking, not the dog. The reader is invited to imagine the manner of barking and, implicitly, to visualize the dog wagging its tail and jumping about. 'Joyeuse' in ST 3 qualifies Léa's state of mind, not the way in which she speaks (although, as we saw, the lack of a comma confers some degree of adverbial force on the adjective).

Where there is a choice in French between adjective and adverb, there is therefore a further possible nuance, as witness a comparison of these five variants of ST 3:

ST 3(a)   – Ça c'est une bonne idée, s'exclama Léa joyeuse.
ST 3(b)   – Ça c'est une bonne idée, s'exclama Léa, joyeuse.
ST 3(c)   – Ça c'est une bonne idée, s'exclama joyeusement Léa.
ST 3(d)   – Ça c'est une bonne idée, s'exclama la jeune fille joyeuse.
ST 3(e)   – Ça c'est une bonne idée, s'exclama la jeune fille, joyeuse.

In STs 3(b) and 3(e), rendering 'joyeuse' by 'joyfully' results in an overlapping translation, losing explicit reference to the subject's state of mind, and adding an explicit reference to the way she speaks. For the same reasons, using 'joyfully' to render the 'joyeuse' of ST 3(a) also gives an overlapping translation: here, however, there is less translation loss in respect of literal meaning, because of the degree of adverbial status conferred on 'joyeuse' by the lack of a comma. In the case of ST 3(c), there is even less translation loss in rendering adverb with adverb; but the impact of 'joyfully' will necessarily be less nuanced than that of 'joyeusement', because (apart from anything else) the adverb is the only option available in English, whereas 'joyeusement' is one of three different possibilities in French. As for ST 3(d), the choice between 'joyful' and 'joyfully' must depend on the context; if the context shows that the girl is joyful by nature, 'joyful' is an accurate choice and involves minimal translation loss; but if she is simply exclaiming joyfully, then the English adverb, as an overlapping translation, incurs a similar loss to that involved in the translation of ST 3(a).

Sometimes, however, English does allow a closer counterpart to a French adjective used in the ways we have been examining. Two examples will make this clear.

First, to return to TTs 3(a) and 3(b), if the context suggested that 'gleeful' would be a more accurate rendering of 'joyeuse', then one could translate 's'exclama Léa joyeuse' as 'Léa exclaimed in glee'. This too, is an overlapping translation (less so in the case of ST 3(a)), *defining Léa's state of mind* as 'glee' rather that *describing Léa* as 'gleeful'. Nevertheless, it does preserve the ST's prime focus on how she feels, instead of switching focus to how she speaks. Indeed, such is the attractiveness of the English *preposition + noun* in cases of this sort that, if 'joyful' were after all more accurate in the context, the translator would want to consider the possibility of using 'joy' ('in/with joy'). The only reason for not choosing 'cried Léa in/with joy' is that neither fits this particular sentence in terms of register or idiomaticity.

Second, take this variant of ST 2:

ST 5   – Rentrer en France? dit Jeanne, incrédule.

This is another case where the option of using *preposition + noun* does exist:

TT 5   'Go back to France?' said Jeanne incredulously/disbelievingly/in disbelief.

The nuance between 'disbelievingly' (way of speaking) and 'in disbelief' (state of mind) is similar to that between 'gleefully' and 'in glee'. In the case of TT 5, however, choosing 'in disbelief' incurs less translation loss, in so far as the comma in ST 5 minimizes any adverbial force that 'incrédule' might have.

It is, then, worth bearing in mind the possibility of using a prepositional phrase in English to translate the type of expression examined here. Nevertheless, it remains true that the most favoured solution is to choose an adverb, the translation loss in terms of literal meaning being out-weighed by that involved in not meeting the demands of idiom and register.

A further point to be borne in mind is that the adverb is sometimes the only option in French, because the adjective would be grotesque for semantic reasons. In such cases, the question of nuance as between French adverb and French adjective does not arise. Compare, for example, the following sets of sentences:

– Je vois, dit le colonel encore plus sèchement.

? – Je vois, dit le colonel (,) encore plus sec.

Elle aimait à le piquer, et il répliquait vertement.

? Elle aimait à le piquer, et il répliquait (,) vert.

Finally, it does sometimes happen that an English *adjective* (or adjectival past participle) is a serious translation option, as in this example:

ST 6   – Alors vous n'avez rien compris à mes explications? observai-je un peu vexé.

TT 6(a) 'Haven't you understood anything I've been telling you?' I said, feeling rather upset.

TT 6(b) Rather upset at this, I said reproachfully: 'Haven't you understood anything I've been telling you?'

TT 6(c) That upset me a bit, and, reproachfully, I said: 'Haven't you understood anything I've been telling you?'

(In TTs 6(b) and 6(c), 'reproachfully' is an example of compensation in kind, conveying the reflected meaning of French 'observation' (in the sense of 'reproche' or 'critique') which the verb 'observai-je' has in this sentence.)

Here, for class discussion and translation, are some more examples inviting comparison of adjective and adverb both intralingually and interlingually:

– Combien d'hommes au travail, ce matin? demanda impérieusement le colonel.

– Combien d'hommes au travail, ce matin? demanda le colonel (,) impérieux.

– Oh, un système ordinaire, dis-je, un peu triste.

[*See sentence 2 in the exercise*] – Faudrait lui parler de la pilule, dit un autre jeune homme en relevant sa tête endormie.

– Faudrait lui parler de la pilule, dit un autre jeune homme en relevant la tête d'un air endormi/somnolent.

Elles se regardaient, perplexes.

Elles se regardaient, indécises.

– Vous avez du feu? me demanda-t-il brusquement.

– Vous avez du feu? me demanda-t-il, brusque.

17.2   Transposition from French *preposition* + *noun* to English adverb

Sentence 4 in the preliminary exercise is notable for two things. The first will
strike any French reader immediately – the weighty adverb 'implacablement', which by its very length gives a kind of 'relentless' emphasis to the
sentence. The second will go unnoticed by most French readers, but is of
interest for us in this section – the prepositional phrase 'à un rythme ralenti'
functioning as an adverbial complement:

ST 7   Pour lui aussi, la durée s'écoule à un rythme implacablement ralenti.

A literal translation might read something like this:

TT 7(a)   For him, too, time is passing at a relentlessly slow pace.

It would, however, be more idiomatic in English to do what French hardly
ever does with adverbs in '-ment', namely to use one such adverb as the
direct modifier of another:

TT 7(b)   For him, too, time was passing relentlessly slowly.

Using 'implacablement lentement' is virtually unthinkable in French. The
phrase 'à un rythme ralenti' is in fact a good example of a much-favoured
structure in French, *preposition* + *noun* in the role of adverbial complement. We looked at some examples of this type of structure in Chapter
16, pp. 205–7, to which the reader is referred. As with those examples,
rendering *preposition* + *noun* with an adverb results in greater dynamism in
the TT. The significant translation loss consists in the fact that the TT is less
in the nature of an analytic *definition of the situation*, and more in the nature
of a *description of the manner in which events unfold*.

In the following sentence (sentence 6 in the preliminary exercise), there
are again two adverbial complements:

ST 8   Ils accomplissaient leur besogne sans hâte, méthodiquement.

Here again, the natural solution in English is to use two adverbs:

TT 8   They were carrying out their task unhurriedly, methodically.

This time, however, one adverb does not qualify the other, but both directly
qualify the verb. It would have been possible in French to say 'ils
accomplissaient leur tâche lentement, méthodiquement', but this option is
unlikely for two reasons. First, juxtaposing two adverbs in '-ment' is
relatively unusual and would, therefore, be rather ponderously emphatic.
Second, the difference between 'lentement' and 'sans hâte' is similar to that

between 'slowly' and 'unhurriedly'. The difference is presumably important to the writer, who is describing unmolested German dive-bombers at Dunkirk. His problem is that there is no adverb in French that conveys the precise notion of unhurriedness (as applicable to aircraft, at any rate), so that he is obliged to use the common *'sans' + noun* construction. 'Without (any) hurry' is, of course, possible in English, and would entail less translation loss in respect of literal meaning; the translator's choice will depend on contextual factors, notably register.

Sentence 5 of the preliminary exercise is another reminder of the homology of French noun-based adverbial phrases and English adverbs:

ST 9   'I've given up trying with Patrick,' said Mavis Mottram studying Eva's vase critically.

TT 9   – Avec Patrick, moi, je n'essaie même plus, dit Mavis Mottram tout en considérant d'un œil critique le bouquet d'Eva.

In this sentence, there is little alternative to the French 'd'un œil critique'. This is an overlapping translation, keeping the notion of critical observation, but adding explicit reference to the look in Mavis Mottram's eye and losing explicit reference to her general disapproving demeanour as she looks at the flowers. In English, of course, there is a choice between 'critically' and 'with a critical eye'. That is, there are nuances available in English which are denied to the French speaker, just as, in French, where there is a choice between adjective and adverb (as in 'joyeuse/joyeusement'), there is usually a greater range of nuance than is possible in English. Coping with the translation loss attendant on these sorts of restriction is the stuff of everyday life for translators, who must resort to some form of compensation if they judge the loss unacceptable.

For further discussion of transposition from French *preposition + noun* to English adverb, see pp. 205–7. Here are some final examples for class discussion and translation:

Il avait parlé bas, presque d'un ton d'excuse.

– Je ne sais pas nager, dit Atkins d'une voix obstinée.

– Je ne sais pas nager, dit Atkins (,) obstiné.

– Je vois, dit le colonel sur un ton glacial.

– Je vois, dit le colonel (,) glacial.

Elle les dévisageait avec une insolence incroyable.

Elle jeta un coup d'œil anxieux autour d'elle, puis, d'un pas mal assuré, se mit à traverser la cour.

17.3   Transposition from French *preposition* + *verb* or relative clause to English adverb

In sentence 7 of the preliminary exercise, an adverb seems to be the most idiomatic way of rendering 'sans se gêner':

ST 10   L'autre reluquait les garçons sans se gêner.
TT 10   The other guy was unashamedly/uninhibitedly ogling the boys.

A *preposition* + *noun* construction is perhaps conceivable here – something like 'with no shame/embarrassment', or 'without any inhibition'. What is most unlikely in translating ST 10 is an adverbial complement containing *preposition* + *verb* – for example, 'without being embarrassed'.

'Unashamedly' and 'uninhibitedly' are as typically English adverbs as 'unhurriedly' (TT 8). It is very easy to form such compounds in English. French, however, very rarely adds the suffix 'ment' – and perhaps just as rarely the prefix 'in' – to an adjectival past participle. Instead, as we have seen, it commonly has recourse to *preposition* + *noun* or – less commonly, but nonetheless regularly – to *preposition* + *verb*. ST 10 is therefore a useful example, because it is a reminder that translators into English have at their disposal possibilities for affixation which it is easy to forget when reading French texts that are devoid of such structures. More often than not, an adverbial complement constructed with *preposition* + *verb* in a French ST can in fact be rendered with the same structure in English. If this is done, it will often be at the cost of some slight translation loss in respect of idiomaticity or register, but the occasional instance of such loss, while regrettable, will probably not be unacceptable. However, as with a consistent absence of phrasal verbs (see p. 214) or unreinforced prepositions (see pp. 236, 238), a consistent lack of compound adverbs like 'uninhibitedly', or 'unhurriedly', or 'unashamedly', will insidiously create an impression, if not of translationese, then at least of 'not-quite-Englishness'.

Sentence 9 in the preliminary exercise contains a good example of an adverbial construction which can be reproduced in English, but which can also be rendered with a single adverb:

ST 11   Tous étaient prêts à mourir, sans poser de questions, pour le IIIᵉ reich.
TT 11(a) All of them were ready to die, without asking (any) questions, for the Third Reich.

Because TT 11(a) is a possibility in English, it may not even occur to the translator that another English option exists, one which has no structural counterpart in French:

TT 11(b) All of them were ready to die unquestioningly for the Third Reich.

'Unquestioningly' entails translation loss in respect of literal meaning, because it is an overlapping translation that loses the element of static analysis and definition of the people's behaviour and adds in its place an element of dynamic description (the eager manner in which they court death). The question, once again, is whether literal meaning should be privileged above such features as idiomaticity and register; and the answer, once again, can only be given in terms of the context.

The impossibility of finding an adverb to translate 'uncomprehendingly' in sentence 8 of the preliminary exercise was intended as a reminder of a further alternative using a verb, namely a correspondence of English adverbs to French relative clauses:

ST 12 'Two bananas?' yelped Sherwood uncomprehendingly.
TT 12 – Deux bananes? glapit Sherwood qui n'y comprenait rien.

Here, for class discussion and translation, are some further cases in which transposition from a French structure containing a verb to an English adverb is an option:

On est en droit de présumer qu'il sait ce qu'il fait.

Mais, sans qu'on ait pu se l'expliquer, il n'était pas au rendez-vous.

– Je viens de me rappeler que je voulais te demander quelque chose, dit-elle. Que veut dire 'diversification transsexuelle'? – Cela veut dire poésie pour invertis, se hâta de répondre Wilt.

La providence s'acharnait à la poursuivre.

Ce noble but, elle le poursuivait depuis onze ans, sans compter, sans s'en laisser détourner.

17.4 Transposition from French adverb

We have looked at three common categories of transposition, from French adverbial expressions constructed round adjectives, nouns or verbs to English adverbs. However, the fact that adverbs are formed and used more frequently in English than in French does not mean that transposition is all one-way traffic. The final category we examine may be said to group together exceptions to the rule – that is, cases where an adverb in French is best transposed into a different part of speech in English.

Sentence 10 in the preliminary exercise is a typical example:

ST 13 Elle gagne difficilement sa vie.
TT 13 She finds it hard to make a living.

'Difficilement' is regularly used in this way, and usually needs to be rendered with a phrase constructed round an adjective. Compare the similar use of 'mal', as in:

ST 14 Je vois mal en quoi consisterait cette prétendue supériorité du rugby anglais.
TT 14 I fail to see just where English rugby is supposed to be so superior.

In TT 14, 'mal' is transposed into a verb, 'I fail to'; a phrase with an adjectival complement would also have been possible: 'I find it hard to.' In the following example, 'mal fait' could be translated as 'badly done', but an adjective is more idiomatic:

ST 15   – C'est du travail mal fait, dit-il d'un ton faussement indifférent.
TT 15   'It's shoddy work/workmanship,' he said in (tones of) feigned indifference.

ST 15 contains an instance of another regular problem case, the adverb 'faussement'. The solution adopted in TT 15, transposition of French *adverb + adjective* to English *preposition + adjective + noun*, is a classic one. Sentence 12 in the preliminary exercise is another example:

ST 16   Les jeunes gens s'éloignèrent sous l'œil faussement désespéré de Raoul.
TT 16   The youngsters walked off as Raoul watched in feigned/mock despair.

The two verbs in sentence 11 of the preliminary exercise can be translated with two verbs in French:

ST 17   You don't laugh at Margaret Thatcher and get away with it.
TT 17(a) Qui se moque de Margaret Thatcher n'en sort pas indemne.

However, just as English has hidden reserves of adverbs on which it can draw in the translation of French adverbial phrases, so, here, French has an adverb which has no structural counterpart in English:

TT 17(b) On ne se moque pas impunément de Margaret Thatcher.

Depending on the demands of register, 'impunément' will usually be translated as 'with impunity', or 'and get away with it', or 'without suffering the consequences'.

The conclusion to be drawn from these examples is, therefore, a simple caveat. Just as, in the case of nominalization (see Chapter 16), the alert translator does not seek as a matter of blind prejudice to minimize the number of nouns in an English TT, so too, in respect of adverbs, there are often cases where the more common procedure is reversed, French adverbs needing to be transposed to different parts of speech in the English TT. Here are some final examples for class discussion and translation:

Il l'avait regardée longuement.

Vous devez obligatoirement composter votre billet avant de monter dans le train.

La démarche a été diversement interprétée par les observateurs.

L'abbé ramena frileusement sur ses genoux la couverture.

Elle ouvrit la fenêtre brutalement.

18

Contrastive topic and practical: 'absolute' constructions

This chapter is intended to provide the material for all or part of a practical. If possible, students should be asked to complete and hand in the following short exercise in advance of the practical. It should, in any case, be completed before passing on to the material in the rest of the chapter.

PRELIMINARY EXERCISE

Translate the following sentences into French.

1 Bad luck is very enriching.
2 [*On the subject of the economy*] The figures are depressing.

3 While you're a student, you'll be travelling abroad.
4 If you'd been a student, you'd have travelled abroad.

5 When she had finished her lunch, she went out.
6 When my brother had left and mother was at prayer, Lucile would shut herself away.

7 Emma fainted and they carried her over to the window.
8 William and Tokor had stopped the car and were sitting gazing at the city.

The preliminary exercise points the way to four types of structure that are highly characteristic of French, and which often give rise to translation problems. In what follows, each of these types of structure will be dealt with in a separate section. What they all have in common is that each type can be interpreted as involving a particular kind of ellipsis, and each can be conveniently described as an 'absolute' construction. As in the case of nominalization, 'absolute' constructions in French also have their structural counterparts in English, but are distinctly less commonly used. Consequently, in translating a French 'absolute' construction into an idiomatic English TT, the translator usually needs to resort to grammatical transposition. As with nominalization, the contrast between French and English 'absolute' constructions usually reveals a preference in English for the particular or concrete as opposed to a preference in French for the generic or abstract.

18.1   Transitive verb with no object

In most cases of this type, it is the absence of a *direct* object that is at issue. French not only allows, but frequently prefers, the use of a transitive verb without an overt direct object, as in this simple example:

ST 1   Ce n'est pas que les éditeurs ne publient plus.
TT 1   It is not that publishers have stopped publishing.

The possibility of using transitive verbs in this 'absolute' way does of course exist for English, and ST 1 offers no translation problems in this respect (compare 'the cup that cheers'; 'thou shalt not kill'). However, the use of such a type of structure is much more common in French, and if such structures were reproduced every time in an English TT, this would quickly lead to translationese. The following typical example is one that does pose such a translation problem:

ST 2   Au risque de scandaliser, j'avoue même qu'une femme en pantalon ne me
          choque pas.

For reasons of English idiom, one is unlikely to choose to translate this as 'At risk of scandalizing/shocking . . .'. Two much more likely candidates are:

TT 2(a)   It may shock/scandalize you, but . . .
TT 2(b)   It may sound shocking, but . . .

Choosing between these options will depend, of course, on such considerations as genre and register, but each option entails translation loss in terms of literal meaning. TT 2(a) is a particularizing translation as a result of the additional specification of 'you' (as distinct from, say, 'them', 'people', and so on). TT 2(b) is a partially overlapping translation: 'shocking', used as an adjective, loses explicit reference to the act of scandalizing somebody, and adds, in its place, an explicit reference to the permanent, inherent quality of scandalousness attributed to not being shocked by a woman wearing trousers.

Similar points could be made about the next two examples, from which the first two sentences of the preliminary exercise were derived:

ST 3   Ça enrichit, les coups durs.
TT 3   Bad luck is very enriching.
        (In this example, 'very' is inserted to compensate for the emphasis given by the word order in the ST.)

ST 4   [*On the subject of the economy*] Les chiffres rendent morose.
TT 4   The figures are depressing.

As in TT 2(b) and TT 3, the absolute use of a transitive verb without a direct object is often idiomatically rendered in English by the use of an adjective. In the following case, there is a choice between a number of constructions, of which we list three:

ST 5   Sa nomination au poste de premier ministre surprit et rassura.
TT 5(a)   His appointment as Prime Minister was (both) surprising and reassuring.
TT 5(b)   His appointment as Prime Minister came as/was a reassuring surprise.
TT 5(c)   When he was appointed Prime Minister, it was/came as a reassuring surprise.

A measure of just how unexceptional the use of transitive verbs without a direct object is in French can be gained from the following colloquial example:

ST 6   Fais voir, donne! Mais dis donc, comment tu fais?
TT 6   Let's have a look, give it here! Hey, how do you do it?
        (Note that 'donne' also exemplifies another common type of phenomenon: the ellipsis of an *indirect* object.)

We offer here another example for discussion and translation:

[*The officer in charge of a blockhaus orders the machine-gunner to fire.*]

– Envoie une giclée!
– On voit pas! (N.B. *not* 'on y voit pas')
– Le taillis dans le fond. Arrose!

In translating all these examples where, in French, a transitive verb is used without an object, the tendency is to resort either to an overlapping translation (if transposition is to an adjective, or to *copula + noun* – for example, 'was a surprise') or to a particularizing translation (if a direct object is supplied in the TT). The latter case, where a direct object is added in the TT, brings out a typical difference between English and French, one which was clearly shown in Chapter 16: English tends often to concretize and particularize where French shows a preference for a less concrete and less specific reference to details.

18.2 Transposition from a verbless phrase, noun or adjective to a clause

Very commonly, a French sentence will contain a verbless phrase, noun or adjective which requires to be rendered with a clause containing a verb in English. The following example is a French ST from which sentences 3 and 4 in the preliminary exercise were derived:

ST 7   Etudiante, vous voyagerez à l'étranger.
TT 7(a)   While you're a student, you'll be travelling abroad.

It is clear that similar remarks apply to the category exemplified above as applied to previous examples of absolute constructions. Depending on context, the item 'étudiante . . .' may be alternatively rendered not only as 'while/when you're a student' but also as 'since/as you're a student . . .'. Transposition into a clause containing the addition of a verb inevitably entails a particularizing translation. In TT 7(a), the general, timeless concept of 'being a student' is particularized by reference to a specific time at which a specific individual is a student.

A further indication of the generic quality of the French verbless construction is the fact that it is consonant with the subsequent use of a number of different tenses, aspects or modalities:

ST 7(b)   Etudiante, vous avez voyagé/aurez voyagé/auriez voyagé/voyagez/ voyageriez à l'étranger.

Like 'lors de mon passage' (see p. 212), 'étudiante . . .' contains no precise temporal, aspectual or modal indication, and will, according to context, be rendered by any one of the following particularizations:

TT 7(b) $\left\{ \begin{array}{l} \left\{ \begin{array}{l} \text{If you had been} \\ \text{If you were} \end{array} \right\} \\ \left. \begin{array}{l} \text{When} \\ \text{While} \\ \text{Whenever} \end{array} \right\} \left\{ \begin{array}{l} \text{you are} \\ \text{you were} \end{array} \right\} \end{array} \right\}$ a student . . .

Similar remarks apply to the following examples, adapted from Astington (1983, p. 52), which should be discussed in class:

Lui président, les prélèvements obligatoires passeront de 42% à 40% du produit intérieur brut.

Lui président, les prélèvements [. . .] $\left\{ \begin{array}{l} \text{passeraient} \\ \text{seraient passés . . .} \\ \text{sont passés} \end{array} \right\}$

Any translation of 'Lui président' that uses a clause with a verb is, once again, an example of transposition from an absolute construction to a relatively specific, particularizing one. In this instance, however, English would allow recourse to a 'timeless' phrase instead of a verbal clause:

With him as President, compulsory contributions will go/would go/have
gone/would have gone/went down . . .

This solution, exploiting the use of 'with', is sometimes a useful one
in translating the type of absolute construction under discussion. The
solution does, however, still entail a degree of particularization: 'with'
seems to establish a clear and explicit *causal* relation within the TT
construction (compare 'with all this snow, there are bound to be accidents'),
whereas the French 'Lui président' leaves the causal implication inexplicit,
and as only one of several possible interpretations. Similar considerations
are raised by two further optional English renderings: 'Under/during
his presidency'. (For a good non-literary example of the use of this
construction, see p. 178: 'Roues au sol, serrez les écrous à fond.')

A type of construction that closely approximates the French absolute construction under discussion does, of course, exist in English, as
witnessed by 'He a scholar, it is surprising to find such a blunder'.
This instance is distinctly old-fashioned and donnish, but it does have
colloquial counterparts, as in 'And him a magistrate, too!'. In general,
however, considerations of idiom and register would seem to militate
against using such a construction for rendering its structural analogue
in French.

The next three examples contain a type of phrasal construction in French
which is related to the category under discussion, and which should be
discussed and translated in class:

Le désir de pouvoir conserver une bonne partie de l'électroménager
existant (parce que pratiquement neuf) dans une cuisine qui est à
refaire [. . .].

[*Of a Prog Rock band*] Leur musique est mûre, parfaite, géniale
réellement, car inspirée à la moindre seconde.

Harris, lui, eut son père fusillé par les Allemands, car travaillant pour
l'Intelligence service.

In the first of these examples, a verb must be supplied in the English TT to
prevent the phrase 'practically new' from being taken as directly qualifying
the owner of the kitchen. In any case, as the other two examples show,
English is more resistant to the omission of a finite verb in a clause
dominated by 'because' than it is to a similar omission in clauses dominated
by 'although' or 'while'.

Verbless absolute constructions are just as likely to be encountered in
everyday or informal French as in literary French, as we see from the
following:

[*From a D.I.Y. book*] Le détachement de la languette de verre se fait soit avec l'outil [. . .] soit avec des tenailles (dans ce cas prudence!).

Et les précautions en cas d'incendie? Hein? (see p. 133)

Et les rapports! Et les enquêtes! (see p. 133)

We have seen that in translating these absolute, timeless formulations into English, particularization is virtually inevitable. The same is true of the absolute use of an adjective in French, as, for instance, in:

Reposée – donc jolie, disaient les magazines – Lucien pourrait encore la désirer.

In this construction, again, 'reposée' could have been accompanied by a main clause containing a future, present, past or conditional verb. It should also be noted that a literal translation of this sentence into English would result in a nonsensical misattributed participle, with 'rested' qualifying 'Lucien'. This kind of misattribution is a common danger in translating such a construction. The problem does not arise for the French reader: gender concord ensures that feminine 'reposée' unambiguously qualifies the object of Lucien's desire. This type of construction is common in French, though it is sometimes criticized, if for no other reason than that in *spoken* French the features of feminine gender are frequently not audibly realized, which can lead to ambiguity.

From this section we can draw two simple conclusions. First, as with the items in the previous section, these types of absolute construction are, even when possible in English, less common in English than in French. Second, if one is to respect the interests of English idiom, such constructions usually need to be translated with some degree of particularization. The challenge to the translator is, first, to have the confidence to use a structure that does not directly imitate the structure of the ST, and second, to ensure that the particularization introduced into the TT is consistent with the context (for instance, to make a contextually appropriate choice between 'as/since/when/while/although', and so on).

18.3 'Ablative absolute'

The type of construction discussed in this section can be helpfully thought of as a survival or imitation of Latin ablative absolute, which, in Latin, takes the form of *noun + participle* in the ablative case. An example is: 'sole oriente, tenebrae abfugiunt' rendered as 'with the sun rising, the darkness flees'; compare '(with) the bridge (having been) built, crossing the river was easy'. One of the examples given in the previous section may perhaps be interpreted as a hidden instance of such a type of construction: 'Lui président' could be construed as an elliptic version of 'lui étant président'; compare 'he (being) a scholar'.

In fact, the 'ablative absolute' type of construction in French can almost always be interpreted as implying ellipsis of 'étant' or 'ayant été'. ST 8 below, for example, may be regarded as a contraction of 'Son déjeuner étant/ayant été terminé . . .' (and TT 8 as a contraction of 'Her lunch being/ having been finished...'). Such a contracted construction is perfectly possible in English, as in 'Arms folded, she listened intently'. Consequently, the following example presents no translation difficulty (see sentence 5 in the preliminary exercise):

ST 8   Son déjeuner terminé, elle sortit.
TT 8   Her lunch finished, she went out.

Nevertheless, as we have seen with other types of absolute construction, the demands of idiom and register will often necessitate a particularizing or overlapping translation of such a construction. The following examples should be discussed in this light:

Réflexion faite, le coup de tête de Botard ne m'étonne pas. (See p. 110.)

Les Catalans relevés, je défends Kirschweiler. (See p. 132.)

Il sera beaucoup plus facile de les hacher, le bol bien rempli. (See p. 187.)

Eux disparus, la librairie ne sera plus qu'un circuit de dépôts à court terme.

As with the earlier cases of 'lors de mon passage' and 'Etudiante, vous . . .', rendering French 'ablative absolutes' by using a clause with a verb in English will inevitably produce a particularizing, or sometimes partially over-lapping, translation. Henri Godin (1964) sees this type of construction as typical of a 'streamlining' tendency in modern French, and cites an early example from Chateaubriand (see sentence 6 in the preliminary exercise), who first wrote:

Lorsque mon frère était parti et que ma mère était en prières, Lucile s'enfermait.

then changed his text to:

Mon frère parti et ma mère en prières, Lucile s'enfermait.

18.4 Transposition from past participle or adjective to noun phrase or relative clause

In this category, too, we are dealing with a type of structure that is extremely common in French, but occurs with much less frequency in English. Take, for example:

ST 9   Ils éditeront à des tirages aussi bas que possible pour réduire le risque encouru.

TT 9   They will publish with the smallest print runs possible, so as to reduce the risk incurred.

Translation by an analogous English structure is possible in the case of ST 9; however, such an option is less likely to be suitable in ST 10:

ST 10   On célébra Rocroi délivré.
TT 10   We celebrated the relief of Rocroi.

Here, a literal translation – 'We celebrated Rocroi (having-been-) relieved' – is out of the question. The idiomatic rendering by 'the relief of' is a virtually obligatory case of overlapping translation.

The type of construction under discussion is very common in French, and often necessitates considerable structural recasting when translated into English, as we can see in the example of ST 11:

ST 11   [*On a bus*] Il se jeta sur une place devenue libre.

Since a literal 'He threw himself onto a having-become-free seat' is unacceptable, more or less drastic ways of recasting the ST structure need to be sought. Some possibilities are:

TT 11(a) He grabbed a seat someone had just vacated.
TT 11(b) Then he saw a free seat and grabbed it.
TT 11(c) Then some people got off and he grabbed a free seat.

In the type of case under discussion, the French structure may be seen as a contracted relative clause with ellipsis of 'être' ('Rocroi qui avait été délivré'; 'une place qui était devenue libre'). Such ellipsis is frequently inadmissible in English, and, as a result, the translator is forced to look for structural alterations for an idiomatic English rendering. The following examples will probably need significant rewriting in translation:

On porta Emma évanouie devant la fenêtre. (See sentence 7 in the preliminary exercise.)

[*William and Tokor are out for a drive. They stop on a hilltop and look at the view.*] William et Tokor arrêtés dans leur voiture contemplaient la ville. (See sentence 8 in the preliminary exercise.)

Michel ahuri se tut.

Our three final examples show another structure which is often encountered. As with other examples in this section, these cases can also be construed as involving ellipsis of the copula 'être', but here the qualifier is not a past participle but an adjective:

Seule dans la pierraille de Nuremberg déserte, une cycliste souriante.

En tout cas, dis-je furieux, tu pourrais cesser de sortir du Baudelaire comme un perroquet.

Oh, un système ordinaire, dis-je, un peu triste.

The adjectives in the last two examples are probably best rendered by adverbs in English; this is a common solution to the problems posed by the structures exemplified here, as we saw in Chapter 17.

19

Contrastive topic and practical: prepositions

This chapter is devoted to a practical problem which, although it requires little discussion, has considerable implications for the translator. The problem is actually more immediately obvious in translating from English into French, because in that case the translator is seen to be forced into grammatical transposition, usually in the form of adding reinforcing elements to the French TT. On the other hand, the problem is more subtle and more insidious in translating from French into English, mainly because the translator may overlook the need for transposition, since the French structures can be replicated in English. To replicate them may, in fact, not result in ungrammatical, or even unidiomatic, constructions in the TT, but merely in a structure that is less compact than that of a 'normal' English text. If this lack of terseness and 'normalcy' persists over a longish stretch of TT, the cumulative effect will be that of an impression of oddness, even foreignness.

The topic at issue is conveniently approached by way of an attempt to translate the following passage. If possible, this passage should be translated and handed in before the topic is discussed in class. It should, in any case, be completed before passing on to the material in the rest of the chapter.

PRELIMINARY EXERCISE

Translate the following passage into English:

Chaque fois qu'Henri promenait son chien [. . .], il suivait invariablement le même chemin. Le chien le prenait docilement, et Henri suivait le chien. Ils descendaient la rue, tournaient devant le bureau de poste, traversaient le terrain de jeu et passaient sous la ligne de chemin de fer pour arriver au sentier qui longeait la rivière. Un kilomètre au bord de l'eau, puis retour au bercail. Ils repassaient le viaduc puis pénétraient dans ces rues où les maisons étaient bien plus grandes que celle d'Henri et il y avait des arbres et des jardins et les voitures étaient toutes des B.M.W. ou des Mercedes.

5

The passage given in the preliminary exercise is, in fact, itself a translation of an English ST, a TT version suitably doctored in order not to give away its English origins, which would have prejudiced translation choices. Here is the original English text:

> Whenever Henry Wilt took the dog for a walk [. . .], he always took the same route. In fact the dog followed the route and Wilt followed the dog. They went down past the Post Office, across the playground, under the railway bridge and out on to the footpath by the river. A mile along the river and then under the railway line again and back through streets where 5 the houses were bigger than Wilt's semi and where there were large trees and gardens and the cars were all Rovers and Mercedes.
>
> (Sharpe, 1978)

The French TT could, of course, be discussed in a number of respects, but we shall concentrate briefly on the specific points that relate to the topic of this chapter, namely the relative weakness of French prepositions in comparison with their English counterparts.

In the English text, the verb 'went' is qualified by a series of eight adverbial complements, each having a preposition as its nucleus. In none of these cases has the translator been able to use a simple French preposition on its own to render the English preposition. In four instances, the TT uses prepositions reinforced with a verb:

past the Post Office	*tournaient devant* le bureau de poste
under the railway bridge	*passaient sous* la ligne de chemin de fer
to the footpath	*pour arriver* au sentier
through the streets	*pénétraient dans* ces rues

In three other cases, the French TT contains no preposition, the English preposition having simply been replaced with a verb of motion:

across the playground	*traversaient* le terrain de jeu
by the river	*qui longeait* la rivière
under the railway line again	*repassaient* le viaduc

In the remaining case, a compound French preposition containing a noun has been substituted for a simple English preposition:

along the river	*au bord de* l'eau

These eight examples of grammatical transposition are typical of a technique to which French translators often have to resort when confronted with English prepositions. Their task is made more difficult still by yet another phenomenon typical of English structure: the use of one preposition as an adverbial modifier of another preposition. The English text contains two examples of this, 'down past' and 'on to'. To these we may add further complications: the possibility of modifying a preposition by an adverb, as in 'back through', or of using an adverb to modify further an expression consisting of a preposition modified by another preposition, as is the case in 'out on to'. In each of these cases, the resulting complex effectively constitutes a compound preposition (as witness the absence of commas after 'down', 'on', 'back' and 'out'). French analogues of such compound prepositions cannot usually be formed for the purposes of French TT, as shown here:

They *went down past* the Post Office	Ils *descendaient la rue, tournaient devant* le bureau de poste
out on to the footpath	*pour arriver au* sentier
then under the railway line again and *back through* streets	puis *retour au bercail*. Ils repassaient la viaduc puis *pénétraient dans* ces rues

What these comparisons reveal is that a 'normal' English text is liable to contain prepositional structures that have no structural counterparts in French. In the light of this we can begin to appreciate what is missing in terms of 'normalcy' from an English text that contains no instances of these extremely common and compact English prepositional structures: such a text would be subtly, but distinctly, odd. The danger of this 'oddness' is all the greater in that, when translating from French to English, it is actually perfectly possible, for the most part, to replicate in the TT the kinds of structure that are used in French (for example, to render 'tournaient devant' as 'turned in front of'). The passage given in the preliminary exercise is almost certain to have been translated in this manner; in fact a typical rendering of it might run along the following lines:

Every time Henri walked his dog [. . .], he invariably took the same route. The dog would set quietly off, and Henri would follow the dog. They *went*

down the street, turned off by the Post Office, *crossed* the playground and
went under the railway line, *coming at last to* the path *that ran alongside* the
river. A kilometre by the water *before returning to the fold*. They *went*   5
back under the viaduct, and *then set off through* streets where the houses
were much bigger than Henri's and there were trees and gardens and the
cars were all B.M.W.s and Mercedes.

A 'back-translation' that rediscovers the original English preposition-based
adverbial complements attached to the verb 'went' is not likely to be found
for the italicized phrases, for the translator would be reluctant to lose the
explicit variety and deliberateness embodied in the accumulated verbs of
motion in the French text. (Conversely, the French text itself has suffered
considerable translation loss in comparison with the *original* version:
compared with the economical and dynamic power of the English prepositions, the succession of verbs seems very plodding.) Needless to say, the
translator's choices must, as ever, be weighed against the demands of
context, idiomaticity, and stylistic considerations such as that of a racy,
punchy and down-to-earth style of narrative. However, a French TT is
almost bound to lose some of these stylistic features of the Tom Sharpe *Wilt*
ST; and a 'back-translation' to English is hardly likely to be able to recover
these features.

In the text we have been examining, the French counterparts to English
prepositions are predominantly verb-based phrases. This is indeed a
common correspondence between the two languages, but it is by no means
the only one. Equally often, an English preposition may correspond to a
compound French preposition containing a noun:

L'éditeur ne peut le vendre que *par l'entremise* d'un libraire.	The publisher can only sell it *through* a bookseller.
C'est *de la part de* qui?	Who's it *from*?

or to a French relative clause or present participle:

J'avais contemplé avec nostalgie le chromo *qui représentait* sa chambre. (See p. 100.)	I had gazed longingly at the coloured picture *of* her room.
Jean-Rostand, un gros établissement *accueillant* plus de 2300 élèves.	Jean-Rostand, a big school *with* over 2300 pupils.

or to a French preposition reinforced by an adjective or past participle:

L'après-midi du vendredi est *consacré à* votre éducation.	Friday afternoons are *for* your education.
C'est les hurlements *venus de* la cuisine qui l'ont réveillée.	It was the screaming *from* the kitchen that woke her.

The practical work that follows is divided into four sections, reflecting the four categories of French–English correspondence illustrated above. Each section comprises two stages. In stage A the task will be to translate English sentences containing prepositions that cannot be directly rendered into French. The function of this is to raise awareness, by practical experience, of the relative weakness of prepositions in French. In stage B, the task is to give alternative translations of each of a set of French sentences, including a translation that renders the italicized material by a single English preposition. *Stage B should be done without a dictionary throughout.*

19.1 English preposition corresponds to French verb or preposition reinforced by a verb

A 1 What's the quickest way to the University, please?
   2 I'll come for you about seven.
   3 I managed to crawl away from the flames.
B 4 Il faudrait téléphoner *pour appeler* un médecin.
   5 On ne peut atteindre le bureau qu'*en traversant* la chambre.
   6 La machine heurta le bureau et *il glissa* jusqu'au mur *qu'il rencontra* d'une force irrésistible.

19.2 English preposition corresponds to French preposition reinforced with a noun, or French compound preposition containing a noun or noun phrase

A 7 She's on the executive committee.
   8 There's only one night crossing from Ostend.
   9 She was calling him from across the street.
B 10 Un maçon laissa tomber une brique *du haut d*'une échelle.
  11 Le résultat de cette politique sera la disparition, *en l'espace de* cinq ans, de la plupart des libraires français.
  12 Une main-d'œuvre bon marché *en provenance des* territoires occupés.

19.3 English preposition corresponds to French relative clause or present participle

A 13 I'm very touched by your concern for me.

14 The headmaster was a batty old man with a literally moth-eaten gown.

15 The houses over the road are much bigger than ours.

B 16 On n'est pas près d'oublier le match *qui a opposé* Agen et Béziers, l'an dernier.

17 Sur les véhicules *dont* les sièges peuvent *être rabattus* [. . .] veillez à ce que ces palettes ne soient pas détériorées.

18 Il est recommandé d'employer cette vitesse pour les produits *contenant* beaucoup d'eau.

19.4 English preposition corresponds to French preposition reinforced by an adjective or past participle

A 19 A young man with AIDS tells us his tragic story.

20 He illustrates his argument with quotations from Shakespeare.

21 In France, passengers with tickets have to date-stamp them before boarding the train.

B 22 Le pasteur, *vêtu de* son habit noir, nous terrifiait.

23 Il ne semblait pas savoir de quel défi, et *lancé par* qui, il s'agissait.

24 Mille rumeurs vagues *relatives aux* trésors enfouis par Kidd et ses associés.

20

Summary and conclusion

The idea of translators as active and responsible agents of the translation process has played a constant and central part throughout this course. Indeed, the personal responsibilities of translators are, in our view, of paramount importance. Although loyalties may genuinely be divided between responsibilities to the author of the ST, to the manifest properties and features of the ST (in particular, with a view to what is there in black and white in a written ST), to the 'paymaster' by whom a TT has been commissioned, and to a putative public for whom the TT is meant, it is, in the end, the translator alone who is responsible for submitting a particular TT. Responsibility entails decisions, and it is with this in mind that we have insisted at every juncture on the key themes of *strategy* and *decisions of detail*, stressing the idea that decisions of detail should be rationally linked to the prior formulation of overall strategy for translating a particular text in a particular set of circumstances.

The formulation of an appropriate translation strategy implicitly means 'ranking' the cultural, formal, semantic, stylistic and genre-related properties of the ST according to their relative textual *relevance*, and the amount of attention these properties should receive in the process of translation. The aim is to deal with translation loss (see especially Chapter 2), and the attendant necessities of compromise and compensation (see the discussion in Chapter 3), in a relatively rational and systematic way: in short, by sanctioning the loss of features that have a low degree of textual relevance, sacrificing less relevant textual details to more relevant ones, and using techniques of compensation to restore features of high textual relevance that cannot be more directly rendered.

To return briefly to the idea of 'textual relevance', this is a qualitative measure of the degree to which, in the translator's judgement, particular properties of a text are held responsible for the overall impact carried in and by that text. In a sense, textually relevant features are those that stand out as features that make the text what it is. This is not as trivial and circular as it might sound. On the contrary, it is the basis for the only reasonably reliable test of textual relevance. No such test can, of course, escape a degree of subjectivity, but the most objective test of textual relevance is to imagine that a particular textual property is omitted from the text and to assess what difference this omission would make to the overall impact of the text as a whole. If the answer is 'little or none', we may take it that the property in question has a very low degree of textual relevance. If, on the other hand, omission of a textual property would imply a loss in either the genre-representative or the individual (perhaps even deliberately idiosyncratic) character of the text, we may attribute a high degree of relevance to the textual property in question.

Ideally, developing a translation strategy by way of assessing textual relevance in a ST entails scanning the text for every *kind* of textual feature that might conceivably be relevant to formulating an appropriate TT. For such scanning to be systematic and speedy, it is vital to have in mind a concrete 'check-list' of the *kinds* of textual feature one needs to look out for. It is with this in view that we suggest the schema of textual 'filters' sketched out on p. 246. The overall schema summarizes practically the entire framework of the course, and, for the most part, follows the order of presentation in the main body of the text. The only exception to this is in the inclusion of 'grammatical transposition' among the options listed in the 'cultural' filter, where it occupies a position between 'calque' and 'communicative translation'. It can be argued that grammatical transposition is, indeed, a cultural matter and has important implications in the presentation of different world-views favoured by SL and TL respectively (for instance, the tendency in French to prefer 'abstract and static' descriptions of events as against the tendency in English to use a 'dynamic and particularizing' mode of expression; see the discussion on 'nominalization' in Chapter 16). It can also be argued that as an option, grammatical transposition is intermediate between the rather more SL-oriented creation of calqued expressions (which retain much of the grammatical flavour of their SL models) and the considerably more TL-oriented choice of communicative translations (which may retain little of the literal meaning of their SL counterparts). Consequently, the position accorded to grammatical transposition in our schema of textual 'filters' can be fully justified. The reason why this does not tally with our presentation in the main body of the text is a tactical one: grammatical transposition forms the subject matter of four contrastive chapters (Chapters 16–19), which we have chosen to use as movable course components, and which, by sheer size alone, could not be accommodated in the chapter on cultural issues (Chapter 3) without disrupting the modular structure of the course. For reasons of practical usefulness, grammatical transposition has been taken out of its logical place in Chapter 3 and given extended treatment in the form of contrastive exercises. The schema of textual 'filters' restores this issue to its logical place.

For the rest, the contents of the 'cultural' filter correspond to issues discussed in Chapter 3. This component calls attention to textual features that present choices between 'extra-cultural' and 'indigenous' elements (see the discussion in Chapter 3). As such, it invites the translator to assess – when considering a ST in this light – the degree to which features of the ST are detachable from their cultural matrix, that is to say, the extent to which their culture-specificity is textually relevant.

The 'formal' filter corresponds in content and organization to Chapters 4–6 and constitutes a component for scanning the formal properties of texts, which are discussed in detail in these chapters.

The 'semantic' filter summarizes the contents of Chapters 7 and 8 and focuses the attention of the translator on the important decisions relating to the translating of literal meaning, as well as of textually relevant features of connotative meaning.

The 'varietal' filter sums up the stylistic aspects inherent in the use of different language varieties, and invites the translator to pay due attention to the textual effects of sociolinguistic variation. The contents of this filter correspond to Chapters 9 and 10 in the course.

Finally, the 'genre' filter serves as a brief and necessarily sketchy reminder of the vital importance of assessing the genre-membership of texts, and discovering their genre-related characteristics. This filter corresponds to the entire contents of Chapters 11–15.

Although analogies can be misleading when used in explanation, we shall risk an analogy by suggesting that the schema visualizes the methodological framework of translation as a 'series of filters' through which texts can be passed in a systematic attempt to determine their translation-worthy properties. In terms of this analogy, textually relevant properties find their level by being 'collected' in the appropriate filter; the importance of the various levels can be ranked according to the nature of the text (for example, the prosodic level will probably rank as minimally important in scientific texts, whereas it may be ranked as maximally important in some poetic genres); and certain filters or levels will be found to contribute no textually relevant features (for example, a particular text may be found to contain no significant allusive meanings).

It should also be said that STs are not the only texts that can be passed through the elements of the proposed series of filters: tentative TTs can be similarly processed before they are finalized, and their features compared with those of the ST, as a means of evaluating their success. It is also possible to evaluate published TTs by the same process. That is to say, the series of filters can serve three related functions: first, the scanning of a ST for a systematic discovery of its textually relevant properties; second, the scanning of a provisional TT as a systematic way of deciding on those elements of detail that are most likely to be successful and appropriate in a finalized version; and, third, the evaluation of existing TTs completed by other translators.

The analogy of filters is a mechanical one, and in this lies a serious danger of misunderstanding. We do not wish to imply that our schema is intended as a means of 'mechanizing' the process of translation: on the contrary, we believe this process to be an intelligent and 'humanistic' one involving personal, and in the final analysis subjective, choices on the part of the translator. The schema of filters is not a mechanical device but a 'mnemonic' one: it reminds the working translator of what features to look for in a ST, as well as of the need to rank these features in order of relative textual relevance, as part and parcel of working out a strategy for translating the ST. It also serves to remind translators of options and choices when tinkering with the details of editing a provisional TT. But the decisions and choices remain entirely non-mechanical: they are for the translator to make.

A further point to be made about the schema of textual filters concerns the time element. Scanning a text in the kind of detail that a full use of the filters would seem to imply is unrealistic when the translator is working against a time limit. In such cases, a more perfunctory use of the schema can still be helpful in speeding up the process of adopting a translation strategy, and in dealing with particularly problematic points of detail. It is worth remembering that the usefulness of the schema is not dependent on making a full and exhaustive use of its scanning potential: it performs a useful function even in speed translation. The translator simply has to make as much, or as little, use of it as time will allow.

Finally, it is worth noting that, through practice, the scanning of texts in the manner suggested by the schema quickly becomes habitual, so that the translator comes to perform the process automatically, without having to consult the 'check-list' contained in the schema.

SCHEMA OF TEXTUAL 'FILTERS'

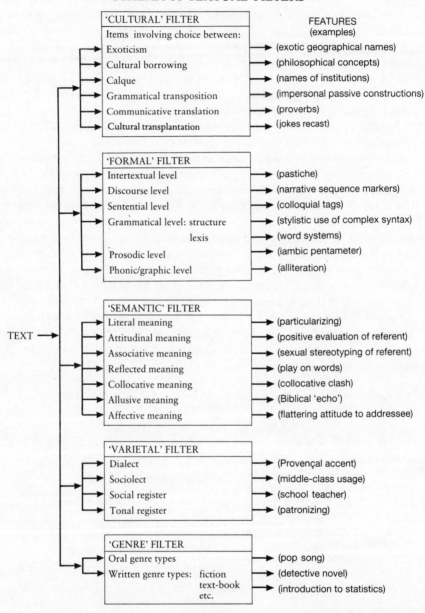

Figure 20.1

Glossary

affective meaning   the emotive effect worked on the addressee by the choice of a particular **linguistic expression**, rather than others that might have been used to express the same literal message; affective meaning is a type of **connotative meaning**.

alliteration   the recurrence of the same sound/letter or sound/letter cluster at the beginning of two or more words occurring near or next to one another in a **text**.

allusive meaning   the **connotative meaning** of a **linguistic expression** which takes the form of evoking the meaning of an entire saying or quotation in which that expression figures. (N.B. If a saying or quotation appears in full within a **text**, that is a case of *citation*; we speak of *allusion* where only a recognizable segment of the saying or quotation occurs in the text, but that segment implicitly carries the meaning of the entire 'reconstructed' saying or quotation.)

anaphora   in *grammar*, the replacement of previously used **linguistic expressions** in a **text** by simpler and less specific expressions (such as pronouns) having the same contextual referent; in *rhetoric*, the repetition of a word or phrase at the beginning of successive clauses.

associative meaning   the **connotative meaning** of a **linguistic expression** which takes the form of attributing to the referent certain stereotypically expected properties culturally associated with that referent.

assonance   the recurrence of a sound/letter or sound/letter cluster in the middle of words occurring near or next to one another in a **text**.

attitudinal meaning   the **connotative meaning** of a **linguistic expression** which takes the form of implicitly conveying a commonly held attitude or value judgement towards the referent of the expression.

calque   a form of **cultural transposition** whereby a TT expression is modelled on the grammatical structure of the corresponding ST expression.

code-switching   the alternating use of two or more recognizably different language variants (varieties of the same language, or different languages) within the same **text**.

cogency   the 'thread' of intellectual interrelatedness of ideas running through a **text**.

coherence   the tacit, yet intellectually discernible, thematic development that characterizes a **cogent** text, as distinct from a random sequence of unrelated sentences.

cohesion   the explicit and transparent linking of sentences and larger sections of **text** by the use of overt linguistic devices that act as 'signposts' for the **cogency** of a text.

collocative meaning   the **connotative meaning** lent to a **linguistic expression** by the meaning of some other expression with which it frequently or typically collocates in a grammatical context; that is, collocative meaning is the 'echo' of expressions that 'partner' a given expression in commonly used phrases.

communicative translation   a style of **free translation** involving the substitution for ST expressions of their contextually/situationally appropriate cultural equivalents in the TL; that is, the TT uses situationally apt target culture equivalents in preference to **literal translation**.

compensation   the technique of making up for the **translation loss** of important ST features by approximating their effects in the TT through means other than those used in the ST – that is, making up for ST effects achieved by one means through using other means in the TT.

compensation in kind   compensating for a particular type of textual effect in the ST by using a textual effect of a different type in the TT.

compensation by merging   condensing the features carried over a relatively longer stretch of the ST into a relatively shorter stretch of TT.

compensation in place   compensating for the loss of a particular textual effect occurring at a given place in the ST by creating a corresponding effect at a different place in the TT.

compensation by splitting   distributing the features carried in a relatively shorter stretch of the ST over a relatively longer stretch of the TT.

connotative meaning the implicit overtones and the nuances that **linguistic expressions** tend to carry over and above their **literal meanings**. (N.B. The overall meaning of an expression in context is compounded of the literal meaning of the expression *plus* its connotative overtones.)

crossover the conversion of a written **text** into a corresponding oral text, or, conversely, of an oral text into a corresponding written text. (N.B. The correspondences are a matter of degree, and are never more than approximate.)

cultural borrowing the process of taking over a SL expression verbatim from the ST into the TT (and, ultimately, into the TL as a whole). The borrowed term may remain unaltered in form or may undergo minor alteration or **transliteration**.

cultural transplantation the highest degree of **cultural transposition**, involving the replacement of source-cultural details mentioned in the ST with cultural details drawn from the target culture in the TT – that is, cultural transplantation deletes from the TT items specific to the source culture, replacing them with items specific to the target culture.

cultural transposition any degree of departure from a maximally **literal translation** – that is, the replacement in a TT of SL-specific features with TL-specific ones; cultural transposition implies a certain degree of TL orientation.

decisions of detail in translating a given **text**, the decisions taken in respect of specific problems of grammar, lexis, and so on; decisions of detail are ideally taken in the light of previously taken **strategic decisions**.

deictic a textual element (for instance, a demonstrative, a pronoun, a temporal expression) designating a specific referent which the hearer/reader is required to identify relative to context of situation.

dialect a language variety with non-standard features of accent, vocabulary, syntax and sentence formation (for example, intonation, **illocutionary particles**) characteristic, and therefore indicative, of the regional provenance of its users.

discourse level the textual level on which whole **texts** (or sections of whole texts) are considered as self-contained, **coherent** and **cohesive** entities; the ultimate discourse structure of texts consists in a number of inter-related sentences, these being the lowest analytic units on the discourse level.

editing   the last stage of the translation process, consisting in checking over the draft of a written TT with a view to correcting errors and polishing up stylistic details.

exegetic translation   a style of translation in which the TT expresses and explains additional details that are not explicitly conveyed in the ST; that is, the TT is, at the same time, an expansion and explanation of the contents of the ST.

exoticism   the lowest degree of **cultural transposition** of a ST feature, whereby that feature (having its roots exclusively in the SL and source culture) is taken over verbatim into the TT; that is, the transposed term is a recognizably and deliberately 'foreign' element in the TT.

foot   a prosodic/metric unit in versification, consisting of a rhythmic pattern of stressed and/or unstressed syllables; in certain languages (for example, English or Latin, but not French), feet are the basic units of poetic rhythm.

free translation   a style of translation in which there is only a global correspondence between units of the ST and units of the TT – for example, a rough sentence-to-sentence correspondence, or an even looser correspondence in terms of even larger sections of text.

generalizing translation   rendering a ST expression by a TL **hyperonym** – that is, the **literal meaning** of the TT expression is wider and less specific than that of the corresponding ST expression; a generalizing translation omits details that are explicitly present in the literal meaning of the ST.

gist translation   a style of translation in which the TT expresses a condensed version of the contents of the ST; that is, the TT is, at the same time, a synopsis of the ST.

grammatical level   the level of linguistic structure concerned with words, the decomposition of complex (inflected, derived or compound) words into their meaningful constituent parts, and the patterned syntactic arrangement of words into phrases, and phrases into yet more complex phrases.

grammatical transposition   the technique of translating a ST expression with a given grammatical structure by a TT expression with a different grammatical structure containing different parts of speech in a different arrangement.

hyperonym   a **linguistic expression** whose **literal meaning** is inclusive of, but wider and less specific than, the range of literal meaning of another expression; for example, 'bread' is a hyperonym of 'cottage loaf'.

hyponym   a **linguistic expression** whose **literal meaning** is included in, but is narrower and more specific than, the range of literal meaning of another expression; for example, 'cottage loaf' is a hyponym of 'bread'.

illocutionary particle   a discrete element which, when added to the syntactic material of a sentence, tells the listener/reader what affective force the utterance is intended to have – for example, 'alas', 'dammit!', 'n'est-ce pas?', 'eh?'.

interlineal translation   a style of translation in which the TT provides a literal rendering for each successive meaningful unit of the ST (including affixes) and arranges these units in their order of occurrence in the ST, regardless of the conventional grammatical order of units in the TL.

inter-semiotic translation   translating from one semiotic system (that is, system for communication) into another. For a translation to be inter-semiotic, either the ST, or the TT, but not both, may be in a human natural language.

intertextual level   the level of shared culture on which **texts** are viewed as bearing significant external relationships to other texts (for example, by allusion, by imitation, by virtue of genre membership).

intralingual translation   the re-expression of a message conveyed in a particular form of words in a given language by means of *another* form of words in the *same* language.

linguistic expression   a self-contained and meaningful item in a given language, such as a word, a phrase, a sentence.

literal meaning   the conventional range of referential meaning attributed to a linguistic expression (as abstracted from its **connotative** overtones and contextual nuances).

literal translation   a word-for-word translation, giving maximally literal rendering to all the words in the ST as far as the grammatical conventions of the TL will allow; that is, literal translation is SL-oriented, and departs from the ST sequence of words only where the TL grammar makes this inevitable.

partially overlapping translation   rendering a ST expression by a TL expression whose range of **literal meaning** partially overlaps with that of the ST expression – that is, the literal meaning of the TT expression both *adds* some detail *not* explicit in the literal meaning of the ST expression, and *omits* some other detail that *is* explicit in the literal meaning of the ST expression;

in this sense, partially overlapping translation simultaneously combines elements of **particularizing** and of **generalizing translation**.

particularizing translation   rendering a ST expression by a TL **hyponym** – that is, the literal meaning of the TT expression is narrower and more specific than that of the corresponding ST expression; a particularizing translation adds details to the TT that are not explicitly expressed in the ST.

phonemic translation   a technique of translation that consists in an attempt to replicate in the TT the sound sequence of the ST, while allowing the sense to remain, at best, a vague and suggested impression.

phonic/graphic level   the level of linguistic structure concerned with the patterned organization of sound-segments (phonemes) in speech, or of letters (graphemes) in writing.

prosodic level   the level of linguistic structure concerned with metrically patterned stretches of speech within which syllables have varying degrees of *prominence* (in terms of such properties as stress and vowel-differentiation) and varying degrees of *pace* (in terms of such properties as length and tempo).

reflected meaning   the **connotative meaning** lent to a **linguistic expression** by the fact that its *form* is reminiscent of a homonymic or near-homonymic expression with a different **literal meaning**; that is, reflected meaning is the 'echo' of the literal meaning of some other expression that sounds or is spelt the same, or nearly the same, as a given expression.

rephrasing   the exact rendering of the message content of a given ST in a TT that is radically different in form, but neither adds nor omits details explicitly conveyed in the ST.

script   a written **text** intended as a basis for the performance of an oral text realized in spontaneous (or apparently spontaneous) form.

sentential level   the level of linguistic structure concerned with the formation of sentences as complete, self-contained linguistic units ready-made to act as vehicles for oral or written communication. (N.B. over and above the basic grammatical units that it contains, a sentence must be endowed with sense-conferring properties of intonation or punctuation, and may in addition contain features of word order, and/or **illocutionary particles**, all of which contribute to the overall meaning, or 'force', of the sentence.)

sentence markers   linguistic devices that, over and above the syntactic basis of words and phrases, endow sentences with a specific type of communicative purpose and intent; the principal types of sentence marker are intonation/punctuation, sequential focusing (that is, word order) and **illocutionary particles**.

social register   a style of speaking/writing that gives grounds for inferring relatively detailed stereotypical information about the social identity of the speaker/writer. (N.B. 'Social identity' refers to the stereotypical labelling that is a constant feature of social intercourse.)

sociolect   a language variety with features of accent, vocabulary, syntax and sentence-formation (for example, intonation, **illocutionary particles**) characteristic, and therefore indicative, of the class affiliations of its users.

source language (SL)   the language in which the **text** requiring translation is expressed.

source text (ST)   the text requiring translation.

strategic decisions   the initial decisions taken, in the light of the nature of the ST and the requirements of the TT, as to what ST properties should have priority in translation; **decisions of detail** are ideally taken in the light of these strategic decisions.

synonymy   the highest degree of semantic equivalence between two or more different linguistic expressions, the expressions having exactly identical ranges of **literal meaning**. (N.B. Synonymous expressions usually differ in **connotative**, and therefore in 'overall', meaning; that is, they are unlikely to have perfectly identical meanings in textual contexts – compare 'automobile' and 'jalopy', for instance.)

target language (TL)   the language into which a given **text** is to be translated.

target text (TT)   the **text** proffered as a translation (that is, a proposed TL rendering) of the ST. (N.B. 'Publishing' a target text is a decisive act that overrides the necessarily relative and tentative success of the target text.)

text   any given stretch of speech or writing produced in a given language (or 'mixture of languages' – compare **code-switching**) and assumed to make a **coherent** whole on the **discourse level**.

textual variables   all the ostensible features contained in a **text**, and which *could* (in another text) have been different; that is, each textual variable constitutes a genuine *option* in the text.

tonal register   a style of speaking/writing adopted as a means of conveying affective attitudes of speakers/writers to their addressees. (N.B. The **connotative meaning** of a feature of tonal register is an **affective meaning**. This connotative meaning is, strictly speaking, conveyed by the *choice* of one out of a range of expressions capable of conveying a particular literal message; for example, 'Give me the money, please.' versus 'Chuck us the dosh, will you?'.)

transcript   a written **text** intended to represent and record (to a relative degree of exactitude) a particular oral text.

translation loss   any feature of inexact correspondence between ST and TT.

transposition   see **grammatical transposition**.

transliteration   the use of TL orthographic conventions for the written representation of SL expressions; for example, Russian 'спутник' transliterated as English 'sputnik'.

word system   a pattern of words (distributed over a **text**) formed by an associative common denominator and having a demonstrable function of enhancing the theme and message of the text (for example, an alliterative pattern emphasizing a particular mood).

References

Anderson, V. 1972. *The Brownie Cookbook*. London: Hodder & Stoughton.
Aphek, E. and Tobin, Y. 1988. *Word Systems; Implications and Applications*. Leiden: E. J. Brill.
Apollinaire, G. 1966. *Calligrammes*. Paris: Gallimard, Coll. Poésie.
Apollinaire, G. 1980. *Calligrammes: Poems of Peace and War*, Hyde Greet, A. (trans.). Berkeley: University of California Press.
Astington, E. 1983. *Equivalences. Translation Difficulties and Devices, French–English, English–French*. Cambridge: Cambridge University Press.
Audisio, G. (ed.) 1945. *Les Ecrivains en prison*. Paris: Seghers.

Ballard, M. 1987. *La Traduction: de l'anglais au français*. Paris: Nathan.
Baudelaire, C. 1961. *Les Fleurs du Mal*, Adam, A. (ed.). Paris: Garnier.
Beaumarchais, P. A. C. de. 1934. *Le Barbier de Séville*. Paris: Larousse, Classiques Larousse.
Beauvais, R. 1970. *L'hexagonal tel qu'on le parle*. Paris: Hachette.
Beauvoir, S. de. 1960. *La Force de l'âge*. Paris: Gallimard.
Beauvoir, S. de. 1973. *The Prime of Life*, Green, P. (trans.). Harmondsworth: Penguin Books.
Beeton, M. 1962. *Mrs Beeton's Family Cookery*. London: Ward, Lock & Company.
Boudard, A. 1981. *Le corbillard de Jules*. Paris: Gallimard, Coll. Folio.
Brassens, G. 1973. 'La marguerite', from *Poèmes et chansons*. Paris: Editions Musicales 57.
Brassens, G. 1985. 'The Daisy', from *Graeme Allwright sings Brassens*, Kelly, A. (trans.). Paris: Phonogram, Philips Record 824 005–1.
Brassens, G. 1973. 'Le testament', from *Poèmes et chansons*. Paris: Editions Musicales 57.

Cadou, R.-G. 1972. *Pleine poitrine et quelques poèmes*. Périgueux: Fanlac.
Cardinal, M. 1975. *Les Mots pour le dire*. Paris: Grasset.
Cardinal, M. 1984. *The Words to Say It*, Goodheart, P. (trans.). London: Pan Books, Picador.
Carton, F. et al. 1983. *Les accents des Français*. Paris: Hachette.
Catullus. 1969. *Gai Valeri Catulli Veronensis Liber*, Zukovsky, C. and L. (trans.). London: Cape Goliard.
Caws, M. A. 1977. *The Surrealist Voice of Robert Desnos*. Amherst: University of Massachusetts Press.
Céline, L.-F. 1976. *D'un château l'autre*. Paris: Gallimard, Coll. Folio.
Chuquet, H. and Paillard, M. 1987. *Approche linguistique des problèmes de traduction. Anglais ←→ français*. Gap, Paris: Ophrys.
The Cookbook for the Braun Multipractic Plus and the Multipractic Plus Electronic; Cuisiner avec Multipractic Plus et Multipractic Plus Electronic de Braun. 1981. Kronberg: Braun A.G.
Cross, T. (ed.) 1988. *The Lost Voices of World War I*. London: Bloomsbury.

Desnos, R. 1968. *Corps et biens*. Paris: Gallimard, Coll. Poésie.
Dutourd, J. 1972. *Au Bon Beurre*. Paris: Gallimard, Coll. Folio.

Euroabstracts Section II. 1987. 'Amélioration des moyens de fermeture des enceintes à confiner en cas de feux ou incendies', Vol. XII, No. 1. Luxembourg: Commission of the European Communities.
Emmanuel, P. 1987. 'Le pain et le livre' in *L'Arbre et le vent*. Paris: Seuil.

Gaulle, C. de. 1945. *Discours de Guerre*, 3 vols, vol. 3. Paris: Egloff.
Gaulle, C. de. 1959. *War Memoirs. Unity: 1942–4. Documents*, Erskine, H. and Murchie, J. (eds. and trans.). London: Weidenfeld & Nicolson.
Gide, A. 1975. *L'Immoraliste*. Paris: Mercure de France.
Gide, A. 1966. *The Immoralist*, Bussy, D. (trans.). London: Cassell.
Godin, H. 1964. *Les Ressources stylistiques du français contemporain*. Oxford: Blackwell.
Goscinny, R. and Uderzo, A. 1961. *Astérix le Gaulois*. Neuilly-sur-Seine: Dargaud Editeur.
Goscinny, R. and Uderzo, A. 1969. *Asterix the Gaul*, Bell, A. and Hockridge, D. (trans.). Leicester: Brockhampton Press.
Goscinny, R. and Uderzo, A. 1965. *Astérix et Cléopâtre*. Neuilly-sur-Seine: Dargaud Editeur.
Goscinny, R. and Uderzo, A. 1973. *Astérix en Corse*. Neuilly-sur-Seine: Dargaud Editeur.
Goscinny, R. and Uderzo, A. 1980. *Asterix in Corsica*, Bell, A. and Hockridge, D. (trans.). London: Hodder Dargaud.
Grainville, P. 1976. *Les Flamboyants*. Paris: Seuil.
Grellet, F. 1985. *'The word against the word'. Initiation à la version anglaise*. Paris: Hachette.
Guillemin-Flescher, J. 1981. *Syntaxe comparée du français et de l'anglais. Problèmes de traduction*. Gap, Paris: Ophrys.

Halliday, M. A. K. and Hasan, R. 1976. *Cohesion in English*. London: Longman, English Language Series.
Hopkins, G. M. 1980. *Poèmes: accompagnés de proses et de dessins*, Leyris, P. (trans.). Paris: Seuil.

Ionesco, E. 1988. *Rhinocéros*. Paris: Gallimard, Coll. Folio.
Ionesco, E. 1960. *Rhinoceros*, Prouse, D. (trans.). Harmondsworth: Penguin Books.

Jakobson, R. 1971. *Selected Writings*, Vol. II. The Hague: Mouton.

Lainé, P. 1974. *La Dentellière*. Paris: Gallimard.
Lanoux, A. 1956. *Le Commandant Watrin*. Paris: Julliard.
Larreguy de Civrieux, M. de. 1926. *La Muse de Sang*. Paris: Librairie du Travail.
Lebesque, M. 1970. *Comment peut-on être Breton? Essai sur la démocratie française*. Paris: Seuil.
Leech. G. 1974. *Semantics*. Harmondsworth: Pelican Books.

McCluskey, B. 1987. 'The chinks in the armour: problems encountered by language graduates entering a large translation department', in Keith, H. and Mason, I. (eds). *Translation in the Modern Languages Degree*. London: Centre for Information on Language Teaching and Research.

Michaux, H. 1927. *Qui je fus*. Paris: Gallimard.
Michel, G. 1967. *La Promenade du dimanche*. Paris: Gallimard.
Michel, G. 1968. *L'Agression*. Paris: Gallimard.
Montesquieu, C. de S. 1960. *Lettres persanes*, Vernière, P. (ed.). Paris: Garnier.

Newmark, P. 1982. *Approaches to Translation*. Oxford: Pergamon.

Pagnol, M. 1971. *Jean de Florette*. Paris: Presses Pocket.
Ponge, F. 1965. *Tome premier*. Paris: Gallimard.
Prévert, J. 1949. *Paroles*. Paris: Gallimard.
Proust, M. 1966. *Swann's Way*, Part One, Scott Moncrieff, C. K. (trans.). London: Chatto & Windus.
Proust, M. 1987. *A la recherche du temps perdu*, Vol. 1. Paris: Gallimard, Bibliothèque de la Pléiade.

Racine, J. 1960. *Théâtre complet*, Rat, M. (ed.). Paris: Garnier.
Rommel, B. 1987. 'Market-orientated translation training', in Keith, H. and Mason, I. (eds). *Translation in the Modern Languages Degree*. London: Centre for Information on Language Teaching and Research.

Sharpe, T. 1978. *Wilt*. London: Pan.
Sharpe, T. 1982. *Wilt 1*, Dupuigrenet-Desroussilles (trans.). Paris: U.G.D., Coll. 10/18.

Tracy, M. 1965. *Modern Casserole Cookery*. London: Studio Vista.

Viguie, J. C. 1983. 'Construction et caractérisation d'un électrolyseur pour la réduction électrochimique de la vapeur d'eau à 850°C. Rapport final.', in *Euroabstracts Section 1*, Vol. XXI, No. 12, Part 2. Luxembourg: Commission of the European Communities.
Vinay, J.-P. and Darbelnet, J. 1958. *Stylistique comparée du français et de l'anglais*. Paris: Didier.
Voltaire. 1961. *Lettres philosophiques*, Taylor, F. A. (ed.). Oxford: Blackwell.
Voltaire. 1960. *'L'Ingénu' and 'Histoire de Jenni'*, Brumfitt, J. H. and Gerard Davis, M. I. (eds). Oxford: Blackwell.
Volvo advertisement. 1986. In *Le Moniteur Automobile*, 859, pp. 28–9.

Index